Whitewater Wanderings

by
Chuck Hines

authorHOUSE®

AuthorHouse™
1663 Liberty Drive, Suite 200
Bloomington, IN 47403
www.authorhouse.com
Phone: 1-800-839-8640

© *2008 Chuck Hines. All rights reserved.*

No part of this book may be reproduced, stored in a retrieval system, or transmitted by any means without the written permission of the author.

First published by AuthorHouse   5/27/2008

ISBN: 978-1-4343-8536-9 (sc)

Printed in the United States of America
Bloomington, Indiana

This book is printed on acid-free paper.

Introduction

As I reflect back on my life from the vantage-point of one who recently turned 75, I find there have been three distinct threads. The first and foremost is Family. While of greatest importance, this is also very personal. The second is Church, which involves my religious convictions, and these I am willing to share with those closest to me. The third is the Young Men's Christian Association, or as it's better known, the YMCA, which has been my career, my calling, my profession.

I have written a book about my YMCA career entitled "A Walk on the Y'ld Side," which has been published by AuthorHouse. The sub-heading of the book informs readers that it is a collection of my "memories from 40 years of teaching and coaching youngsters through the auspices of the YMCA."

My specialty while working for the YMCA in Minnesota, Iowa, Illinois, and North Carolina was aquatics, and this can be broken into two components. During the first 20 years of my Y career, I was involved locally and nationally with swimming and water polo. I was the chairman of national committees for the American Swimming Coaches Association and the Amateur Athletic Union, and I was an officer of the U.S. Olympic Men's Water Polo Committee, helping devise a strategy whereby our men's team earned the bronze medal at the 1972 Games in Munich, Germany. The YMCA girls team that I coached won the Gold medal at the Junior Olympics and then represented the Eastern U.S. at the 1977 World Women's Water Polo Club Championships at Quebec City, Canada. That event ended the first half of my Y career.

The second half took me out of the pool and onto the rivers for the next 20 years. I was given an opportunity to create a national whitewater kayaking program for the YMCA. Eventually I became involved again with the Olympics and the Junior Olympics, this time in the sport of whitewater racing in the 1990s. I then served as president of the Nantahala Whitewater Racing Club, helping devise a strategy that enabled the Racin' Rhinos to win four consecutive U.S. championships in 1997, 1998, 1999, and 2000.

It is the YMCA, where I still go swimming thrice weekly, that has provided the foundation for my participation in various aquatic activities. It is still the YMCA that means the most to me after Family and Church. And yet ... and yet ...

The river is a special place, and whitewater kayaking is a wonderful way to become closer to God's Great Outdoors. Whitewater slalom racing is a very unique sport, with ever-changing conditions and challenges that demand the utmost in physical and mental dexterity. So I have written this book about the YMCA *and my whitewater wanderings. I am not sure they can be separated.*

Hopefully you will enjoy reading this book as much as I've enjoyed writing it. In the doing, I have been able to re-live some of the most exciting moments of my life. Ah, what memories.

                Chuck Hines, Asheville, North Carolina, April, 2008

Chapter One

It was raining. Hard. For the past 24 hours, the Nantahala River Gorge in Western North Carolina had been besieged by a raging October rainstorm. The bright leaves that normally colored the trees each autumn had been blown into the river, which itself was swollen by water cascading from the surrounding creeks and streams. Rocks and ridges in the river were covered by the swirling and spiraling current. It was a dangerous place to be, and yet there I was, a novice kayaker, striving to make my way down the river.

"Let's grab some lunch," instructor Kathy Bolyn had told us a few hours earlier, "and then we'll hit the river."

After a morning of practicing in the downpour at nearby Queens Lake, our group gathered at a shed, where we dried off and enjoyed sandwiches and soft drinks. Then we were led by our instructors to the river. We were all relative beginners, and of our group of about a dozen, I was at the very bottom in ability, or so it seemed to me.

"Just follow us," Kathy said, as we placed ourselves into the small, cramped kayaks, adjusted our life-jackets, tightened our spray-skirts, donned our helmets, and grabbed our twin-bladed paddles. Anyone passing by on the highway might have thought we knew what we were doing. But we didn't. At least I didn't. Kathy and the two other instructors pushed off into the crazy current, and I followed, with the rain obscuring everything farther down the river.

As I overturned for the third time – or was it the fourth? – and ended up swimming through the rapids in one direction while my kayak headed off in the opposite direction, I asked myself, What am I doing here?

It had all started innocently enough. I was on the staff of the nearby Asheville YMCA, halfway through my 40-year career with the organization. A specialist in aquatics, I was responsible for operating the Y's indoor swimming pool. I taught learn-to-swim classes, coached the swimming and water polo teams, lifeguarded from time to time, and supervised various other programs which we conducted at the Y and in several rented pools. It came easy for me. In my younger days, I'd been a Midwest champion in competitive swimming and an All-America performer in water polo. The water was my element, my home, and now, having passed the age of 40, I was being recognized for coaching national champions in those two sports. I felt comfy.

But in the summer of 1976, I'd received a letter from the YMCA's National Physical Education Management Team that turned my life around. It said: "We are looking for someone or some YMCA to design a physical education program that appeals to the adventurous nature of youth, preferably an activity that can be done outdoors. There is even a small stipend available in the amount of $300."

The YMCA was founded in London, England, in 1844 by a gentleman named George Williams. The Y came to the United States in 1851. It has been a major presence in our country and in 120 other countries ever since. At present, the organization has over 40 million members globally. Half are here in the U.S. The YMCA always is seeking new activities for its participants and for the communities it serves, and it was the Y that invented basketball way back in 1891 and volleyball in 1895. The Y opened its initial pool in 1885 and began offering swimming lessons in 1906 and playing water polo in 1908. The YMCA was the first organization to create a national scuba diving program in 1959. I had been involved with Y swimming and water polo and scuba diving at the highest levels. Now the YMCA was looking for someone to develop a new outdoor adventure activity for youth.

Just up my alley! I was growing a bit weary from coaching swimming and water polo, and as I approached middle age, I was ready for a change. Could the letter I received be the answer? I'd enjoyed some previous experiences in a canoe, starting at age 12, when I was attending Camp Little Scorpion in my home state of Minnesota. Some years later, my wife Lee and I went canoeing frequently on the St. Croix River, and we took two week-long canoe/camping trips to the famed Boundary Waters of Minnesota and Manitoba. I even had joined the American Canoe Association (member #13,904), the American Whitewater Affiliation, and the U.S. Canoe Association while teaching basic canoeing skills to over 100 youngsters in my previous YMCA jobs in Minnesota, Iowa, and Illinois.

Furthermore, we had a kayak club that was renting out our Asheville YMCA pool on Saturday nights, and I had watched them from time to time. The sleek, slender, and highly maneuverable boats appealed to me. I actually sat in a kayak a couple of times and paddled around in the pool, receiving instruction and encouragement from my friend John Bayless. Nothing to it. Thus I signed up for a two-day kayak clinic on the Nantahala River in October of 1976, figuring it would be as easy as a walk in the park.

I was wrong.

The rain kept on pouring down. It was an absolutely miserable day. The Nantahala River's Class II rapids were now – I later learned – at a Class III level, making them almost impossible for beginners to paddle successfully. I was somewhat stable in my kayak when headed down the river, carried along at a swift pace by the churning current. But whenever there was an obstacle to be avoided or an eddy to be caught – a calm spot, usually hidden behind the rocks – I immediately flipped and exited from my boat. I did not yet know how to perform the Eskimo roll, with which kayakers can upright themselves whenever they overturn. I lost count of how many times I flipped and swam. I do know I spent more time swimming and emptying water out of my kayak than actually paddling.

"Don't lean upstream," the instructors repeatedly told us, "or you'll flip for sure." Their advice was either lost in the clamor of the rain and rushing rapids or ignored. When I finally reached home, feeling defeated and dejected, I told my wife, "That's a really dumb sport."

What had happened? I was a reasonably good athlete, in great shape physically, with many years of recreational canoeing to my credit, and eager to succeed at whitewater kayaking. Yet the two days had been a disaster. I slept on it. I thought about it for the next several weeks. I wondered how many others like me were encountering the same sad situation when striving to learn whitewater kayaking. I came to the conclusion that it was important for the YMCA to create a whitewater kayaking curriculum that would offer our members a safe and enjoyable introduction to the sport, while at the same time fulfilling the Physical Education Management Team's directive to develop a new national program that could be done outdoors. But how to go about it?

I phoned Bunny Johns, the director of instruction for the Nantahala Outdoor Center, and told her we were interested in creating a YMCA kayaking curriculum, perhaps using the Y pool. The Nantahala Outdoor Center, or NOC, was just making its mark in Western North Carolina. It had opened in 1972, which was the year that whitewater paddling exploded on the national scene. For the first time, the sport was contested at the Olympic Games held in Munich, Germany, and that had captured the public's attention. This was fortified by the release of an exciting movie, "Deliverance," featuring Burt Reynolds and John Voight, which showed canoeists battling rapids and robbers on the Chattooga River here in the South. There was even a picture of a kayaker on the cover of "Sports Illustrated" magazine. Suddenly everyone was interested in whitewater activities, and the Nantahala Outdoor Center was leading the way. I felt the YMCA needed to plunge into the sport, too, despite my woeful experience on the Nantahala, or perhaps because of it.

Bunny Johns, a champion canoeist herself who later became president of NOC, sent four good instructors to the Asheville YMCA in 1977. They were Micki Piras, Bruce Sager, Steve Holmes, and Dave Mason. All were not only proficient paddlers but also outstanding racers.

We conducted classes for adults on Thursday evenings at the YMCA, and they were jammed from the beginning – we had 15 enrolled in each and every course, which was the maximum we could handle. I participated myself as a student in the instruction, gradually learning the basics of kayaking. This included the strokes, braces, wet exits, and eventually the Eskimo roll.

One day a YMCA member came into the aquatic office adjacent to the pool, where I was seated at my desk. "I see you're teaching kayaking," he said.

"Yup," I replied. "Are you interested in signing up?"

"I've already been kayaking for a few years, but I have a daughter who'd like to learn. If you can conduct a course for her and other youngsters, I can help."

That was a special moment which now, 30 years later, still reverberates with me. The gentleman who came into my office with his inquiry was Will Pruett. A sixth generation Ashevillean, he had grown up in our fair city, served for six years in the Air Force in the big bombers, and graduated from Western Carolina University. He was now a community leader in the new field of computer programming. I discovered that he had canoed down the Nantahala and other WNC rivers in his younger days and then, after viewing "Deliverance," had taught himself to kayak. He was married and had two daughters, one of whom wanted to learn how to kayak.

Although I was an athlete myself, my forte was actually teaching and coaching youngsters, and this is what the YMCA was paying me to do. I had 500 children in my swimming classes, plus those in other activities. With what I was now learning for myself in our adult kayaking classes, and with Will Pruett's assistance, I was ready to move ahead and create a youth program in whitewater kayaking.

We set aside two afternoons weekly, Tuesdays and Thursdays, 4:15 to 5:30, for conducting the youth kayaking program in the YMCA pool. As with the adult classes, our youth course filled up immediately with 16 participants, half boys and half girls. This included Will Pruett's daughter, Amy, 14, and my daughter, Heather, 12.

The curriculum I was devising consisted of six sessions at the YMCA, with each session having a classroom meeting followed by pool instruction. In the classroom, we discussed equipment and river safety. We showed the several good films about whitewater kayaking and canoeing that were available. I handled the adult classroom instruction myself. Then I sent the adults to the pool, where the NOC instructors took over. When it came to the kids, Will and I did it ourselves.

After the six sessions at the YMCA, we took our adult students out to the French Broad River for a practice. This river flows through Asheville and contains everything from flat water to challenging Class IV rapids. We put our students into a gently flowing current, where they transferred their pool-learned skills onto moving water. Then we scheduled a real river trip down some other nearby river such as the Green, Tuckaseigee, Little Tennessee, or Nolichucky. On the trip, they tackled Class II rapids. At the conclusion of the six sessions at the YMCA and the practice on the French Broad and the river trip, the adult class was concluded, and we started another course with a new group.

For the youngsters, however, our program was continuous. It didn't end. It was like a club or a team, with ongoing adventures and opportunities. More on this later.

As 1977 came to an end, I was satisfied that we were making good progress, both with our own kayaking instructional efforts at the Asheville YMCA and with creating a new national program for the YMCA of the USA. And better things lay ahead.

Chapter Two

"Warning! Class III, IV, and V rapids ahead – only guided or experienced boaters should attempt the run to Hot Springs. These rapids must be scouted!"

So said the French Broad River Guide prepared by the Land-of-Sky Regional Council in the 1970s. This referred to an eight-mile stretch of the river just north of Asheville. The guide continued: "This section is generally recognized as one of the toughest whitewater runs in Western North Carolina. The water moves very swiftly through rock gardens and over ledges which require constant maneuvering and vigilance. There are nine major sets of more difficult rapids – six Class IIIs, two Class IVs, and one Class V, none of them easy."

Our party of six kayakers and five canoeists met at the YMCA on a Saturday morning in March of 1978. We departed at 9:30 a.m. and returned home 11 hours later, around 8:15 p.m., almost totally exhausted.

Charles White was our trip leader. A long-time canoeist, he had taken one of our recent YMCA kayak courses, and we felt comfortable with him leading the way. I had been learning to kayak for the past year, and I was ready to try my luck on this challenging stretch of river. It was a beautiful, sunny day, and as the river flows through a gorge in the Cherokee National Forest, the scenery was spectacular. Everyone reached the take-out without serious mishap, although two of the canoeists and four of the kayakers overturned. The canoeists ended up swimming. The kayakers had a choice between coming out of their boats and swimming OR performing an Eskimo roll and uprighting themselves. This is one of the advantages of kayaking over canoeing.

I flipped twice myself but rolled up both times. My practices in the YMCA pool were paying off. Doug Brooks also did a couple of Eskimo rolls. Mike Clevenger overturned and did an unbelievable hands-only roll when his paddle became trapped in some rocks. Rob Kern flipped once while negotiating an eight-foot waterfall and was unable to roll up, his only error of an otherwise splendid day. Jerry Mills and Greg Weldon, the other kayakers, looked smooth and classy from start to finish.

We were all paddling low-volume Phoenix Slippers or Perception Spirits. These were constructed of fiberglass, and while they were light in weight, they were prone to being destroyed by the rocks that lurked in every river. We had to be careful, and we all carried duct tape in our boats so we could patch the holes that were inevitably poked in our boats as we kayaked down the river. At 6' and 185 pounds, I found that my bright orange Spirit tended to nosedive in the steeper drops and chutes, angling down instead of riding up, and this resulted in my two flips, the first of which was a bad head-banger at the bottom of a rough, rocky Class III. Whew – glad I was wearing a sturdy helmet!

For me, this was a satisfying day. After my first humiliating attempt at kayaking on the Nantahala River in October of 1976, I had spent most of 1977 properly learning the sport through the auspices of our YMCA program. I also had taken a Nantahala Outdoor Center course, taught by Bunny Johns. We paddled sections of the Tuckaseigee and Little Tennessee Rivers. I ran several other rivers around WNC – the Davidson, lower Green, Swannanoa, East and West Forks of the Pigeon – but this trip in the spring of 1978, on the most difficult section of the French Broad River, was my first real test. As I drove home, I definitely was NOT feeling dejected and defeated, as had been the case on my initial effort. No indeed. I was feeling reassured that this was a sport I could enjoy and perhaps even master.

*****

A large tree had fallen across the river, and its extended limbs clawed out, blocking all but a thin three-foot passage on the extreme left side of the rushing rapids. Trip leader Lorri Cameron eddied out, turned, and pointed directions to the seven of us who were following. Rob Kern, the next in line, zipped through the narrow passageway, but disaster struck moments later when the next three kayakers all became entangled in the tree branches, forcing me, too, into the limbs. There we were, four of us –Debbie Childs, Jack Clement, Ernie Thurston, and me – demonstrating the way NOT to paddle down a river.

Luckily, Will Pruett came to our rescue. As calm and capable as ever, he smiled as he parted the branches and allowed us, one at a time, to maneuver free.

Nothing is more dangerous on a river than strainers, which are tree limbs and branches that permit water to flow through but which can snag unwary boaters. This one, halfway through our trip on the Oconaluftee River, hadn't been bad, and thanks to Will, we had suffered no severe consequences.

We'd come to the Oconaluftee in the early spring and discovered this small river to be running fast and cold, with Class II-III rapids. There were rocks to be dodged and some three- and four-foot drops to be negotiated. And the outstretched tree limbs to be avoided, if possible.

Along the way, we found many good spots for surfing, and at first we did a lot of this, playing in the waves, but as the sun began dropping and then disappeared behind the gathering clouds, we moved on. By the time we finished our three-hour trip, a rainstorm was in progress. We had frozen fingers and numb toes as we dressed, lifted the kayaks onto our cars, and headed back to Asheville, with the heavens still pouring down upon us. It had been an enjoyable outing.

*****

Easter Sunday was bright and beautiful, and as usual, I attended church with my wife Lee and our daughter Heather. The service at West Asheville Presbyterian, where I also taught a children's Sunday school class, was inspirational. Easter Monday remained sunny but a bit on the cool side. Most people had the day off, as Easter Monday was traditionally a holiday in the South. Therefore we'd scheduled the previously postponed Tuckaseigee River trip for this day. Unfortunately the list of participants dwindled down to just three of us – Rick McGinnis, Denise Laursen, and myself – and at the put-in, we picked up a fourth. He was Pat Bowen, who was from Washington, DC, but was attending Western Carolina University.

It was early afternoon when we entered the Tuckaseigee at the Dillsboro put-in, just below the dam. The water was up, and Rick, who'd scouted the river while shuttling his car, said that we could expect some good-sized waves and grabby holes. The wind was blowing fiercely in our faces as we headed downriver, and sure enough, as the Class I entranceway opened into the gorge, we began bouncing through a series of three- and four-foot curlers. Most of the rocks and boulders were submerged by the swift, high water, but we managed to do some eddy turns and peel-outs from time to time, as well as ferrying from one side of the river to the other. It was good practicing.

The run was short, less than two hours, but we had fun. It was still sunny at the take-out as we relaxed and feasted on Denise's chocolate chip cookies. Yummy. Too bad more paddlers hadn't shown up to enjoy the Tuck and the cookies.

*****

"Now that is a rapid," whispered Al Agle, as he and I and our instructor, Jim Snyder, squatted atop a large boulder and looked down at Lower Keeney Rapid in the New River Gorge of West Virginia. It was a lovely day in July, 1978, and neither Al nor I had planned to spend it challenging Lower Keeney or the other tough rapids we were scouting and running. Al, from Pennsylvania, and I, from the mountains of Western North Carolina, had come to West Virginia to improve our kayaking techniques at Appalachian Wildwater's kayak school.

Under the direction of Jim Snyder, an expert, we'd devoted several days to practicing on an easier section of the New River, successfully sailing through Class II and III rapids, in which we surfed and rolled with some semblance of skill.

Jim was so pleased with our progress that he suggested we run the Gorge on Friday, our final day. This was recognized as one of the roughest stretches of whitewater on the East Coast, and I had read in a guidebook that "this is a big, powerful river with heavy water, for experts only, and taking all safety precautions … the seven-mile stretch from the C&O railroad bridge to Fayette Station contains rapid after rapid that will tax the skill of every boater … with at least four rapids being Class IV or higher …"

One of those listed as Class IV or higher was Lower Keeney, which Al and Jim and I were now eyeing. "Yes," Jim said, "it's a Class IV, but that's all. You guys have done well all week, so let's take a crack at it."

With big boulders on the right side, a huge hole on the left, and a narrow tongue leading down the middle into honest-to-goodness five-foot waves, we knew it was going to be difficult. In my small Perception Spirit, a low-volume fiberglass kayak not really suited for such big water, I followed Jim down the middle. Stroking and bracing hard, we made it through safely. Al was less fortunate. Trailing behind us, he veered off to one side and plowed into the deep hole, which demolished him. Thirty yards and three unsuccessful roll attempts later, he bailed out and was swept downriver for a quarter of a mile before finding an eddy. As Jim looked after Al and made sure he was all right, I paddled farther down and pushed Al's boat into an eddy. The guidebook had mentioned the river's "jet current," and it certainly felt like that to me.

Al took another couple of swims as we proceeded down the New River Gorge, and I joined him on one. Otherwise I was able to roll up when necessary. An airline pilot by profession, Al panted after one particularly nasty swim, "This is tougher than any landing I've ever made."

Al decided to skip the final big rapid, about which the guidebook said, "The last Class V is right at Fayette Station. Most kayakers will want to end their trips above this rapid and watch only the experts run it."

Although no expert, I wanted to try my luck, and I followed Jim down a steep drop into the huge waves. At mid-summer's level, it wasn't a Class V, but it was a solid IV. I rode it like a wild-west bronco buster, and then suddenly I flipped over into the turbulence. I relaxed, felt myself being bounced up and down, positioned my paddle patiently and properly, lashed out, leaned back, and popped up into the froth and foam with a near-perfect Eskimo roll. Yea!

Below the rapid, Al rejoined us, and we paddled our way through several smaller rapids to the take-out. For six hours, fear had ridden the New River Gorge with us. We had lost some battles along the way, but we had survived, and in so doing, we had won the war – the war that each whitewater enthusiast wages within himself when he hears the roar of the rapids ahead and must dig down deep inside to find courage and perseverance.

This is what the sport is all about, and for me, in the summer of 1978 and at the end of the New River Gorge run, it gave me a feeling of real exhilaration and satisfaction.

*****

Nearly knocking off the two kayaks atop my aging Buick, the first full blast of icy winter weather greeted me as I drove to the Nantahala River for a weekend of mid-autumn whitewater excitement. That night, the wind brought with it some snow flurries, and when we awakened the next day, it was cold.

It was October of 1978, almost exactly two years from the day I first floundered my way down the Nantahala in a rainstorm. That day in 1976 had been very discouraging, and I had wondered whether my athletic abilities in the pool could be transferred to the river. Now, after working hard to improve my skills, I was feeling more confident, and I had run the Nantahala several times over the summer months.

When we put our boats into the water on Saturday afternoon, it was overcast and windy, but we were determined to make the best of it, as were the few other paddlers we encountered from as far away as Alabama, Florida, Illinois, and Massachusetts.

Despite frozen fingers, we took our time and did some playing, especially at Surfer's Rapid, and four of us took a spill. Not only that, but I was unable to roll and ended up swimming. Shades of 1976! Here I was, floundering again on the Nantahala. I was embarrassed. Shaking slightly as the wind picked up, we reached Nantahala Falls, a Class III which offered a strong cross-current through standing waves at the top, a large boulder and keeper hole on the right side, a few small, hidden rocks on the left, and a double drop down the middle into a sea of continuing waves. All seven of us – Charles, Fred, Lorri, Jerry, Debbie, Will, and I – made it down the Falls successfully. It had been a "fun run" and definitely better for me than two years previously.

We spent the night at the Nantahala Outdoor Center, which, after half-a-dozen years of operation, was becoming nationally-known. At this stage in its development, NOC had offices, an outfitter's store, a restaurant, and a rustic motel, all situated on the right side of the river along highway 19W. The next morning, we ate a leisurely breakfast at the restaurant, waiting for the upriver dam to release water and for the sun to climb above the surrounding peaks. The word "Nantahala" is a Cherokee word meaning "land of the noonday sun," referring to the fact that the peaks are so high in the Nantahala Gorge that it's practically mid-day before you can see the sun.

Finally we put our boats into the river, right at noon, and Jerry exclaimed, "Look at that lovely sky!" It was a bright, clear blue, and the hills and peaks were colored by shades of green, red, yellow, and orange. It was a sensational autumn day. But it was cold. Even before we began, my fingers were becoming numb. Our group included Debbie and Jerry and me from the preceding day, plus kayaker Rob Kern and open canoeists Randy Hanson and Dana Worley. Unlike the warm-weather months, when the Nantahala becomes extremely crowded, it was almost empty on this day.

The first rapid, just past the put-in, was the fast, bumpy, rocky Patton's Run, a Class II-III that demanded immediate attention and ability. It's always a heckuva way to start out, and Randy overturned and swam. When he returned to the river in his canoe, he let the current push him into the tree-lined bank, and he hit it so hard that his helmet was jolted from his head. We watched as it floated downstream and disappeared. "Not a good beginning," somebody stated.

We eddied out, waiting for Randy to get his act together, and then we headed into a series of Class II rapids – Tumble Dry, Pop 'n Run, Pyramid. The water was swift and very cold, and we laughed as we continued dashing around the Nantahala's continuing curves and through an endless array of one- and two-foot waves.

After an hour, we stopped to rest at the park. "Looks like the water's going down," Rob observed. "Didn't you hear?" said someone in the park. "They shut the dam."

Wow! Within another hour the river bed would be practically dry and impassable. We hastened back into our boats and raced down the river. Hurry, hurry. The water kept dropping inch by inch. Once, leading the way, I flipped at an exposed ledge I'd never seen before, and I bounced along the bottom a bit, waiting it out for 10 seconds, 15, 20, until the water deepened, and I rolled back up, gasping for breath.

We reached Nantahala Falls just as the concluding cascade of water reached it, and without hesitation we plummeted over the Falls into the usual chasm of chaos. We all made it through, I'm pleased to say.

The "race" to the Falls, to the finish line, had warmed us up, and after changing clothes, we headed back to Asheville. As my ol' car eased past 115,000 miles, I relaxed at the end of an enjoyable whitewater weekend, realizing how much progress I'd made over the past two years.

*****

"Nantahala, YMCA Kayak Teams Win." That was the headline in the Asheville Citizen-Times. Following was an article about the first-ever Kayak Polo Championships sponsored by the Nantahala Outdoor Center on Thanksgiving Weekend of 1978.

I had been coaching champion swimmers and water poloists at the Asheville YMCA, but now we were switching our emphasis to whitewater kayaking. Will Pruett and I had a good group of about 16 youngsters. Most knew how to play water polo, so they could handle a ball, and they understood the importance of teamwork. They were becoming competent young kayakers. NOC's Kayak Polo Championships offered an ideal opportunity for our YMCA kaYak kids to demonstrate their skills both at water polo and kayaking.

It was a bitterly cold day when we reached Queens Lake, just up the road from NOC, and we were told that several of the expected teams had backed out at the last minute because of the weather. Bunny Johns said, "I'm very impressed you're here with the Asheville youngsters. Shows a lot of determination." She and her NOC staffers had designed a nice kayak polo course at the lake, and she gathered the teams around her and explained the rules. We already knew the rules, as we'd borrowed NOC's unique snub-nosed kayak polo boats for practicing in the YMCA pool a couple of times. I was sure our team of teenaged girls was ready to play.

The article in the Citizen-Times told the story. It reported that "Nantahala Outdoor Center teams won both the men's and women's divisions of the Kayak Polo Championships held on Queens Lake here Sunday as cold water conditions caused a number of teams to drop out of the competition. Nantahala defeated Aiken, South Carolina, for the men's title, with Steve Holmes leading the way. Bunny Johns led Nantahala past the Asheville YMCA girls for the women's crown, but the YMCA girls came back to take first place in the junior division. The Y team was comprised of Tandy Beck, Rhonda Burleson, Sidney Bradfield, Deanna Davis, Heather Hines, and Karen Miller."

Yes, we were moving forward in developing our own strong youth paddling program at the Asheville YMCA, and in the process we were forging ahead in "designing a physical education program that appeals to the adventurous nature of youth, preferably an activity that can be done outdoors."

I notified the YMCA's National Physical Education Management Team of our efforts. They sent back a letter saying that our program "looked good" and that we should "keep working on it." They said we had earned the $300 stipend, and their letter contained a check in that amount, which we used to purchase new kayaking equipment. What else?

Chapter Three

The spring of 1979 was one of the wettest in Western North Carolina history. It began with a severe February snowstorm and a week-long rainfall that raised all river levels impressively and caused me impulsively to do something rather foolish – to run a river which was at flood stage.

I'd now been kayaking for two years or slightly more if you counted my first fumbling effort on the Nantahala, and I'd learned to paddle correctly and safely. As the new season approached, I was eager to get going again on our local rivers.

On a sullen Saturday afternoon in February, open canoeists Lorri Cameron and Al Preston and I, with my kayak, accompanied by a non-paddling friend, drove the 38 miles to the Green River. The lower section of the Green is one of the best and most popular training sites in the South, and although it boasts a very difficult upstream section, with Class IV-V rapids, most kayak and canoe enthusiasts settle for the lower section, which is located in a deep, scenic valley. Fed by water from the upstream dam, there are fairly continuous Class II rapids with one, Little Corky, a possible III. Nowadays, when I look back into the past, I realize that I paddled the lower Green at least 40 times, usually with our YMCA instructional classes, but none of those trips can compare to that special day in February of 1979.

It was a *cold* day, with the air temperature in the 20s. It was *snowing*. The wind was *blowing*. The river was *overflowing*. We stood around, debating what to do. "Can we do it?" "Should we do it?" "What's the sense of doing it?"

Our non-paddling friend, shivering despite wearing a heavy coat, said, "If you decide to do it, I'll follow you in my car, so if anything happens, you can leave the river and get into my car and warm up quickly."

That settled it. Lorri and Al and I look at each other and laughed nervously. "Let's do it."

Within minutes, we were in our boats and pushing off into the excitement of the swirling waves. I hadn't intended to lead the way, but the quick current caught my kayak and propelled me downriver, and before I knew what was happening, I was *gone*. Lorri and Al never caught up with me, and for all practical purposes, I was heading down a swollen, flooded river by myself. *Alone.*

There wasn't a rock or boulder in sight. Even those that normally stood three or four feet above the river were totally inundated. There wasn't an eddy anywhere. It was a washout from one side of the river to the other, with the rampaging water up into the trees along the shoreline. It was a river trip that went so *fast* I've never been able to remember all the details, and yet I'll never forget it.

The Green was a contortion of sizeable waves. Logs, tree limbs, and other debris bumped against my boat and impeded my paddling. The snow stung my eyes. The cold numbed my fingers. In less than 15 minutes, I was swept beneath the first bridge, as I struggled to maintain my balance. In another five minutes, I was zipping down Big Corky where, finally, I found and squeezed into an eddy, pausing briefly to catch my breath.

But it was freezing cold just sitting there. *Let's go, Chuck!* I was again stroking and bracing my way along. Jacob's Ladder was a downhill dive through a series of gigantic waves, and I realized what a poor place this would be to take a swim. Probably life-threatening.

The island in mid-river that separates Little Corky into left-side and right-side channels had vanished, leaving just a few bare-limbed treetops sticking up from the throbbing and rushing river. Normally this rapid required careful maneuvering. Not on this day. I was hurtled by the waves around the protruding trees at breakneck speed. A few more minutes took me to the second bridge. I was perspiring and shivering at the same time. That's enough, I decided.

Our non-paddling friend pulled up in his car. "How was it?"

I chuckled. "Piece of cake."

"Not for me," declared Al Preston, who I noticed was sitting in the car. "I flipped my canoe and swam. I just about froze. It was scary. I don't know what I'd have done without this nice warm car."

"What about Lorri?" I asked, and as I did so, she came paddling into view, joining us at the take-out beneath the second bridge, an expression of pure delight framing her reddened face.

"Wheeee!" she exclaimed. "The best ride I've ever had. I don't suppose anyone will believe us, but there were honest-to-goodness four-foot waves on the Green today, and a lot of 'em. What a thrill!"

Truly, it had been a remarkable experience. After dressing in the whistling wind, we drove upriver to the starting point, and as we passed challenging Little Corky, we saw that the river was beginning to flow across the road. "Within an hour," I said, "this road will be impassable." The others nodded.

At the time, it didn't register on us just how high the lower Green was running, but on the numerous occasions I returned to the river thereafter, I discovered that the road is six or seven feet above the river. Wow. Six feet higher than usual, that's what the Green offered us on that day in February of 1979, *providing me with a natural high that's remained with me ever since.*

*****

"Kayaking: Daring Sport Gains Popularity." Thus read the headline in a March edition of the Citizen-Times newspaper. The sub-heading said, "Champion Gives Demonstrations." This was followed by three photos of U.S. women's slalom titlist Linda Harrison negotiating the slalom gates we'd hung in the Asheville YMCA pool.

I had invited Linda to spend a week with us. After the experts at the Nantahala Outdoor Center had helped us create a kayaking instructional curriculum in 1977, we had assumed operational responsibility for the program ourselves. For the adults enrolled in our courses, I was teaching in the classroom while Will Pruett, Jim Maynor, and Rocky Meadows were teaching in the pool. Then we would take our adult students to a practice on the French Broad River and on a concluding river trip. We were continuing to fill up every class we offered at the YMCA.

Will and I were doing the youth kayaking program, with an occasional assist from Jim Maynor. As one who possessed a competitive urge since my childhood days and who had been competing in and coaching such sports as swimming and water polo, I definitely wanted our new YMCA kayak program to contain a competitive component. This included the kayak polo we had done, but more importantly, I wanted us to focus on slalom and wildwater racing. In slalom, athletes maneuver through "gates" hung above the river. This, I felt, was the prime competitive activity for kayakers, requiring a combination of speed and maneuverability. It was the event that had been contested in the 1972 Olympic Games at Munich, Germany.

Thus I invited Linda Harrison to visit us and work with our young kayakers. She came and bunked at our house. Each morning she practiced on the French Broad River, and each afternoon or evening she taught slalom racing techniques in the YMCA pool. It was informative for all of us, and the newspaper article reported: "Kayak champion Linda Harrison goes paddling two or three times per day, an hour each time, no matter how chilly and wet the weather. She lifts weights for strength, and she runs for endurance…

"The bronze medalist at the 1977 World Championships, she's in training now with hopes to be No. 1 in this year's (1979) World Championships planned for Quebec, Canada, in July. To have gotten this far, Linda has concentrated on kayaking and not much else for the past two years. Her specialty is slalom racing. She admits she is probably the fastest woman in the world right now and is concentrating less on speed and more on negotiating the gates cleanly, as each touch of a slalom gate adds seconds to the time it takes to run the slalom course…

"On Monday, Tuesday, Wednesday, and Thursday, Linda was at the YMCA in Asheville to give kayaking demonstrations and to encourage the promising young kayakers at the Y…

"Chuck Hines, the YMCA's Vice-President for Aquatics, said Linda had seen the Y girls on the Nantahala River and thought they were good, so he invited her to come here and teach the girls about slalom racing…

"Hines said some of his 12-, 13- and 14-year-old kayakers already are showing skills that most adults can't do. He explained that the YMCA's kayaking program has gained the importance that water polo once held earlier in the 1970s, when Asheville teams won 10 national tournaments…

"Last year, over 90 adults and 30 youngsters took the YMCA kayaking instruction. Graduates of the Y's courses have organized a club that schedules weekend trips to various WNC rivers that are known as among the most challenging in the East."

After Linda's visit and two more months of additional practicing, our YMCA youngsters were ready to enter the second annual French Broad River races. The Citizen-Times said that "three of the nation's best canoeists and two top kayakers have filed entries … the downriver races Saturday will start at 10:00 a.m. at the Long Shoals bridge, with junior competitors racing three miles and the adult competitors 12 miles … the slalom event will start at 2:00 p.m. on a 16-gate course near the Amboy Bridge road."

The newspaper also printed a lengthy follow-up article. "With whitewater sport becoming so popular throughout WNC, it's no wonder many youngsters have taken an interest in paddling, and 15 of them have been enrolled in the Asheville YMCA's junior kayak racing program for the past three months. They have been training twice weekly on the slalom gates at the YMCA pool and have enjoyed trips down the Green, Tuckaseigee, Little Tennessee, and Nantahala Rivers under the supervision of coaches Chuck Hines and Will Pruett...

"Hines explained that whitewater racing is divided into two categories, one for kayaks and one for canoes. The kayakers, who sit in their boats, use a double-bladed paddle. They compete solo and take part in the K-1 class for men or the K-1W class for women. The canoeists, who kneel in their boats, use a single-bladed paddle. They can compete solo in the C-1 class for men or with a partner in the C-2 class for two men or the C-2M (mixed) class for one man and one woman. Furthermore, the canoes can be open or decked. Hines admitted that it can be confusing at times, but that the objective was to attract as many different individuals as possible to the sport...

"The YMCA youngsters, who are all kayakers, will be competing in the French Broad downriver and slalom races this Saturday, May 26. As at most races, there will be junior competition for those 17-and-younger, along with Masters racing for those 40-and-older. Hines, who also is Vice-President of Aquatics at the Asheville YMCA, said that with all the various categories of competition, whitewater paddling is a good family activity."

A week later, the newspaper reported the results of the 1979 French Broad River Races. The downriver winners – those who raced as fast as they could down a lengthy stretch of the river – included Dave Mason, Tom Popp, Sam Fowlkes, Ed McGinnis, Nick Meyers, Ken and Fran Strickland, Jim Green, and four representatives of the YMCA – Jim Maynor, Betsy Warner, and juniors Nathan Brown and Amy Pruett.

The slalom winners – those who maneuvered through a series of gates hung above the river on a shorter section – were Steve Epps, Julie Downs, Rick McGinnis, Fran Strickland, and YMCA juniors Mark Sheppard and Karen Miller. In the Men's Masters competition, I finished first, closely followed by Will Pruett.

An even larger competition was held a few weeks later on the Nantahala River. The Citizen-Times informed us that "the 11th annual Southeastern Championships for canoeists and kayakers, combined with the Age Group Nationals, are expected to attract over 300 participants and will consist of slalom races on Saturday and wildwater races on Sunday. The slalom will be conducted at Nantahala Falls, while the wildwater will run along an eight-mile course paralleling U.S. 19W."

In those days, racing on the river was much more popular than it is nowadays, as I write this in 2008. There were indeed 300 or more competitors at the Nantahala on that weekend, coming from at least a dozen states. I was entered in two kayaking events, the Masters slalom and the Cruising Class slalom. In the former, I had an exceptional race, running the course at the Nantahala Falls site without clipping a single gate or pole, and I finished in a time of 2:18. This gave me first place by a whopping 27-second margin. I was overjoyed. Truly I was becoming a GREAT kayaker, right?

Then came the Cruising Class slalom. I bombed. My run was an abysmal failure. A total disaster, reminiscent of my first attempt on the Nantahala back in October, 1976. I didn't flip. I didn't swim. But I must have hit every gate on the slalom course, at least those I didn't miss completely. My friend Will Pruett did just the opposite. After a poor performance in the Masters, he climbed to second place in the Cruising Class, followed by Jim Maynor in third and several others ... including myself ... last ... in a time of 4:58. I went from first to worst in just a few hours. The river will humble you!

We also had three YMCA teenagers entered in the K-1W junior slalom. Karen Miller was second, Amy Pruett third, and Tandy Beck fifth.

All in all, our Y contingent didn't fare too badly. Of course, the best performers were those in their 20s – like Linda Harrison and her national teammates – who were the real champions. Yet we were satisfied as we drove home to Asheville. "Ya know," said Will, "if we build a permanent slalom course on the French Broad River where we can practice more often, we could become pretty good at racing." So that's what we did.

We constructed a 12-gate course on the French Broad. It was at the Firefighters Camp in south Asheville. Hung from stout cables, the gates with their red, white, and green poles looked pretty. There was a gentle current down the middle of the 50-yard-long course, with some rocks on the right side and a shallow shoal on the left. We placed the gates so as to require forward, reverse, and upstream maneuvering. It was only Class I+, maybe a weak II when the water was higher than usual, but it gave us a place to practice. Those who spent a weekend creating the course were Sean Devereux, Mike Harper, Harold Mathews, Jim Maynor, Will Pruett, this writer, and four of our YMCA junior kayakers.

Perhaps most importantly, the course was well-protected by being at the site of the Firefighters Camp, where a caretaker resided in a small house. There was ample parking space and even a pavilion. Not bad. On the negative side, we were allowed to enter the property and use the course just twice weekly. We arranged for Tuesday and Thursday afternoons, usually from 4:00 to 7:00 p.m. I worked this into my schedule as the YMCA's Vice-President of Aquatics. It became another outreach effort, away from our downtown facility, into the community, which had become a priority for the YMCA .

We were also permitted to use the slalom course one or two weekends monthly if we made proper arrangements through the Firefighters Association. So we were set. We were now conducting adult and youth kayaking classes at the YMCA, running frequent weekend river cruises through the auspices of our new Asheville YMCA Kayak Club, and operating a slalom course. But I still had a lot more to learn about the sport, so I headed north.

*****

"Spread your hands wider apart and keep your elbows higher," shouted Jerry, one of my instructors, as I struggled to maneuver my kayak through the slalom gates on the Madawaska River in northern Ontario. I had come to Canada to spend a week at the Madawaska Kanu Camp, owned and operated by Hermann and Christa Kerckhoff. A number of last-minute "pressures" at home almost kept me from making the trip and then prevented me from concentrating completely on my paddling after I arrived. But while my kayaking wasn't up to par, I enjoyed myself at MKC.

Situated in a wilderness area near the Algonquin Provincial Park and a l-o-n-g 22-hour drive from Asheville, the Madawaska Kanu Camp was internationally recognized and attracted participants from around the world. Traveling alone, I was weary when I got there, what with the problems back home weighing me down and the fact that we were having a gas shortage in the U.S. I encountered great difficulty keeping my tank filled as I made the northern trek.

Nonetheless the camaraderie of the group at MKC helped rejuvenate me. There were 33 of us adult kayakers on hand, 17 classified as beginners and 16, myself included, as intermediates. Those of us in the intermediate section were further divided into three smaller classes, each with its own instructor. In my class were:

* Jim, a professional photographer from Wisconsin, a big-water kayaker adept at surfing, with a super roll.

* Bob, a university professor from Missouri, also a big-water kayaker, with many previous trips to western rivers.

* George, an orthopedic surgeon from Toronto, in his fourth year at MKC, with strong strokes and a pleasant personality.

* Paul, a young IBM trainee from Toronto, having returned recently from a rugged Outward Bound program, with more enthusiasm than experience in kayaking.

* Mike, a young outdoorsman from Ottawa, who possessed great expertise in open canoeing and a desire to improve his kayaking competence.

Although I was progressing nicely on my own path to paddling proficiency, I felt I would be hard-pressed to keep up with my five classmates, particularly since I was the oldest, at 46. After I had won the Masters race on the Nantahala, I'd been included in an article in the Citizen-Times which was headlined "Adults Can Participate in Athletics at Any Age." The concept of Masters competition for adults was just gaining national popularity, and the article said, "The average adult used to sit and cheer while his or her youngsters competed in athletic events. Not any longer. More and more older adults are participating in Masters competition. Participants range in age from 25 to 90. The sport can be anything from swimming to powerlifting. Each sport has its own age requirements…

"Most Masters athletes compete in the sport in which they excelled when they were younger, said Chuck Hines, Vice-President of the Asheville YMCA and a specialist in aquatics. A former All-America water poloist and already a Masters champion in swimming, Hines tackled whitewater kayaking when he was 43. He admitted it isn't easy learning a sport when you're older, but that it's fun, healthy, and challenging."

The article also reported on two other Masters athletes, Debbie Robinson and Dr. Kemp Battle.

The article then concluded with comments from Carl Mumpower, a YMCA member and friend of mine. "According to Mumpower, a psychologist with the Asheville Counseling Center, there are several reasons why older adults return to sports. He said that we as a society are losing the fables and fantasies about growing old. We no longer believe that as you age, your body fades away whether you like it or not, and that you have a decreasing energy level. Mumpower said we are now heading in a more realistic direction, which he sees as a nice trend."

Returning to the Madawaska Kanu Camp, our initial instructor was Jerry, from Cleveland, Ohio, who was a technician, one who was interested primarily in the "technicalities" of the sport. He helped improve my forward stroke, my sweep stroke, and my left-side duffek stroke. To do this, he had us working endless hours in the slalom gates. None of us had small and sleek slalom racing kayaks. We were all using cruising-style boats. So it was difficult squeezing through the slalom gates.

Be that as it may, I appreciated Jerry's efforts, which were supplemented on two occasions by another instructor. He was Norbert Sattler, from Austria, who had been the world champion in K-1 or men's slalom. Three other world-class slalom racers were at MKC: Canadian Claudia Kerckhoff and Austrian Peter Fauster and American Linda Harrison, whom I knew from her visit to Asheville.

Apart from our morning and afternoon paddling practices, the week at camp was enjoyable. We had a choice of staying in a dormitory, which I did, or outside in tents. The weather was warm and comfortable. The food was superb. But there was a shortage of water, which became a major inconvenience, and an abundance of annoying black flies.

Overshadowing everything, in my opinion, was the camaraderie and fellowship. I benefited immensely from meeting so many fine men and women and from sharing ideas and experiences. While this book is about kayaking and being on the river and weaving through the waves and into the surging rapids, which is the sport's main attraction, I must say that the participants help make it such a wonderful activity.

Two afternoons, upon completion of our slalom practicing, we left the gates and went upriver to Staircase Rapid. This was a long, challenging Class III, over a couple of drops into big holes and then down a very narrow tongue into a cascade of four-foot waves. Running straight through was tough enough, but we were asked to catch eddies on both sides of the river as we made our way down.

The first time we tried it, Bob was the only one to catch the very evasive eddy on the right side. I caught an easier eddy on the left side. George and Mike missed all the eddies but paddled through the rapid safely. Jim, supposedly the big-water man with the never-fail roll, dived into a deep hole and flipped and came up swimming. Paul also took a swim. The second time, the water level was higher, making it even more difficult. George was the only one to catch the eddy on the right side. The rest of us caught easier eddies farther down. No one swam.

On our last day, we did more river-running. We had a choice of visiting the Class III-IV Petawawa River or doing the Class II Palmer Rapids. Of the 33 adult students, 13 of us chose the Petawawa, which flows leisurely through the Algonquin Provincial Park, providing an easy and scenic cruise for open canoeists. But as it moves eastward, the river's characteristics change. At the put-in, just below a railroad bridge, we discovered a 10-foot waterfall. "This is a worrisome way to start a trip!" exclaimed Nick, and the rest of us nodded. "Don't worry," laughed Jerry. "We are NOT running the waterfall."

However, the rapid immediately below the waterfall quickly caught our attention. It was a quarter-mile long and a definite Class IV. The put-in was so splashy and churning that just getting over the eddy-line and into the main flow would be difficult. The eddy-line, caused by the washout from the waterfall, was a foot high. Once making it from the eddy into the rushing river, there were two possible paths, one a sneak route along the right bank with occasional eddies, the other a mad dash down the middle through three- and four-foot waves and around big boulders and hidden holes.

Jim, from Wisconsin, was the first to go, and he looked good until suddenly flipping. But he rolled up and continued downriver, passing from sight. Others followed, some sneaking down the right side and some maneuvering through the mid-river maelstrom. Finally it was my turn. I muscled my way out of the eddy and felt the swift swells catch my Perception Spirit and propel it forward. It was an up and down ride. I was swept sideways over a five-foot ledge into a waist-deep hole. I leaned downstream and braced, feeling torrents of water ravaging my body and my boat. Gradually, oh so gradually, I worked my way backwards out of the hole into calmer water, breathing a sigh of relief and inwardly applauding my performance.

When I reached an eddy farther along, instructor Jerry said, "I thought you were going over for sure, but you handled it well." Others were less fortunate. Paul came swimming past us, as half of our group of 13 took unwanted swims.

The next two miles saw us paddling through a series of Class II-III rapids, having fun, but as the river disappeared around a bend, George said, "Here's the next big one. Lover's Rapid." We eddied out and scouted. It was a big one indeed. Short. But the water cascaded downward into a washing-machine of four- and five-foot waves. It reminded me of Bull Sluice on the Chattooga River, but with larger waves at the bottom. A Class IV+. At higher levels, probably a Class V. So I decided to walk around. My boat was leaking, and at the end of a week of strenuous paddling, I was tired.

Several others also walked around, and we sat together and watched as Jim, Bob, Brenda, George, Charlene, Paul, Russ, and Mike tried their luck. Three made it through cleanly, including the two ladies. No surprise there. This is a sport in which the women can do as well as the men, if not better. Two others flipped but rolled up. Three ended up swimming. Mike, the young outdoorsman from Ottawa, plunged into the washing-machine at the wrong angle, vanished into the foam, and reappeared doing a spectacular rear ender. His boat jutted skyward, then collapsed back into the froth. Upsidedown, he tried several times to roll, but failed. The instructors went to his rescue. I went to retrieve his paddle, 200 yards downriver. Later he said, "I really got slammed. If I hadn't been wearing a good life-jacket, I would have had some broken ribs, for sure."

After easing through a series of Class IIs, we reached Swimmers Rapid, the last one, a Class III with some good spots for surfing. We stayed there for an hour, playing, before loading up and returning to the Madawaska Kanu Camp.

The next day, with a couple of Canadians as passengers, I departed from MKC and drove to Toronto, where they gave me a three-hour tour of the city. I had been to other communities in Canada while coaching YMCA water polo teams – Montreal, Quebec City, Winnipeg – but this was my first time in Toronto. Then my friends bid me adieu, and I aimed my aging Buick in the direction of home in Western North Carolina.

It was a 22-hour drive, allowing me ample time to reflect on my week at MKC. It had been a good change of pace, which I needed, and I had thoroughly enjoyed the company of the paddlers I had met. I'd improved my skills. I was now ready to put the finishing touches on the new YMCA whitewater curriculum and work harder with our Y kaYak kids. Life was good.

Chapter Four

"Where's your helmet, Darrell?"

"I dunno."

"Find it and put it on."

"Awwwww," the 12-year-old boy grumbled. But 10 minutes later, he was fully outfitted and pushing off into the slow current. Five other 12-, 13- and 14-year-olds joined him, and we set off on our seven-mile trip down Section Two of the Chattooga River. Sam Fowlkes was leading the way. Tall, lithe, bearded, and athletic, Sam was paddling a C-1, or decked canoe, the same boat in which he had won a race recently on the Nantahala. The rest of us were in kayaks.

We had hired Sam to help us with our Asheville YMCA youth program, making sure it met the standards of the American Canoe Association. It was comforting to have a paddler of such talent up front. The six youngsters followed – Darrell and Deanna Davis, Tandy Beck, Brian Finny, Karen Miller, Amy Pruett – and were given directions from time to time by Will Pruett.

Jim Maynor and I brought up the rear. Jim had been in one of our first adult kayaking courses. He had been the "star" of the class, and he'd returned soon thereafter and asked if he could help teach others. I was surprised, but pleased. Every YMCA relies heavily on volunteers, who serve on various boards and committees and assist with the wide variety of programs. Jim was a wiry fellow, still single at the age of 34, who drove a truck for a living. Not the type you'd think would want to teach others.

But Jim had proven to be a tremendous asset to our Y kayaking. He was very good at teaching other adults, patient and personable, and he knew his stuff – he could demonstrate all the techniques and critique others as they learned. He was very safety-conscious. He was on his way to becoming a terrific wildwater racer, winning many events and ranking as one of the "top 5" in the country in that category of competition.

Jim also started helping out with our YMCA kaYak kids on their river excursions. On this day, he and I found ourselves lazing along as we paddled down the Chattooga. The water was running abnormally high for that time of the year, at 2.4 on the gauge, but the section we were running was not difficult. Tomorrow, I realized, we'd have to suck it up when we did Section Three with a YMCA adult group, but today would be a breeze.

The Chattooga heads up in the higher mountains of Western North Carolina and then flows southward, forming the border between South Carolina and Georgia. Depending on the amount of rain, the water level can vary from .5 to 3.5 or higher, and a level of 2.4 was considered ideal. Without much effort, we followed Sam through several Class II rapids, all comprised of chutes that plummeted over two- and three-foot ledges into fields of small standing waves. The youngsters were good at following a competent leader, but soon we'd be challenging them to pick their own routes down the river.

I hung back, chatting with a group of young married couples from a South Carolina city who were paddling open canoes. For most of them, it was their first time on moving water, and wisely they had hired an experienced guide. Even so, they remained cautious. I observed that the teamwork between their bow (front) and stern (rear) paddlers was not very coordinated.

Up ahead, the river disappeared over a wide ledge, and I watched as our group stopped at a mammoth mid-stream boulder to scout. One by one, they lifted their boats out. I joined them, and from the boulder we could see a jumbled mass of rocks extending across the river from one side to the other. There was one passage on the left, maybe a Class III. There was another passage on the right, definitely a Class IV. We dismissed the latter as being too tough for the youngsters, but we urged them all to try the Class III rather than carrying around.

They were hesitant. The rapid required a well-planned approach down a three-foot chute into a three-foot curling wave, through that and over a three-foot dead-drop ledge into a series of smaller waves, and then a sharp eddy turn to avoid hitting some overhanging branches.

Sam ran this rapid with ease. The kids remained reluctant. I ran it next and with my usual skill angled awkwardly into the curler, punched through it, plunged over the ledge with no finesse whatsoever, and did a sloppy turn into the eddy. There I sat while Will, still sitting on the boulder with the kids, gave them his best pep talk. Whatever he said must have worked, because moments later Deanna came sailing through and then Amy, Brian, Karen, Tandy, and Darrell. All hit the chute right on target, swept down, and eddied out. Super!

When Will joined us, I ferried over to him and asked, "What did you say to motivate the kids?"

He looked at me and smiled and stroked his beard. Finally he said, "I told them that if *you* could run it, so could they." We both chuckled.

Sam carried his C-1 back up and crossed to the extreme right side of the river and came hurtling down the Class IV. There was a big hydraulic, or hole, at the bottom which caught him, but he braced, braced hard, and was thrown free. He lifted his eyebrows in half joking, half serious relief.

The remainder of Section Two offered additional Class II rapids. Sam and Jim did a lot of playing, while Will and I continued to coach the kids, urging them to practice their surfing skills. Deanna and Amy were the only two who really stuck the noses of their kayaks into the foam, however, and eventually Amy became caught. She was turned sideways and almost overturned, but she maintained a strong downstream lean and worked her way out. Her dad, Will, clapped his hands in approval.

As I wrote in a later report, Section Two can be paddled by just about any canoeist or kayaker with some experience in easy rapids. It is very scenic, and when the water level is 2.4 or close to it, the current clips along at a reasonable rate. The rapids are Class II, except at the one major ledge across the river, and anyone not wishing to try the Class IV on the right side or the Class III on the left can simply walk over the ledge. The remaining rapids offer ample opportunities for eddy-hopping, ferrying, and surfing. The seven-mile distance can take anywhere from two to four hours.

The take-out for Section Two, as you'd expect, is also the put-in for Section Three, which is more difficult. It has a bunch of Class III and IV rapids and concludes with Bull Sluice, a Class IV, which on the Sunday that we were there with a YMCA adult group was a 10-foot plunge into a deep hydraulic. Sam Fowlkes ran it in his C-1, flipped, and fought his way upright again. Charles White ran it in his Perception Quest and looked very smooth. Then Rick McGinnis, probably the best kayaker in our YMCA program at that time, displayed his amazing ability by running Bull Sluice *backwards*, without blinking an eye. The rest of us shook our heads in admiration.

It had been a highly-successful weekend for our YMCA contingent. We'd had a good youth trip on Saturday and a good time with the adults on Sunday. In-between, some of us spent the night in the small Georgia town of Clayton, eating dinner at a restaurant that served us a heaping family-style meal – salad, three meats, two veggies, rice, hot biscuits with apple butter, a choice of beverages, dessert – AND ALL YOU COULD EAT OF IT – for $5.95. Of course, that was in 1979. Have things improved since then? What do *you* think??

*****

There was much apprehension amongst our six youthful kayakers as we drove from Asheville to Burnsville and then onward to a remote corner of Mitchell County in the mountains of Western North Carolina. Our destination was the Toe River Gorge, a challenging stretch of water decorated by hundreds of medium-sized rocks and boulders, requiring "technical" maneuvering.

School had started and now, in mid-September, this was our last scheduled youth trip of the year. With Will Pruett's van and Doug Brook's Toyota providing transportation, and with nine kayaks on top and six 12-, 13- and 14-year-olds squeezed inside, we eased over the narrow and hilly mountain roads to the site of our adventure.

The Toe Gorge lay sparkling beneath the bright autumn sun. As Will and Doug shuttled, our six kaYak kids slid their boats down a steep incline and scrambled after them, clad in helmets, life-jackets and spray-skirts, and clutching their twin-bladed paddles. One by one, they entered a calm patch of water beneath a big bridge. The first one out was Karen Miller, 13, who already owned a reliable pool roll on both sides. She was a Southeastern champion in age group swimming, having joined Sidney Bradfield, Heidi Jones, and my daughter Heather Hines to win the 200-yard medley relay in the girls 13-14 competition at the Southeasterns held at Oak Ridge, Tennessee, in the spring of 1979. With Mary Walton replacing Heidi, they repeated as champions in 1980.

Karen and Sidney and Heather also played water polo and were progressing in the sport of whitewater kayaking. As Vice-President of Aquatics for the Asheville YMCA, I aimed at three accomplishments. First, I wanted us to have the best all-around aquatic program in our area. It was my opinion that we were doing this. Second, I wanted us to have one activity in which we would be the best among all YMCAs in the entire United States. We had achieved this goal in the 1970s with our winning water polo teams. Now we were hoping to become tops in the 1980s with our paddling program.

Third, I wanted our various aquatic endeavors to have a religious content, to be based on the YMCA's philosophy of improving each person's body, mind, and *spirit*. For our pool programs, we usually had a devotional planned once weekly, and many of our youngsters were doing a yearly service project to benefit others. In the newsletters I mailed out to participating families, there was almost always a reference to the Y's Judeo-Christian principles.

Now, going out to the rivers, I had to come up with other ideas. On this day, I asked the youngsters to pick up sticks from the river and river bank and shape them into makeshift crosses and to think about what this might mean to them. We kept doing this from time to time on future trips and once or twice asked the kids to share their thoughts, their religious beliefs and commitments, with the rest of us. My friend Will Pruett, who eventually would sell his successful computer business and become a minister for the Methodist Church, was continually prodding me to remember the spiritual part of our kayaking program.

Back on the Toe Gorge, Karen was joined by Deanna and Darrell Davis, Brian Finney, Tandy Beck, and Will's daughter, Amy. They formed a colorful brigade of boats – red, blue, green, yellow, white, and orange. After a brief warm-up, consisting of easy ferrying, we headed down the river. Will and Doug led the way, and I trailed behind. The water level was low, and we wound our way through continuing rock gardens, over ledges, and down small chutes, paddling not so much swiftly as carefully in our breakable fiberglass kayaks. I saw a couple of the kids reaching out and picking up floating sticks and fashioning them into crosses, as I had asked, and I hoped this would produce some meaningful results.

Halfway down the Gorge, we stopped, and all the youngsters deliberately SWAM down several Class II rapids, on their backs, with feet up and arms outstretched. This was the proper way to do it whenever you flipped, failed to roll, and ended up swimming. We wanted to make sure the kids were able to do it ... just in case. There had been reports of a few paddlers drowning on various rivers when they became swimmers and tried to stand up in the rapids. Their feet became caught in submerged rocks that held them firmly, and the current pushed their heads underwater, and they drowned. So we were teaching our YMCA youngsters this important "lifesaving" skill.

After 40 minutes of swim practicing, we continued kayaking down the river, coming to the one tough rapid of the day, a Class III at best. I ran the rapid and then parked in an eddy on the right side of the river, taking out my trusty 8mm camera to film the proceedings. Will came next, breezing through the three drops, doing a dandy duffek, and eddying out on the opposite side of the river from me. Deanna was almost as nifty until she bumped over the last drop and carelessly drifted with the current into some boulders. "Sloppy!" I shouted at her.

Karen and Brian bounced off the same boulders and joined Deanna farther downstream. "Not good!" Will yelled at them. Our attention was drawn back to the rapid, through which Doug was making a fancy run. He did a draw at exactly the right place, duffeked at the bottom, and joined Will in the eddy. "Very nice," I whispered to myself.

Darrell was paddling weakly, barely pulling at all, not in control of his boat, and he caromed off a rock and slid backwards down the final drop, coming to a stop there and completely blocking the passageway for Amy, who was behind him. Fortunately, Amy WAS in control, and when she saw Darrell's boat blocking her way, she quickly swept out to the left and turned her kayak into the seldom-used right side of the drop, squeezing down a narrow chute. It was a skillful maneuver, and maybe it took a bit of luck, but Amy made it happen.

Tandy, bringing up the rear, was as hesitant as always. She neglected to stroke or draw or brace or do anything else except ride the waves, which pushed her into the big boulder at the end. She flipped, bailed out, and then did something correctly – she demonstrated the right way to swim, on her back, with feet raised and arms outstretched. I guess our swimming lesson had been worthwhile.

There were more rocky Class II rapids as we hustled down the river, and we had to pick our way through. It took continuing concentration. Darrell was the only one to encounter difficulty. While trying to surf at a small ledge, he overturned, exited his boat, and was swept downstream for 50 yards. He too exhibited correct and safe swimming ability, as Tandy had done. I was pleased.

It was late afternoon by the time we reached the take-out, and we feasted on fried chicken and soft drinks. Eventually we began loading up for the drive back to Asheville.

"The kids did well," Will commented, as he started hoisting kayaks onto the top of his van.

"They certainly did," Doug agreed.

"Better than expected," I added.

"Deanna was really smooth," said Doug.

"Amy, too," I stated.

"Hey, you guys," frowned hard-working Will, "how about giving me some help with these boats?"

"Karen was classy," Doug continued.

"Brian and Darrell showed some potential for 12-year-olds," I said.

"Tandy's also coming along," Doug declared, although he may have been stretching it a bit.

"Hey, you guys…" sputtered Will, carrying kayaks on both shoulders, balancing paddles on his head, holding spray-skirts beneath his arms, and kicking helmets across the ground toward his van.

Doug and I smiled at each other. It was pleasant watching Will work so hard, especially at the end of an enjoyable day of whitewater paddling, made even more satisfactory by the fact that we had helped some of the YMCA's youngsters expand their horizons and gain more experience on the Toe River Gorge.

*****

We huddled in a small circle, squinting into the sprinkle of rain, answering to a roll call and receiving our numbered bibs. Danny Pyatt was there from Raleigh. Lee Reading was there from Brevard. So was Steve Thomas from Atlanta. And Doug Cameron from somewhere in Tennessee. I looked at the other whitewater kayak competitors and wondered what I was doing there, with such an elite group, preparing for the Nantahala Outdoor Center's 1979 Thanksgiving Weekend slalom race.

Along with Danny, Lee, Steve, and Doug, there were three dozen others representing most of the Southern states. "It's a smaller field of contestants than we expected, but a good one," said Linda Aponte of NOC, who was not only directing the race but also competing herself.

Surrounded by the other athletes, I stumbled down the path to the water's edge. Bending over my Perception Spirit kayak, I fumbled with the foot pegs inside. Out of the corner of one eye, I watched the experts squeezing into their sleek, needle-nosed, gate-sneaking, low-volume racing kayaks. I'm getting good enough, I told myself, to try the swift, small, unstable racing boats next year. But on this day I was entered in the K-1 Cruising Class, for those of us using the somewhat larger boats.

Wasn't it in the Cruising Class that I had performed so poorly in another slalom race a few months previously? Who would show up today, the Masters winner or the Cruising Class loser? We would see.

"Get it on, dad," shouted my 13-year-old daughter Heather from the cliff above. A promising young paddler, she and our other Asheville YMCA youngsters were currently involved in the Y's indoor competitive swimming program. We would get them back into their boats and on the rivers in a few months. I had been the coach of the YMCA swimming and water polo teams since arriving in Asheville 10 years ago, in 1969. Over that period of time, our Y swimmers had posted a commendable record of 80 victories, eight losses, and one tie in their dual and triangular meets. Our water poloists had done even better, winning a number of national championships. Our Y girls had brought home the Gold medal from the Junior Olympics and then had represented the Eastern U.S. at the World Women's Water Polo Club Championships, finishing fifth despite being the youngest team there.

There wasn't much more we could accomplish in water polo. I was becoming "burned out" on the sport. So in 1976, when the YMCA's National Physical Education Management Team sent me a letter about "designing a physical education program that appeals to the adventurous nature of youth, preferably an activity that can be done outdoors," I was ready for the challenge and set out to develop a new Y kayaking curriculum. Over the past three years, I'd personally advanced from being a bumbling beginner on the river to being a … well, we'd see today exactly how much I had improved.

No guts, no glory, I muttered the popular phrase to myself as I lowered my 6', 185-pound frame into my kayak. As always, the water of the Nantahala was icy cold. I was prepared for it, but nonetheless my fingers quickly became chilled, numbed, as I swept my paddle back and forth, pulling upstream toward gate No. 1 for a practice run.

The 20-gate course had been laid out on a lower section of the Nantahala River, just below the Class V Wesser Falls. We didn't have to run Wesser, but the first three gates were right at the foot of the Falls, amidst the turmoil of the cascading water, with tricky cross-currents. Not easy, especially with the two days of rain bringing the river level up, Up, UP. I worked the three-gate sequence at the foot of the Falls once. Twice. Then I continued down the course. The water became smoother, less difficult, but the gates were tight, tough. I banged a bunch of them before reaching the bottom, where I eddied out and rested.

Concentrate, I told myself. If I can concentrate and the rain doesn't pick up again, I'll be okay. I paddled upstream and found my place in the long line of racers near the starting point. I took off my helmet, readjusted my bib, and sat quietly, closing my eyes and running the course mentally. It was called "visualization." I'll need a brace there, then a pivot, then a strong stroke to the left… Suddenly it was my turn. I jammed on my helmet and lurched forward. The adrenaline pumped through my body. Five. Four. Three. Two. One. GO!

With my right-hand blade I dug in, easing through upstream gate No. 1. Ferrying across the swirling current, I caught the eddy perfectly and muscled into gate No. 2, pulling hard, HARD, driving the bow of my boat into the pulsating deluge at the bottom of Wesser Falls. Momentarily I was yanked even closer to the downpour. It was a dangerous position but a necessity for lining up for the next gate. The current caught my stern, and with a brace I maneuvered backwards through reverse gate No. 3, clearing it successfully but losing my concentration briefly as I heard my wife and daughter and a few friends cheering me on.

Then downriver. Precision paddling. Controlled speed. Man, I missed that gate completely. Can't afford a 50-second penalty. I swung around, powered back upstream, and passed through the gate I had missed. It cost me 10 seconds to do so, maybe 15, but it was better than picking up a 50. Sweat was forming on my brow, running down my face, steaming up my eye-glasses. Both arms were aching. My breath was coming in short gasps. The end was in sight. One more gate to go, a tricky upstream, designed to catch the weary, the careless. I was tired but made sure I was extra careful, and I sneaked through, turned, and stroked hard across the finish line. Whew. What a relief.

"How'd you do?" asked Lee Reading, who had preceded me.

"Fine," I panted, "but I think I touched three poles."

"Your time, Chuck," shouted the timer from riverside, "was 2:46."

"How does that measure up?"

"Some of the fastest racing boats are finishing in the 2:20s, but nobody's clean. Everyone's taking a few penalties. It's a surprisingly tough course."

Half an hour later, I took my second run. I concentrated hard, and I was five seconds faster. I emptied the water out of my kayak and walked up the path alongside the river, joining my wife and daughter to watch the final K-1s and K-1Ws complete their second runs. As we watched, two of the kayakers, one from Florida and the other from Mississippi, flipped in the cross-current below Wesser Falls. Both swam their way down the frigid river.

"They should've rolled," I told Lee and Heather, remembering how one of our YMCA youngsters, Sidney Bradfield, had rolled at that same spot during one of our summertime practices. As I said it, the open canoeists started their category of competition, and the first one dumped at the Falls and swam. This was turning into a swim meet.

"Well, dad," laughed my daughter, "you're not the worst one here."

I wasn't the best, either. The results, posted later, showed me being the fastest Masters (40 and older) kayak racer, which was unofficial as there was no separate Masters category at this event, and officially placing third in the Men's Cruising Class and seventh overall, counting those who competed in the sleek, swifter racing boats.

"Not bad for an old man," said Lee Reading, pointing a congratulatory finger in my direction.

Yes, it had been a good day. Despite the inclement weather, I had enjoyed the competition and benefited from the exercise. I had renewed old friendships while spending the weekend with my wife and daughter in God's Great Outdoors. Together we had dined at NOC's riverside restaurant. What more could anyone ask?

Chapter Five

In March of 1980, an article appeared in the Asheville Citizen-Times. It said, "YMCA kayak coaches and instructors from Georgia, Tennessee, Indiana, Illinois, Ohio, Wisconsin, South Carolina, and North Carolina will be attending a whitewater institute Saturday and Sunday at the Asheville YMCA...

"The purpose of the institute is to study the latest instructional methods, with special attention being given to the use of YMCA pools for teaching beginning kayakers. Time also will be devoted to classroom instruction and on-the-river techniques...

"The institute is the culmination of a three-year project of the YMCA's National Physical Education Management Team, which in 1976 asked Asheville YMCA aquatic specialist Chuck Hines to develop a kayak curriculum that can be used by YMCAs around the country for teaching the sport...

"Hines' curriculum has been developed with the assistance of whitewater experts from the nearby Nantahala Outdoor Center and several local kayakers. An article about the Asheville YMCA kayaking curriculum has been published recently in 'The Journal of Physical Education.'"

So there we were, 18 of us from eight states, on the second day of the YMCA institute, and...

The wind caught the smoke and pushed it in my direction, and my eyes watered momentarily. I backed away from the small fire, sacrificing its warmth for a taste of cool, wet, sweet spring air. The water in the river beside us bubbled busily, and I glanced upstream at the Class III rapid we had just encountered. Its deep hole had provided some of the best paddlers in our group with an opportunity for surfing and one or two enders. It also had torn off the spray-skirt from Jim Maynor's boat, and Jim, a crack kayaker with a very reliable river roll, had taken a rare swim down the icy current.

We were back on the Toe River Gorge, six months after we'd been there with some of our YMCA youngsters. This time it was a band of brothers, 18 of us men, who were working together to become the first certified instructors in the Y's new kayaking program. The early spring rainstorms had brought river levels in the area to exciting heights. The Toe was at least a foot higher than it had been on our previous visit with the kaYak kids. The weather was quite a bit cooler, with the air temperature and water temperature both registering 51 degrees. The wind whistling down the gorge caused the chill factor to drop even lower.

Much lower, I muttered to myself, as I stood near the fire. Nevertheless we were enjoying ourselves immensely. After a full day in the Asheville YMCA classroom and pool, it was refreshing to be back on the river, even though our trip leader, Ray McLain from the Green Bay YMCA in Wisconsin, was a tough taskmaster. Ray was one of the American Canoe Association's finest instructors, and he was making sure those of us hoping to become certified as YMCA instructors were fully qualified.

So this was no casual cruise. It already had taken us more than two hours to run just the first two miles, as we practiced and played our way through a continuing series of Class II and III rapids. Not only had we covered on-the-river teaching techniques for scouting, eddy-hopping, ferrying, and surfing, but Ray also had made arrangements for one of the participants, Willis Simpson, to deliberately come out of his boat and take a swim. This would test the reactions of those nearest to him. I wasn't in the immediate vicinity when Willis pulled his stunt, but later he said that he'd swallowed more than a small amount of water while swimming through three-foot waves before being pulled ashore.

Now, as we gathered around the fire, it was question-and-answer time. Bob Wahl, a student from Miami University in Ohio and the son of veteran paddler Heinz Wahl of Fort Wayne, Indiana, was asking about using a roll "to escape from a keeper hole." Another collegian, Chris Lechner, a pre-med student at Indiana University, where he was a star swimmer, was responding to the question. Chris had just demonstrated a hands-only roll on the river, bringing smiles of admiration from all the onlookers, especially those of us whose college days were long past.

Author's Note: Chris Lechner moved to Asheville several years later and is now, as I write this, a practicing physician here in town. He once performed a surgical operation on my wife's hand. His children are on the Asheville YMCA swimming squad.

Back on the Toe Gorge, I told Mike King that "I don't even want to think about hitting those holes today, much less throwing away my paddle and doing a hands-only roll." Mike, a soft-spoken Georgian who had coached many state champion swimmers and thus could appreciate Chris Lechner's dual talents in the pool and on the river, nodded a quiet assent.

Still, there were paddlers in our group who willingly dug the bows of their boats into the deepest holes and hydraulics, the best of whom were the Asheville YMCA's Rick McGinnis and Jim Maynor and Tennessean Tommy Parham and the Wisconsin tandem team of Ray McLain and Donny Percy, who were paddling a C-2, or two-man decked canoe.

We doused the fire, sanded it, and re-entered our boats, ready to attack the final rapids of the Toe Gorge. As I started paddling again, my eyeglasses fogged up, and I wheeled into a small eddy where, fumbling with frozen fingers, I accidentally let my paddle blade dip into the swirling current. I flipped. Wow! It was too cold to think. Automatically I swept out with my paddle and popped up. My glasses were now clear. But my mind was foggy.

Luckily, the remaining rapids were all Class IIs, with maybe one being a III, none as difficult as those we'd encountered upstream. I settled into an easy pace to conserve strength, chatting with Russ Oldfather, who had organized one of the leading YMCA kayak and canoe clubs in the country at Elkhart, Indiana. Before long, we reached the take-out, and one by one we shouldered our boats up the hill to the waiting vans and cars. As we began loading up, the sun peeked out. "You're too late!" I shouted at it. Chagrined, the sun quickly hid again behind the thick grey clouds.

It had been a good two days. Chris Skjold spoke for all of us when he wrote a letter later, saying, "We thought it was a huge success, and we are looking forward to continuing progress with the YMCA's new kayaking program."

I wrote a more formal report for the YMCA's National Physical Education Management Team, which read, "We had a very successful kayak instructors institute here in Asheville, attended by 18 participants from North and South Carolina, Georgia, Tennessee, Ohio, Indiana, Illinois, and Wisconsin. Several of the visiting paddlers arrived early so they could go out on our various WNC rivers…

"After spending Saturday in the YMCA classroom and pool, evaluating the kayaking curriculum which we have developed in Asheville, we gathered for a devotional on Sunday morning and then headed out to the Toe River Gorge. There we exchanged teaching techniques and covered such items as trip planning, shuttling, scouting, eddying, peeling out, ferrying, surfing, rolling, and rescuing…

"As we progressed downriver, we paddled our way through two- and three-foot waves, deep holes, tricky cross-currents, and boiling eddies. The cool conditions and a powerful wind made this a challenging and exciting trip. The 18 participants who all successfully completed the weekend institute have been presented certificates for becoming YMCA kayaking instructors. This is a definite FIRST for our organization."

*****

We had done all we could do, at least for the moment, when it came to developing this new YMCA program. We had spent three years working on it, and I had written an article about it for "The Journal of Physical Education," which was one of the YMCA's national publications. We had held an institute to certify our initial instructors. Now it was the PEMT's turn to do whatever was necessary to make the program truly national in scope.

We were free to do our own thing when it came to kayaking at the Asheville YMCA. For me, this meant even more paddling and racing. We were practicing two afternoons weekly at our slalom course on the French Broad River, and my teaching teammates, Will Pruett and Jim Maynor, were stretching their wings. Will won a wildwater race on the Dan River, which took him and the other contestants through four miles of Class II and III rapids. Jim won the Carolina Cup's wildwater competition on the Mayo River, in which over 200 paddlers participated, also paddling through Class II and III rapids.

We sent two of our younger athletes to the Chattahoochee River races in Helen, Georgia. Brent Lawson, 16, and Rick Hensley, 15, took first and second, respectively, in the K-1 junior slalom. Their positions were reversed the next day in the downriver sprint, with Rick placing second and Brent fourth.

Closer to home, I was working with the Buncombe County Parks and Recreation Department to conduct a first-ever event, the Southern Regional Special Olympics Canoe Races. These were held on the French Broad River. There were 28 competitors from North and South Carolina, Tennessee, and Mississippi. The newspaper gave this event excellent coverage and concluded a lengthy article by asking, "Who won? Well, this is a Special Olympics story, and as they say, everyone is a winner, and the winners were announced at a banquet held at Skyland Recreation Center with all the trimmings. Table cloths and floral arrangements highlighted every table. After dinner, a dance topped off the festivities. No one went home disappointed."

I was facing a decision, several decisions, in fact, and I didn't want to disappoint myself by making a wrong choice. I'd been offered step-up-the-ladder and better-paying jobs by a large YMCA in another state, by a small but booming YMCA in a different North Carolina city, and by a non-Y organization here in Asheville. I visited the YMCA in the other state, which happened to be in New Orleans, and I considered the YMCA opportunity elsewhere in North Carolina, which happened to be in Hendersonville, and I thought seriously about the non-Y possibility, which was with a popular private club in town.

I also thought about going to work for the Nantahala Outdoor Center, which was in the process of blossoming into the world's best outdoor education and recreation organization, and I talked with NOC's co-founder and president, Payson Kennedy. I liked working with the NOC people, and I absolutely loved visiting NOC's expanding campus about 70 miles from Asheville.

After much thought and prayer, I decided to stay put with the YMCA in Asheville. As I've stated previously, the Y was my calling in life, my career, my profession. In addition, my wife Lee and daughter Heather wanted to remain in Asheville, and who could blame them? Lastly, whitewater kayaking was becoming a vital part of my life and my lifestyle, and this played an important role in my decision.

Author's Note: Throughout my life, from childhood through adulthood, I've had an approach to my athletic activities that's fivefold. First, I become interested in a sport and read about it. Second, I learn to do the sport reasonably well. Third, I compete in the sport, usually with success. Fourth, I teach and coach the sport, frequently producing champions. Fifth, I write about the sport. You know what? I'm still doing this at the age of 75.

*****

Puddles of water decorated the roadside ditches. "The river's gotta be up," insisted Burt Butler, "after the heavy rain of last night." And the equally heavy rain of the night before, and the night before that, I added silently.

Still, we remained unsure of what we'd find. Several other paddlers had been pessimistic and had taken off for another river, the Obed in northern Tennessee. But we had decided to take our chances on the Conasauga, and here we were, approaching the Georgia border in extreme southern Tennessee, where the Conasauga wanders back and forth from state to state as it winds its way down the Cohutta Mountains.

A report we had received from a friend told us "the Conasauga is a beautiful river, mainly Class II ledges and boulder fields, with a couple of rapids that might be classified as IIIs. The water quality is exceptional, and the water is often crystal clear." In addition, I had read in the new text, Canoeing and Kayaking Guide to the Streams of Tennessee, that "this is an absolutely superb river run, a beautiful expression of Nature's bounty."

Burt, our leader for this YMCA-sponsored trip, came to a sudden halt on the backwoodsy road and pointed to the right. "That path leads to the take-out. Let's go for a look." He and his wife Diane, who form a fine tandem canoeing team, led the way. I followed expectantly. Behind us came Pete Raboin and Ellen Rogers, a couple of Georgians, and a family from Indiana comprised of Max Gilpin, a competent canoeist, and his children, Kathy and Mark, who would be kayaking.

These people and a dozen more from several states had come to YMCA Camp Ocoee in eastern Tennessee, where we were conducting another weekend institute to introduce and promote the new Y kayaking curriculum. After a day of classroom work, we had split into two groups on the second day, one going to the Obed and the other to the Conasauga.

"It's up all right," said Burt impassively. Indeed it was. "It's higher than I've ever seen it," he said. "Should be fun."

Leaving one car at the take-out, we crowded into the two other vehicles and drove up a winding mountain road to the put-in. At one point, we stopped and looked down about 500' to the river valley, chuckling nervously as we watched a pair of men in an aluminum canoe crash into a big boulder and capsize. "Don't laugh," Burt warned us. "That's the start of the toughest section, and it's not easy."

Two hours later, his words came back to haunt us. We had reached the same rapid, following Burt and Diane in their canoe. We had scouted the rapid, which was called Taylors Branch, from riverside, and had discovered it to be a rocky Class III. Disdaining the usual route on the left side, I eddied out behind a huge boulder in mid-river, ferried across to the right, found my path blocked, peeled out down the middle into three-foot waves, and tried my luck cutting back against the strong, splashing current.

It worked well until I reached the rapid's bottom, where the river pushed me broadside into a rock. I leaned downstream, but it was too late. The rushing current upended me, and I was swept swiftly along a shallow ledge, bumping against the bottom with my twin-bladed paddle trapped beneath me. Reluctantly I bailed out. My first swim of the year, I thought disgustedly. Oh, well, everyone swims sooner or later.

"You'll have a chance to redeem yourself later," Burt consoled me. "We have a harder rapid just ahead."

"It's all right," I replied. "My goal is to be the best 47-year-old kayaker on the river each trip I take, and despite my swim, I feel confident I'm going to achieve my goal today."

The two youngsters in our group smiled. "I guess there aren't too many other paddlers your age, are there?" one of them observed brightly.

"Not many," I admitted, "and whenever I see Payson Kennedy of the Nantahala Outdoor Center on a river, I head somewhere else. He happens to be just about my age, and he's a whole lot better than I am, having won numerous national championships."

Such small talk gradually gave way to silence as we neared The Falls, which on that particular day was a definite Class III+. There was a long, technical approach which snared Pete and Ellen in their canoe. It took them two minutes to work their way free. Eddying out on the right bank, we contemplated the lower half of the rapid. To run it, we'd have to angle completely across the river, through two-foot waves and over two ledges, past one rock formation and then around a giant boulder, and into a fast-water chute where a pushy cross-current would make the final turn and dip difficult. The text I had read previously said it was a three-foot chute with a pool below, but that must have been at a normal water level. I could see on this day that it was a five-foot chute with churning waves below.

Max and young Mark decided to walk around. So did Pete and Ellen. I couldn't blame them. But Burt and Diane had run it before at a normal level, and they wanted to give it a try. They shoved off in their canoe, bounced over the ledges, caromed off the rock formation, careened around the big boulder, and plunged into the chute, buffeted from side to side by the cross-current. Only a quick brace by Diane kept them going, and they reached the bottom with a boatload of water. But they'd remained upright.

Kathy, a cute 17-year-old with plenty of pluck, pushed off next in her high-volume kayak. She was in control all the way and made it look easy.

I brought up the rear, and determined to compensate for my earlier swim, I concentrated all the way and breezed through. "Nice run," Burt shouted.

Thereafter we encountered only Class II rapids, and we let Mark, 13, lead the way for a while. Like his older sister, he was competent and oozing with confidence, and I felt their father, Max, deserved credit for introducing them to kayaking at such a young age.

Along the 10-mile route, we ran into a dozen other kayakers and canoeists from Georgia, South Carolina, and Ohio. They all passed us with a wave and a nod. We took our time, playing and having fun. It was quiet and scenic. Satisfying. The sun sparkled. The trout jumped. The leaves at riverside whispered. The river glistened. I glanced down. The bottom was clearly visible five or six feet below. I cupped my hand and grabbed a swallow of fresh water. I leaned back and relaxed, going with the flow.

How much like life the river is, I was thinking. A crisis (rapid) arises and throws you, but you struggle back. You're no quitter. Another crisis (rapid) appears. You overcome this one, earning a rest. You drift along. Life is sweet. But on the horizon looms another crisis (rapid). You can't drift on forever, whether it's life or the river. I sensed the Conasauga's quickening pace. I heard the dull roar ahead. I sat up, tightened my grip, and took a deep breath. I smiled, ready for the next challenge on the river. And in life.

Chapter Six

"YMCA Paddlers Set for Nantahala Races" read the large headline on the sports page of the Citizen-Times. The summer of 1980 had arrived, and we had been asked by our friends at the Nantahala Outdoor Center to conduct a slalom race at their venue. "We're too busy with our rafting activities," said one of NOC's leaders, "but there's still a lot of interest in racing. Could you help us out?"

"We're busy, too," I told them. "We have 500 kids in our summer swimming classes, if you count the day campers we're teaching, and we have our own kayaking and scuba diving programs."

"We'll give you some help," the NOC people said, "if you'll help us." They offered to provide all the necessary equipment plus an Olympic athlete, Carrie Ashton, to work with me and our other Asheville YMCA representatives.

"Okay," I finally consented. "Let's do it."

I had directed hundreds of small swim meets and dozens of larger water polo tournaments, several of them international in scope, while working for the YMCA, so I wasn't overly concerned about organizing a slalom race. How hard could it be? As usual, I underestimated the problems involved.

We hurriedly gathered together our resources, and after spending two weeks cajoling every Asheville paddler I knew into coming to help as boat inspectors and gate judges and timers and everything else, we seemed prepared to host the race in mid-summer on the Nantahala. We called our event the U.S. Invitational, and it became the precursor for what is now the U.S. Open held annually on the Nantahala.

The Citizen-Times publicized our efforts, saying, "Kayakers and canoeists from the Carolinas, Georgia, Tennessee, Florida, and Virginia have pre-registered for the Asheville YMCA Kayak Club's races on the Nantahala River near Bryson City...

"Most whitewater races are conducted during the spring and fall months. This one, according to the YMCA's Chuck Hines, is the only one being held in the Southeast this summer...

"The Nantahala River is dam-fed, and a reasonable amount of water is released daily by the Tennessee Valley Authority, enabling the YMCA to set up a Class II slalom course at a time when most rivers are drying up. The course will start with a 50-yard dash through two- and three-foot waves, after which the competitors will weave through 15 slalom gates. Some of the gates will require forward paddling, some reverse stroking, and some an upstream effort against the current...

"The racers will be timed, and whenever they touch a slalom pole with their boat or paddle or body, a penalty will be added to their time. Head judge Lorri Cameron of Asheville said it was unusual for anyone to have a clean run."

Carrie Ashton, a 1972 Olympian in slalom racing, had done a good job of setting up the course, and then she turned it over to us for the actual handling of the event itself. We were expecting 50 or 60 competitors. But many more showed up on the Saturday of the race, and we were overwhelmed. It took us an extra hour to sign them up, and when we were done, we had nearly 100 participants from 10 states and the District of Columbia.

Then the rain came, a downpour, which caused an additional delay.

Then some rafters yanked down a couple of the slalom gates, which caused another delay.

I had hoped to compete but became so busy keeping things going that I never got into my boat. Because we were running late, several helpers had to leave before we finished, and I ended up doing the concluding award ceremony myself. Finally, when it was all over in the evening, my car failed to start, and I had to call a mechanic to fix it so I could return to Asheville. What a day!

But the Asheville YMCA Kayak Club had succeeded somehow in conducting a major race for the benefit of many whitewater competitors. Three of our Y athletes won events. Brent Lawson, 16, took top honors in the K-1 junior slalom. Curtis Bull, 13, who had come from Florida to train with us over the summer months, finished first in the K-1 beginners slalom, beating several adults in the process. Will Pruett, that wily whitewater whiz, whipped all his opponents in the K-1 Masters slalom. His daughter Amy, 16, was third in the K-1W junior slalom. Several other YMCA racers placed fourth, fifth, and sixth in the various events. As I lay awake at home that night, I acknowledged that it had been a rewarding experience, but not one I was anxious to repeat anytime soon.

*****

Monday was beautiful. As I drove back to work at the YMCA in downtown Asheville from an early-afternoon lunch break, the October sky overhead sparkled with clarity. Not a cloud anywhere. The sun's rays felt good on my shoulder. I opened the car window and inhaled the clean, brisk air, and I shook my head in dismay as I remembered the completely different conditions that had existed just 24 hours earlier.

We had gathered in the YMCA's parking lot on Sunday morning, shivering in the rain. The cold front from the Midwest had stalled in the mountains around us, and it was not only wet and windy but also cold. An unpleasant day, for sure. Had this been a YMCA Kayak Club cruise, conducted for fun, we might have cancelled it. But this was different. This was an instructional trip, the culmination of the Y's second autumn adult kayaking course, and we had paying customers to serve.

Being a whitewater instructor for the YMCA or the Nantahala Outdoor Center or any other organization isn't all fun and games and "a great way to make a living," as so many believe. Most of the time it's plain old hard work, just like every other job. On this particular Sunday – as much as I enjoy paddling – I winced at the thought of shepherding our beginning adult students down the lower section of the Nolichucky River.

"We're going, aren't we?" queried Bill.

"I'm ready for anything!" insisted Don.

"I was awake all night in anticipation of today's trip," said Patti.

"Sure. Of course," I replied, forcing a smile. There was no backing out. Jim Maynor and Anne Terrell, two of our instructors, had gone on ahead with most of the equipment, and they were waiting for me and another instructor, Rocky Meadows, to follow with the students.

"Where's Scott? Linda?" asked Debbie, a vivacious young woman I had coached in swimming and water polo and who would go on to become a U.S. champion in triathlon. On this day, though, she was a beginning kayaker, another example of the Y's emphasis on all-around programming.

"Scott called and said he wasn't coming," I responded. "I guess it's too cold for him ... and here comes Linda now." A peppery young lady jumped out of her car and said, "I kept waiting and waiting for the phone to ring, hoping to hear your voice, Chuck, saying the trip had been postponed because of this awful weather."

"Sweat or shiver, we paddle the river," I told her with a grin. "That's our motto."

A bit more than an hour later, having driven to the Nolichucky, we were indeed ready to paddle an intermediate section of the river. Jim and Anne greeted us as we reached the put-in. Both were subdued. Jim looked at me as if to say, Are YOU the one responsible for this absurdity?

I was. I had made the decision to conduct this day's instructional lesson on the river. For better or worse.

We huddled beneath a shelter, changing into paddling apparel. We had wet suits and gloves for the students who requested them. The rest of us wore wool sweaters covered by paddle jackets. I longed to put on my pogies (gloves), but I didn't. It wouldn't be right. I needed to suffer for making the others suffer.

We stalled around for a while, feeling better as the downpour dwindled to a drizzle and then disappeared. "Let's go!" I shouted.

The students had received six lessons in the YMCA's pool and classroom and had spent time on a slow section of the French Broad River in Asheville and also practicing at our slalom course, so they knew the basics, but this was their first time on faster-moving water. We had them paddle upstream for several hundred yards, focusing on the forward stroke. The current caused some problems. "How do you get this @!$#&+%*# boat to go straight?" Linda grimaced. Jim coached her patiently. We spent an hour working on the strokes, catching eddies, peeling out, and ferrying. Linda swam. Bill swam. Frances swam.

The weather wasn't getting any warmer, and I looked up to see more storm clouds approaching above the mountain peaks. "Roll 'em!" I shouted again, and we headed downriver. The first rapid was a Class II+, requiring some maneuvering through a rock garden, then down a fast, narrow chute into a field of three-foot waves. I led the way, eddying out below the chute, and held my breath as the students, one after another, tried their luck. Bill. Debbie. Patti. Whew. Jerry. Frances. Yea. Don. Linda. Not a single spill. What great teachers we were!

Numerous Class IIs followed. For the most part, the students ran them successfully. Jerry rolled. Don rolled. The rain returned.

"We have two rapids remaining," I said, clenching and unclenching my frozen fingers and peering through my misty eye-glasses at the other paddlers. "Both require some maneuvering. Then we'll finish with Surfer's Ledge near the take-out."

Halfway through the first remaining rapid, Frances became pinned. The current held her tight. "I'll get Frances," Jim yelled over the rapid's roar. He helped her to shore. I eddied out behind her overturned boat and worked a full five minutes pushing it free. It banged down the rest of the rapid. At the bottom, I watched closely to see Frances' reaction. At 50, she showed a lot of courage by immediately hopping back into her kayak. "Ready?" I asked. "Sure," she smiled. Atta girl!

Next it was Debbie's turn. At the very bottom of the last remaining rapid, she became pinned between two big boulders. It was a treacherous situation, but she, like Frances, remained calm and collected despite being unable to move at all. Jim jumped out of his boat, waded over to her, and pushed her free. As she splashed into the current, she executed a perfect brace and was swept into an eddy, where she laughed with relief.

Jerry, a dermatologist, was the final victim. Knifing into Surfer's Ledge, he was rudely flipped, and his roll failed him. As he struggled to shore, I taunted him. "You turkey!" I can't recall the last time I addressed a physician that way. It felt good. Whitewater is the great equalizer. Jerry, who previously had learned scuba diving at the YMCA, frowned with professional expertise, then broke into a loud laugh. Physicians are people, too.

It was cold as we changed into warm clothes at the take-out and loaded up the boats. The students, as usual, were too weary and excited to be of much help. They chattered away, sharing each other's experiences. I lifted four kayaks onto the roof racks atop my old Buick and tied them securely. Jim lifted seven onto his new van and fastened then down. Anne and Rocky gathered the paddles, spray-skirts, helmets, and life-jackets.

"When's the next trip?" someone asked.

I smiled wanly, too tired to reply. This had been my sixth instructional trip of the year in wet, cold, miserable weather. Wouldn't we ever catch some sunshine? Maybe next time. Next month. Next year. But we'd be back, rain or shine, with another YMCA kayaking class. With more eager students. You know our motto. "Sweat or shiver, we paddle the river."

*****

"Asheville Y Team Wins," said the headline in the Citizen-Times. Each autumn since its opening, the Nantahala Outdoor Center had conducted a triathlon event. This sport was brand-new and was just becoming popular. We were training a handful of tri-athletes at the YMCA. Will Pruett said, "Why don't we enter this year's NOC triathlon?"

"Who?" I asked, raising my eyebrows. "You mean you and me?"

"No," Will laughed, "but maybe we can put together a relay team of younger guys."

"I'll find a swimmer and a canoeist, if you can find a runner."

The aforementioned newspaper article reported on our efforts. "The Asheville YMCA team of Jay Sly (swimming), Dave Culp (running), and Rob Harkness (canoeing) won the men's division of the eighth annual National Outdoorsmen's Triathlon hosted by the Nantahala Outdoor Center of Bryson City last weekend…

"The event consisted of a one-mile swim, a four-mile run, and an eight-mile paddle contested in relay fashion between nearly 100 contestants."

Our three athletes received nice tee-shirts from NOC for participating, and Jay gave his to me. I wore it around the YMCA for the next few months. It was another good example of the Y's willingness to explore new activities and opportunities.

*****

Finally Charlie Walbridge got what was coming to him.

"It's about time," somebody said.

"He deserves it," someone else stated.

Everybody nodded in agreement.

Charlie stood before us, as our applause washed over him, just as the waves have washed over him on countless rivers.

A tall, energetic resident of Pennsylvania, who now lives in West Virginia as this is being written, he had served as chairman of the River Safety Task Force in 1978, 1979, and 1980, doing more than anyone else to promote river safety. He had worked with half a dozen different organizations, written articles in various magazines, and edited a quarterly newsletter that he sent out free of charge.

Now he was one of a dozen speakers from coast to coast who had come to Columbus, Ohio, on October 29-31 for the National River Rescue Conference. In the process, he received a nice award for his past efforts, for which he received a standing round of applause. Will Pruett and I, representing the YMCA, were among the 100 in attendance. Sponsored by the Ohio Department of Natural Resources, the conference saw us spending the first morning in a classroom and the afternoon and evening in two pool sessions, the last one at the bubbler pool – with simulated waves – at Ohio State University.

The second day was spent on the river, where rescue techniques were demonstrated by the American Red Cross, Rescue 3 of California, Dive Rescue Specialists of Colorado, and the U.S. Coast Guard. The third day took us back to the classroom, where the speakers and demonstrators showed films and slides, fielded questions, and summarized matters.

Conference registrants each received a textbook and a vast array of informative pamphlets and flyers. As Will and I returned to Asheville in his van, he said, "We can put this information to good use in our Y program. Let's make sure we pass out copies to all our instructors."

I nodded. We had hoped to paddle one or two rivers in Kentucky on the way home, but time didn't permit, which was a disappointment. Nonetheless it had been a worthwhile weekend. One of the primary reasons we were teaching YMCA kayaking was to make sure our students, young and older, could go out on the rivers safely. What we had learned at the conference would enable us to be even more effective and knowledgeable instructors.

*****

It was eight degrees outside, with a brisk wind whipping down from the mountain peaks, creating a chill factor in the minus digits. Mid-winter. Too cold to heat the schools, so the youngsters, my daughter included, were enjoying a day off.

The postal people kept working, though, and in the morning mail I received whitewater newsletters from California and Chicago, a rafting brochure from Colorado, correspondence from four top national leaders in the sport of kayaking, and, at the bottom of the pile, the January issue of a popular canoeing magazine.

In the afternoon, YMCA instructors Jim Maynor and Will Pruett walked into the aquatic office adjacent to the pool, where I was seated at my desk. We spent a few minutes discussing the new equipment we had just purchased. When we started teaching our whitewater curriculum, we were dependent on NOC for equipment. Then Will himself bought and donated four boats to the Y, along with a large assembly of accessories such as helmets, paddles, spray-skirts, and life-jackets. Without him, our program probably would not have survived. But it had, and thanks to the income it was bringing in, we were now able to purchase what we needed out of the Y budget.

Toward evening, as I was preparing to leave my job and head home, the phone rang with an inquiry about our next adult kayak course. It made me anxious for winter to end so we could "kick off" another year of river revelry.

Later that night, sitting at home in front of a sparkling fire, my thoughts flew back to the previous year's escapades, focusing for some unknown reason on a trip we'd taken down Section Three of the Chattooga River. There had been 10 of us, led by former Army helicopter pilot Chuck Baker. He and I had become good friends. We had similar names, and both of us had served in the military – I was an Army veteran of the Korean War, having served there with the occupation troops immediately after the conflict ended – and we were whitewater enthusiasts, and we had teenaged children who also were paddlers.

Chuck Baker had run Sections Three and Four of the Chattooga a dozen times, and we were fortunate to have him as our trip leader. Even so, we'd delayed our departure from the YMCA, procrastinating about the possibility of the water level on the river being too low. Then, halfway to the Chattooga, one of our vehicles, a jeep, suffered a flat tire in a backwoodsy area that reminded us of scenes from "Deliverance."

Eventually we reached the put-in and found it deserted, a rare occurrence. "Oh, oh," said Lorri, "it must be too low."

"I don't care," replied Luther Lawson, the father of Brent, one of our best Y youngsters, "I've come this far, and I intend to run it."

We dilly-dallied around some more, soaking up the summer sun's warm rays, and finally we agreed to give it a try. The shuttle took another hour but brought good news. "The level's okay. The gauge shows it a bit above 1.7, which isn't bad for this time of the year."

Considering that we had several open canoeists in our group, along with the kayakers, and that six of the 10 had never been to the Chattooga before, I figured 1.7 would be perfect. Not too high. Not too low. I remembered a previous trip I had done when the level was a more challenging 2.6. As I came whizzing around an S-turn into a Class III rapid, I'd found my path blocked by a stalled canoeist. I had done a quick draw to the left, pulling myself into a pile of rocks, flipping where the depth was shallow and the current swift, and in trying to roll, I'd busted my paddle in half. As a result, I'd walked out with my boat on my shoulder.

Now, as I was sitting in front of the fire at home with the wind rattling the windows on that chilly winter night, I grimaced at the memory, but then I smiled as I recalled the more recent trip, which had been so successful.

With the water level just about right, with the sun shining, and with the river to ourselves, we shoved off. Chuck Baker led the way in his kayak, followed by fellow kayakers Rocky Meadows, Richard Isaac, Debbie Angel, 16-year-old Brent Lawson, and myself, and then by canoeists Lorri Cameron, Al Preston, Luther Lawson, and Mike Harper.

The Chattooga is one of the prettiest whitewater rivers in the country, and on that day, it was gorgeous. We eased into the first major rapid, called Warwoman, a Class III. The kayakers had no trouble, but two of the canoeists seemed to be struggling. Only after banging into some big boulders did they reach the bottom.

Section Three is a 12½ mile stretch that contains continuous Class IIs and 10 tougher Class IIIs and IVs. At the Rock Garden, one of the canoeists capsized and suffered through an unpleasant swim, and the rest of us eddied out, waiting patiently. Dicks Creek Ledge looked more formidable at this level than at higher levels, with a lot of exposed rock, and while some ran it, others carried around.

Another canoeist swam shortly thereafter, as we maneuvered through an unnamed Class II, and we approached The Narrows with caution. However, it was less swirly than usual, and we all weaved through this long, tight passage without mishap, although Rocky was forced to demonstrate his outstanding roll. Second Ledge offered its normal eight-foot drop, and we all ran it cleanly except for Al, who, paddling an old aluminum canoe unsuited for this type of whitewater, decided to carry.

So far I'd been running smoothly, but Eye of the Needle, a Class IV, did me in. I came at it from the wrong direction – from the right instead of the left – and was smashed by a twisting six-foot wave. My brace was obliterated by the river's force, and I was jerked upsidedown and swept through three- and four-foot waves by the current. Only after a strenuous effort at keeping calm was I able to roll up. The procedure was duplicated a minute later by Rocky, but Debbie wasn't so lucky, as her roll failed her and she took a short swim. One of the canoeists broached on top, and three of us struggled for 10 minutes pushing him loose.

More Class IIs followed. Then Roller Coaster, a III. More IIs. Then Keyhole, a difficult IV, and I, becoming tired, was fortunate to make it through, banging badly into several boulders but maintaining my balance. Hounds Tooth was next, a III. Finally the rapids disappeared, and the river became smooth and calm – the calm before the storm – and we took time to study the beautiful scenery and to talk with each other.

"Bull Sluice ahead!" Chuck Baker warned us.

"How far?"

"Around the next bend, I think."

We rounded the bend. Still smooth water. Another bend. Another. Still smooth. Then the current began picking up again. Rocks and boulders appeared. Waves. It was Class II, gradually increasing to III. I knew the Bull was coming up. We stopped and scouted. On that day, at that level, it was a Class IV. Young Brent, as cocky as ever, shrugged and hopped into his low-volume kayak and pushed off. He caught the eddy at the top, waved to us, and headed into the pulsating current which pushed him over the first drop, where he braced, and then over the second drop, a longer one. He plunged into a throbbing, convulsive hydraulic, disappearing momentarily. Then he bobbed back up and stroked out, smiling.

The kayakers followed, some of us running it cleanly, others needing a roll at the bottom. The canoeists all carried around, wisely.

We had been on the Chattooga for nearly six hours, and because of our late start, it was becoming dark as we ran the rapid below Bull Sluice to the take-out. Slowly we changed clothes and loaded up our boats. "Did y'all run Section Four?" somebody asked. "No," answered Al, "but it felt like it."

We chuckled until we heard the bad news. A young female kayaker had drowned a few hours earlier on Section Four, which is harder, more dangerous than Section Three. We drove back to Asheville in a subdued atmosphere.

Now as I sat reminiscing at home, staring into the dying embers in front of me, I remembered not only the trip to the Chattooga but also the lessons we had learned at the River Rescue Conference. I resolved to be more careful and conservative in 1981. As Chuck Baker said when he heard about the death on Section Four, "It isn't worth it." No, it isn't, and I was glad we had developed our YMCA program so those wishing to participate in the exciting sport of whitewater kayaking could learn from us and enjoy the sport in a safe and controlled manner. When all was said and done, that was the bottom line.

Chapter Seven

Wearily I rapped on the door of the men's restroom. "Just a minute," came a high-pitched voice from inside. Moments later, the door opened and out came Kathy McLaughlin, a charming young lady. I stared. She smiled. "Sorry," she said, "but there isn't a separate restroom for women here." I looked. She was right. So we shared a laugh back in those days when women were just starting to be treated fairly and equally.

For many women and girls, it was the YMCA that first opened doors for them. I remember using the sport of water polo for that purpose. At the Minneapolis, Minnesota, and Des Moines, Iowa, YMCAs, two of my places of employment when I started my Y career, we had brought teenaged girls into the "male only" swimming pools to play polo. There weren't any separate dressing rooms for women and girls in those days, so we had to improvise. When I was at the Canton, Illinois, YMCA, I had supervised the first-ever Y women's water polo championships. That occurred in 1968.

During the 1970s, the teen girls I coached at the Asheville YMCA won numerous national tournaments, and we were part of the national and international development of the sport for women, which eventually resulted in women's water polo being admitted to the Olympic Games. That took a l-o-n-g time, however, and I had moved on into the sport of whitewater kayaking and racing after receiving a letter about "designing a physical education program that appeals to the adventurous nature of youth, preferably one that can be done outdoors." The letter, which came to me in 1976 from the YMCA's National Physical Education Management Team, had changed the direction of my life.

And now, on an afternoon in February of 1981, Kathy McLaughlin and I were sharing both a restroom and a river, running the Toe Gorge in the mountains of Western North Carolina with several of our paddling partners, thus "kicking off" another season of whitewater excitement.

Will Pruett and Jim Maynor and I had studied the materials brought home from the National River Rescue Conference, and we wanted to make sure we were incorporating the latest and safest ideas into our YMCA kayaking curriculum. So we arranged to conduct this "practice trip" before starting our spring classes for adults at the Y.

In Jim's van, we'd set out on the one-hour trip from Asheville to Burnsville and thence to the mountains beyond. Our group included Will, a 10-year veteran of Carolina's finest whitewater; Jim, the Carolina Cup wildwater racing champion; Rocky Meadows, one of our teaching assistants at the YMCA; Kathy Koon, one of our former students who was becoming an outstanding kayaker; Kathy McLaughlin, a competent open canoeist; and myself.

It was overcast, with a slight sprinkle, but we maintained our exuberance as we parked, unloaded, and bundled up. At the put-in, the water level looked acceptable. "I've seen it higher by several inches," said Jim. I nodded. "Yes, but I've also paddled it lower by several inches," stated Will. Again I nodded. "It appears to be perfect for me," affirmed Kathy Koon. "And I'm sure it's going to be a challenge for me in my canoe," added Kathy McLaughlin.

I'd forgotten how icy-cold the river can be at that time of the year until I pushed off into the gentle current in my Spirit and began warming-up beneath the put-in bridge. My fingers numbed quickly as I ferried easily, did a couple of deep braces, and headed downriver, with the others following. The water trickling down my spine caused me to shiver. But you know our motto. "Sweat or shiver, we paddle the river."

The put-in rapid was easy at this level, and we kept on going, rounding the bend and slipping into the continuing series of rapids running through the Gorge. The first was a Class II+, not as difficult as usual.

The second was more technical, carrying us through a stretch of two-foot waves into a left-side eddy, from which we ferried across the river into a mini-eddy, and then peeled out into the swift current. Just ahead was a ledge which had just a single opening. I ran it correctly, plunging down the four-foot drop, and swerved to avoid a nasty undercut rock. Eddying out, I watched Jim and Rocky throw out braces as they plowed through. The others had no problems.

The following rapids were all Class IIs, and we stopped and surfed on our way downriver, enjoying ourselves and chatting amiably. After a while, we stopped for lunch. Ashore, we nibbled on our food, stomped in the sand to keep warm, and expressed our admiration for God's Great Outdoors. We were alone and yet together … with no one else in sight … here in the mountain wilderness … but mere minutes from civilization … a unique experience available only to river runners.

"Let's go with the flow," someone said, and we were back on the water, weaving a path through more Class IIs. With 17 others, including some of our Asheville YMCA instructors, I had done this same stretch of river, the Toe Gorge, a year ago as part of our Y institute. Top kayakers from the East, South, and Midwest had participated. It had been cold, and the water level had been higher, more challenging. But it was cold on this day, as well. I hunched over as we maneuvered through one- and two-foot waves, over ledges, and around small boulders.

Eventually we reached the take-out. While the rest of us hauled our boats up a steep incline, Jim plucked his 10-speed bicycle out of the bushes and began peddling back to the put-in, where he had left his van. Forty minutes later, he was back, and soon we were stopping for a snack and a restroom visit, with Kathy McLaughlin pulling her surprise exit from the men's room.

During the ride home, she said, "It was a good run today. I was anxious at the start. Tense. But now I feel happy that I made it down the river without any trouble."

"It was just what I needed after a four-month layoff," stated Rocky.

"Maybe Jim will turn into a tri-athlete," Kathy Koon laughed. "He's a great paddler, and now he's also biking, and I'm sure he can add running to his repertoire."

The small talk continued as we drove home, but nobody bothered to mention the obvious. It had been a safe and enjoyable trip because we'd followed all the proper safety precautions:

* Pre-planning, which meant selecting the proper river to visit and the time and place of departure.

* Having a competent and clear-headed group of participants.

* Trustworthy boats, with each containing a throw-bag.

* Every participant outfitted in a wet suit or other protective apparel.

* Careful, relaxed paddling from start to finish, with the absence of any hot-dogging or trickery.

* Teamwork, with each person staying in the group and being his brother's or sister's keeper.

* A shuttle procedure that was inexpensive and workable and quick enough to keep us from getting too cold at the end of this trip on a cold, overcast, wintry afternoon.

These are some of the essentials of successful river-running, as necessary as performing the strokes, braces, and Eskimo roll. I felt we were doing things the right way in our Asheville program as we prepared for another year of pool and classroom instruction, river cruises, and yes, racing.

*****

By the time we reached the river, it was snowing heavily. There we stood, three dozen of us, debating what to do. We'd come to the Ocoee in mid-March from Atlanta and Chattanooga and Bryson City and Asheville and several other Southern cities to do some racing on the Ocoee's challenging Class III-IV rapids. I'd driven over from Asheville with my daughter Heather, 15, the day before, and I'd enjoyed 90 minutes of practicing on the river in my brand-new slalom racing kayak.

Heather kept a watchful eye on me from the bank. There were no gates set as yet, but I enjoyed whizzing around. In such a small, tippy boat, this was just about my limit, because the Ocoee is not an easy river.

Afterwards, Heather and I drove into the nearby town of Cleveland, Tennessee, where we spent the night. When we arose the next morning, it was snowing lightly, and by the time we reached the river, it was snowing heavily. So there we stood.

"What'll we do?" someone asked.

"Well, the racing itself wouldn't be too bad," somebody else responded, "but it's not going to be fun hanging the gates, standing around timing and judging for a couple of hours, and then having to remove all the gates before heading home."

"It could get a little hairy out there on the river, too, if anyone takes a swim. We don't want to do anything dumb."

I didn't say much. As usual, I was the oldest athlete there and one of the least proficient in the field which included four or five U.S. Team members.

By now the wind was whipping up a pretty fierce storm, and I was sure I wasn't the only one who was shivering and shaking. I thought of our motto. But maybe this day should be the exception.

"Heck with it," said one of the race promoters. "I'm calling it off. Instead of racing, why don't we just paddle the river for fun?"

YEAH, everyone quickly agreed. Not me. I'd brought only my little slalom racer, and I wasn't about to tackle the Ocoee from start to finish in a snowstorm, leaving my young daughter by herself on the riverbank for an hour or more. So as a few of the hotshots drove to the put-in, I suggested to Heather, "Why don't we head home, and on the way, we can stop and have a nice meal at NOC."

YEAH, she said. So that's what we did. In retrospect, it was a terrific weekend even though the race was cancelled because of the unexpected snowstorm. Common sense had prevailed. I'd practiced on the Ocoee, spent two full days with my daughter, and wolfed down a great meal at NOC. And we returned home safely. Isn't that what whitewater kayaking is all about? YEAH.

*****

Rarely did I earn headlines in the Asheville Citizen-Times, so it was with much surprise that I awakened one day to find a small heading that said, "Hines Kayak Team Wins in Georgia." Holy smoke!

It was a press release issued by the Georgia Canoeing Association from Helen, Georgia. "The father-daughter team of Chuck and Heather Hines of Asheville, representing the YMCA, won two first places, a second, and a fifth in the seventh annual Chattahoochee River Races held last weekend…

"Hines finished first in the K-1 Masters slalom kayak competition and fifth overall in the men's slalom…

"His 15-year-old daughter, Heather, finished first in the K-1W junior downriver sprint and second in the women's downriver sprint…

"Kayakers and canoeists from Georgia, Alabama, Tennessee, Florida, North and South Carolina competed."

Okay, since you insist, here's the full story. Nestled in the mountains of northern Georgia is the quaint, enchanting Alpine/Bavarian resort town of Helen. At the time we were there in April of 1981, it was still small, comprised of a few motels and restaurants and about 20 shops that featured everything from waxed-while-you-wait candles to glassblowing to homemade fudge.

Flowing through the heart of this little village is the Chattahoochee River, which since 1975 had been the scene of the annual and highly-popular whitewater races. We arrived in Helen – my wife Lee and daughter Heather and I – on a Friday evening, just in time to scout the slalom course, which consisted of 16 gates tightly placed over 300 yards of shallow but rocky current. It was tougher than I had anticipated, and I was worried, especially about a five-foot chute in the middle of the course which had to be done backwards, with a gate above and a gate below.

After a sleepless night in a comfy motel, I awakened at 6:25 a.m. on Saturday and beat the crowd to the river for a couple of practice runs. In my new low-volume slalom kayak, I worked up a good sweat, discovering in the process that this was a course I should be able to navigate successfully. I set a goal for myself of hitting no more than three of the 16 gates.

By 8:30, the river was jammed with kayakers and canoeists who were practicing, so I grabbed a hasty breakfast with Lee and Heather. I was feeling a bit nervous as all the competitors gathered at the starting point by 10:00, and I became even more edgy when I learned the kayak category would be going first and that I would be the lead-off racer. In whitewater racing, it is the s-l-o-w-e-s-t competitors who go first with those following in descending order until you reach the last, or fastest, entrant. So you can see what the race directors thought of my skills.

Most of the athletes on that day were canoeists, about 60 of them, but there were 21 kayakers, half of them collegians from the nearby universities. There were three of us in the K-1 Masters classification who would be competing against each other. I didn't know one of the other "old timers," but one I did know was the swimming and water polo coach at Georgia Southern University, where some of my YMCA swimmers had gone to school. I knew he was a good kayaker.

Promptly at 10:00, right on schedule, I received the countdown. Five. Four. Three. Two. One. Go! I pushed off against the current into upstream gate No. 1, then ferried to the left and slid through reverse gate No. 2. Cutting sharply across the small river, I avoided some rocks and squeezed through gate No. 3. I continued down the slalom course, and at gate No. 4, I carelessly tipped one of the poles with the snout of my boat. Drats! Then it was onward, more carefully, eventually reaching the chute. I whipped around and backed through gate No. 9, feeling the rushing current sweeping me backwards down the five-foot drop. Whooosh! I braced as I bounced backwards through gate No. 10. Yes. Clean as a whistle.

Stroking through the remaining six gates, I paddled hard across the finish line in a burst of fatigue, definitely feeling my age. Puffing and panting, I sat and watched the other kayakers coming down the course. Some looked good, some not-so-good. I felt satisfied. To my knowledge, I had nipped only two poles, although the judges might have detected one or two more hits, each of which would add seconds to my time.

I changed clothes and watched the various canoe classes running the red, white, and green gates while the green-shirted judges scribbled furiously. No doubt about it, this was a well-organized operation, and the sponsor – the Wildewood Shop of Helen – deserved credit. I was impressed by how well the canoeists squeezed their bulky boats through the gates.

Later, with Lee and Heather, I ate a leisurely lunch. It was a bright and sunny day, and this was a great place to spend it. A Bavarian band was playing a polka, and I found myself humming along. Eventually I donned my paddling apparel again and made my way back to the starting point, where I discovered that I'd indeed hit only two of the poles on my initial run and that, amazingly, I was sitting in third place. My time of 4:25

was well ahead of the Georgia Southern University coach who came in at 5:28. The other Masters kayaker had flipped and hadn't finished the race. So those two were out of the competition.

Just five of us in the men's kayak class – the fastest five – lined up for the second runs, or the finals, and again I was the lead-off racer. This time my adrenaline wasn't flowing. I knew I'd already won the Masters category. Thus I paddled calmly and confidently. Smoothly and efficiently. Cleanly. I ran the whole course without a touch anywhere.

Disappointment hit me later, however, when I found that a judge had given me a penalty at gate No. 10 – the reverse gate at the bottom of the five-foot chute – which I was sure I had negotiated properly. Because of the five seconds added to my time for that supposed touch, I had been passed by two more of the collegiate hotshots. "Don't feel badly," my wife consoled me, as good wives are inclined to do. "You did 14 gates cleanly this morning and 15 cleanly this afternoon, and that's better than the goal you set for yourself. You easily beat your competition in the Masters."

"And fifth out of 21 kayakers overall isn't too shabby," my daughter added.

On Sunday, it was Heather's turn. She grew up as a "Y brat," spending hundreds of days with me at the YMCA and learning various Y aquatic activities. She was a swimmer, a lifeguard, a water poloist, and a skin-diver who, the next year when she turned 16, would become a certified scuba diver. Then at 17, as a student at Asheville's suburban Erwin High School, she'd make the All-State Chorale, and she'd go to Europe on a 15-day trip to sing in England, Belgium, Netherlands, Germany, and France. The highlight of that trip for her and the chorale would be performing at Notre Dame Cathedral in Paris.

Heather had started kayaking when she was 12. It wasn't her favorite sport and she never became a slalom racer, but she paddled a dozen rivers around the Southeast and tackled Class II and occasionally Class III rapids with, well, I guess the correct word would be verve. On that weekend, at Helen, Georgia, she entered the downriver sprint on Sunday. There were no gates. The competitors simply raced as fast as they could down the river from the starting point to the finish line. It was a short race over a distance of only 300 yards, sort of a sprint through some easy rapids, plus the five-foot chute.

However, instead of going one after another down the course, starting at one-minute intervals, as slalom racers do, the downriver racers had a "mass" start. All the entrants took off at the same time from the starting point. It was a get-out-of-my-way, elbowing-each-other-aside madhouse. In the years to come, it would be called a "boater-cross." In the girls race that day, Heather outsprinted the three other young teens at the beginning and led all the way to the finish. Yea. In the women's race, she wasn't quite as quick, but she still took second in a field of six ladies. Yea again.

We enjoyed our family trip to Georgia, and a few weeks later, the Citizen-Times reported on another event in which our YMCA was represented. This time it was the Southeastern Championships of the United States Canoe Association. Once again the newspaper reported the results: "Asheville YMCA entries dominated the kayak competition at the USCA's Southeastern Wildwater Championships held last weekend on the Mayo River near Greensboro...

"Jim Maynor of Asheville won first place in the men's kayak race, and Will Pruett placed fourth. Kathy Koon was the winner in the women's kayak race, with Amy Pruett second and Anne Terrell fourth...

"In the junior kayak contest, the Asheville YMCA team swept the first five places. Doug Baker took top honors, followed by John Sherman, Rick Hensley, Chase Ambler, and Chris Teague...

"Another Ashevillean, Kathy McLaughlin, finished fourth in the women's canoe race...

"In team scoring, Asheville was an easy winner in the kayak division and placed second overall in the combined kayak and canoe competition, trailing a Virginia club for the title."

If I remember correctly, there were about 200 paddlers from seven or eight states entered at that event. No small stuff. While our intent in developing a YMCA kayaking program locally and nationally was never to overdo the competitive component, we were making our mark in racing. And the best was yet to come.

*****

Our youth paddling program was now in full swing. We had about two dozen teenagers participating, with pool practices at the YMCA and slalom sessions on the French Broad and twice-monthly river cruises. I remember that Will Pruett and I took Chase Ambler, Doug Baker, Rick Hensley, Heather Hines, Brent Lawson, John Sherman, and Chris Teague, all of them ages 15 and 16, to the lower Green one Saturday, where we joined a Hendersonville YMCA youth group led by John Bayless and Jim Sheppard that included Kenny Davenport, Mark Sheppard, and half-a-dozen other teens. It was a relaxing Class II cruise with plenty of time taken for socializing.

A YMCA in Florida had heard about our new Y kayaking program, and they contacted me about coming to Asheville for a weekend of instruction. I told them we would do one day for them if they came. This would be morning instruction in the classroom and pool, followed by an afternoon cruise on an easy river. We should have taken them to a Class I section of the French Broad. Instead I let my arm be twisted into taking them to the Class II lower Green. "Oh," said the Florida boys and their adult supervisors, "this is simple stuff to us." Sure it was. I still have horrid memories of chasing flailing youngsters and errant boats down the river in a light rain. We had played the Floridians previously in water polo and knew them to be extremely capable in the pool. But on the river and amidst the rapids, which was an entirely different scenario, they were almost totally inept. Luckily, because of their water polo capabilities, they were strong swimmers. When it was over, I realized I had done an inept job myself by allowing this group to dictate where we would go for their river trip, thereby placing them in a perilous situation. What was I thinking? It was an important lesson for me. I would be more strict in the future.

We were conducting other youth trips, and I wrote an article about one of them, which was published in a national magazine. It went like this:

"A clap of thunder echoed down the river and was answered, surprisingly, by a loud laugh coming up from the other direction. I peered ahead, squinting into the mist, but I could see nothing. So I maneuvered down the Class II rapids slowly, carefully. At the bottom, on the left bank, I spotted three young kayakers who were gathered around a fourth, who had overturned. The fourth, I discovered as I drew nearer, was my daughter Heather. When she saw me, she shouted, 'I took a swim!'

"Nothing strange about that, you say? Well, for Heather, 15, this was her very first swim. She started kayaking at 12, and for three years she paddled on an assortment of rivers – the French Broad, Green, Little Tennessee, Tuckaseigee, Nantahala, Nolichucky, even the New in West Virginia – without flipping. As a result, taking a swim on the river became an obsession with her. She grew increasingly worried about it happening, even though she had a 99% reliable pool roll. When would it happen? WHEN??

"It happened on a rainy June day. Nine of us had driven to a remote corner of the mountains, to an obscure, little-known stream not mentioned in any of the guidebooks. It was the type of stream that usually was too low to paddle, but which, after a heavy rainfall, turned into a swift, splashing, spirited downhill dash. I had been there once before, with Chicago's famous "river mom," Marge Cline, who had come to visit us the previous year and study our YMCA instructional curriculum. More about Marge later...

"As Will, in his van, and I, in my aging Buick, rounded the mountain curves en route to this hidden gem, the rain kept pouring down. It had been a dry winter and spring, but suddenly the skies had opened up, and we were enjoying a week of continuing rain. It was almost too much of a good thing, I muttered to myself, slowing down as Will pulled off the road. He hopped out into the downpour and said, 'Becky's sick.'

"A slender, attractive but pale 13-year-old followed him into the bushes, lurching and heaving. He returned with a smile on his bearded face. 'She's not used to our hills and curves, I guess.'

"The girl about whom he was speaking was Becky Weis, the daughter of Chuck Weis, past-president of the United States Canoe Association and the first director of communications for the American Canoe Association. Our YMCA program has been affiliated with the American Canoe Association and the United States Canoe Association and also a third organization, the American Whitewater Affiliation. All three have contributed a lot to the various phases of the sport, and they have worked well together...

"Becky had come from her home in Lafayette, Indiana, to spend several weeks training with our YMCA kaYak kids. She was staying at our house and sharing a room with my daughter Heather. Now she was heading out to the river with us. If her stomach rebelled at being twisted and dipped on our mountain roads, it was excusable. Eventually she returned to our waiting vehicles, her eyes glazed, and we drove onward to the put-in beneath a rickety wooden bridge...

"The rain had subsided, but Becky still wasn't feeling well and moaned that she didn't think she could paddle. I tried to talk her into giving it a try, but failed. Will ambled over and gave her his best pep talk. Whereas my motivational efforts failed, his succeeded, and Becky joined the rest of us as we donned our paddling apparel...

"This was primarily a youth trip, led by Will and myself and another Y instructor, Anne Terrell. Our group included Becky, Heather, Chase Ambler, Tricia Derrough, John Sherman, and Amy Pruett. At the start, I led the way as we eased down the narrow, bubbling stream which was no more than 30' wide. Both banks were heavily forested, with bushes and limbs extending over the water. There were rocks and boulders to be skirted as the swift current carried us single-file downstream. The rain returned, vanished, reappeared, disappeared. We moved in a misty, eerie, quiet world, unable to see paddlers more than a few yards ahead or behind...

"It's like kayaking in the clouds," someone whispered. The tall trees seemed to close in on us from both sides...

"This was not big water. Not at all. But it was continuous, never-ending Class II and III, requiring much maneuvering to avoid the bushes, limbs, boulders. Occasionally a paddler would get hung up on a rock, shoving and struggling, huffing and puffing and cursing. But no major mishaps occurred...

"We kept on descending at a steady pace. One hour became two. Then I found it. As the leader, I bounced into it first: a stream-wide ledge forming a beautiful three-foot surfing wave. For 10 minutes, I played to my heart's content, until my arms grew leaden. Then the others took their turns. Will whizzed in and out, deftly diving into the trough, balancing, sliding across the crest from one side to the other. His daughter Amy, 16, followed, nosing into the deep drop, feeling the curl beneath her as she was yanked down, down, then spit back up. 'Ooooooo,' she gasped...

"Becky, still pale, was next, and she didn't hesitate. She stuck her boat into the wave, over it, down into the froth and foam, smiling as she was prodded and pummeled by the surging surf. She rode the wave like a pro. John was next, then Chase, and both did well. Tricia and Heather were more hesitant, so we headed downriver in the drizzle...

"Will moved to the front, and I held back, helping my daughter surf a smaller ledge. She did so with success, and then sped away. It was shortly after she vanished in the mist that I heard laughter and discovered that she had taken her first-ever swim...

"I broadsided into a boulder!" she exclaimed breathlessly...

"She must have set a world record getting out of her boat," Chase commented...

"I think I chipped an inch off my rear end bouncing over the rocks!" Heather said...

"You should've seen her gasping for air when she came up," Amy chuckled...

"Well, the water is cold!"

"Lift your bow up onto my boat, and I'll help you empty out," Becky volunteered...

"Look ... I lost one of my river shoes," Heather sputtered. But she was smiling and laughing, the type of laughter that comes easily when you have survived something that scared you to death. When you have overcome an obstacle that you have built up in your mind, your imagination. When you have taken your first river swim and, after being swept along, have stumbled ashore and are standing there in the shallows as your heartbeat returns to normal, feeling both silly and satisfied, dismayed and jubilant...

"As I sat in my kayak and watched my daughter, I knew this had been a growing experience for her. As much as she feared the prospect of flipping on the river one day, she had faced her fear. She had not stayed home. She had kept coming on our river trips and paddling through the rapids. Throughout life, she – like all of us – would face hobgoblins of her own making, creating fear and indecision. She would hear that little voice which dwells within us all and says, "You can't ... can't ... can't ...

"But of course we CAN. We CAN if we have enough trust and faith. And each time we discover that we CAN, we are able to push ahead to something bigger and better, harder and more challenging. It's called growing, maturing, expanding our horizons. It's what Jonathon Livingston Seagull was talking about in the best-selling book of that name. Remember him? Whether flying like Jonathon or paddling down the river like most of us, the opportunity for growth is there. Grab it when it comes along, using trust and faith to overcome your fears. Go for it!

"My daughter, having learned that she could flip and survive in the rapids, wasted no time rejoining us as we continued cruising down this lovely backwoodsy mountain stream. The youngsters displayed increasing adeptness at maneuvering in the narrow, bumpy channels..."

"How're you feeling, Becky?"

"I'm okay now."

"How do you like this river?"

"It's beautiful. I'm impressed. Delighted. Excited."

"She moved ahead with confidence, competence. With trust, faith. With a gracefulness in her boat that belied her young age. With a lifetime of adventure, attainment, accomplishment ahead of her. I sighed, feeling my age, and followed along."

*****

"Not as much interest in racing this year, is there," observed Anne Terrell.

It was a rhetorical question, and she didn't expect an answer, but I replied anyway. "I believe it's due to the low river levels, but there are other factors, as well."

"Such as?"

"Oh, a lot of the race sponsors aren't doing a very good job of promoting their races, in my opinion. The entry forms aren't being sent out soon enough. The slalom gates aren't being hung on time, and they often lack numbers. The Junior and Masters categories too often are omitted. The awards aren't satisfactory. I could go on, but you get my drift."

Anne grimaced. We were sitting on the bank of the French Broad River as it flows through Asheville. Along with 27 others, we were preparing to take part in the fourth annual French Broad slalom races held each year on a 12-gate Class I+ course designed to attract almost anyone with a little whitewater experience.

The slalom was the second part of a two-day competition, with the first day devoted to a five-mile downriver race for kayakers and canoeists. In the past, the downriver had drawn as many as 70 or 80 entries. This year, though, it had attracted just three dozen. Our YMCA participants had turned back all challengers and emerged victorious – Jim Maynor in K-1, Kathy Koon in K-1W, Doug Baker in K-1 Junior, Amy Pruett in K-1W Junior, and the duo of Mike Hill and Kathy McLaughlin in the open canoe event.

Now it was time for the slalom, and we had about half as many registrants as in the past. Most were from Western North Carolina, but we had a few from South Carolina and Tennessee and one, young Becky Weis, from Indiana.

The French Broad starts out as four small streams in the higher mountains of Transylvania County, each tumbling over jagged rocks and ledges and cascading waterfalls before joining together to form a wide, broad river. Early settlers called it the Broad, and then to distinguish it from another river just to the east with the same name, they renamed it the French Broad because it flows north and then west into what was once French-occupied territory.

There are stretches of Class III-IV rapids on this river, run regularly by several commercial rafting companies and by skilled kayakers and canoeists. Our YMCA slalom course was on a much easier section, just to the south of Asheville at the Firefighters Camp. I looked up from my spot on the river bank at the course. The gates were hanging from cables that stretched from the bank to a mid-river island. Each gate was properly numbered. The dangling red, white, and green poles ended approximately 4" above the gently flowing and somewhat brownish water.

Although a relatively obscure event, the French Broad slalom races were always well-organized. We had officials – a starter, timers, gate judges – who would not be competing themselves and thus could concentrate on their duties. We had a dozen beautiful trophies for presentation to the winners and runners-up in the various categories.

"Time to begin!" shouted starter Debbie Robinson, a champion swimmer, water polo player, and tri-athlete from our YMCA program, who also was a novice kayaker. "If you haven't had a practice run, it's too late, so please assemble at that big rock in mid-river, about 20 yards above the first gate. That's the start."

One by one, chatting amiably with each other, we hopped into our kayaks and decked canoes and paddled against the current to the starting point. I was sweating beneath the bright summer sun.

"The older people will go first," Debbie laughed, "as it'll probably take them longer to run the course. Let's see … we have three entries in the K-1 Masters … Chuck Hines and Will Pruett and Chuck Baker … and we'll go in that order."

As the initial racer, I moved to the front of the line, my heart beating faster. It looked like this would be my only race over the summer months, and as the defending Masters champion, I wanted to do well. I knew I'd be hard-pressed to win because of my classy opponents. Will Pruett had won many races, and Chuck Baker, who was a terrific river-runner, had just turned 40 and moved up into the Masters class.

Debbie waved at the timers and judges, making sure they were ready. Then she grabbed the rear end of my sleek 19-pound slalom racing kayak and commenced with the countdown. I took a deep breath, hunched forward, held my paddle more firmly, and squinted through my dark glasses at the narrow channel of rushing water which squirted between two rocks just ahead. It was there that I needed to slam into a sharp turn in order to ride the current into the first gate.

"...three ... two ... one ... go!" Debbie released my boat with a blast of her whistle, and I dug in. I pivoted in the channel and caught the current, stroking smoothly. Ah, this was MY course, relatively easy, on which I did most of my practicing, and I felt comfortable. The tension vanished. Gate No. 1 was simple, but No. 2 was an upstream, so I did a quick 180 degree turn and eased through. This was followed by a sideways ferry around some exposed rocks into a couple of reverse gates set in a chute which, due to the low water level, was abnormally shallow and bumpy. This was my favorite portion of the course, situated near the mid-river island, beneath over-hanging limbs, and I slid backwards down the chute and squeezed successfully through the gates and rocks. Then I was zigzagging through the remaining gates and sprinting to the finish line.

"Your time was 2:04!" shouted one of the timers.

"With a single touch," stated one of the gate judges, which added five seconds to my time, giving me a 2:09.

SLOW! The extremely low water level had turned our raceway into a rocky road, a bumpy boulevard, and my speedy slalom boat into a sluggish sedan. Once, at a higher water level with the river moving faster, I had completed the course in 1:49. Not on this day.

Luckily, my second run was a couple of seconds faster and completely clean, and I managed to hang on to my Masters crown with a 2:02. Only Jim Maynor in the K-1 class was able to post a time under two minutes, leaving the rest of us dissatisfied with our pokey performances. But that's the unique challenge of whitewater cruising and racing. As someone said, "You never set foot in the same river twice." Rivers are changing constantly. If the water level goes up or down even an inch or two, it makes a difference. Heavy water pushes rocks and boulders around. Trees fall into the river, creating new barriers. And of course there's the weather, with seasonal changes becoming important. Finally, slalom courses are all different, all special in their own way. Our course on the French Broad bore no resemblance to the ones at the Chattahoochee or Nantahala or Ocoee or elsewhere.

Unlike most athletes, who generally perform on a standard-sized playing field and/or at a set distance, the whitewater paddler faces a constantly-shifting field of play. Nothing on the river stays the same. There's always something new. That's what causes the excitement, and yes, the danger. As somebody else once said, "Ours is a 21st century sport. Outdoors. An adventure. And action packed."

Eventually it was time at our French Broad races for a new event – as I said, there's always something new – which involved a male kayaker and a female kayaker paddling the slalom course one after the other, as a team. My partner was Becky Weis, the visitor from Indiana. A precocious 13-year-old, Becky had surprised us by winning the K-1W slalom competition, beating several older Ashevilleans. She had come from her home in Lafayette, Indiana, to train with our YMCA kaYak kids. I had taken her on trips to a number of rivers – the lower Green, Tuckaseigee, Nantahala, Nolichucky, plus others – and had introduced her to slalom at our YMCA course.

I was sure Becky and I would win. I thought so before the race began. I thought so as we whizzed through the gates, she first and I following closely, and I thought so at the end, even though I was slow backing through the final reverse gate. And my slowness cost us dearly, as we lost by ONE SECOND to the duo of Jim Maynor and Anne Terrell. Drats! The father-daughter team of Will and Amy Pruett placed a close third.

"Gee!" exclaimed Anne. "There should be more co-ed races. That was fun!"

We all nodded. But we weren't done yet, as we had another new event awaiting us. This time it was an upriver sprint, against the current, over a distance of about 100 yards. Some of the timers and judges wanted to participate, so I took my turn on the riverbank, handling a stopwatch. We winced and laughed as the paddlers struggled against the current. It wasn't easy.

As dusk arrived, we packed up and prepared to leave. Trophies had been awarded to the top slalom racers and homemade plaques to all the others. Everyone who'd taken part in the day's activities had been a winner of sorts by striving, seeking, sharing, smiling, surviving. What a great day it had been.

Chapter Eight

"Eat water!"

As we stood above the Arkansas River in central Colorado, looking down from roadside at the rapids, a van from Echo Canyon River Expeditions sped past, and a voice from within shouted the organization's slogan at us. "Eat water!"

My wife Lee and daughter Heather and I chuckled. "That must have been Craig," said Heather, 15. We watched as the van disappeared around a bend, pulling behind it a trailer loaded with three large rafts. Echo Canyon's afternoon expedition on the Arkansas that bright, sunny summer day was about to begin.

A few hours earlier, I had kayaked that same section of the river with Dave Burch, Echo Canyon's personable young owner, and one of his raft guides, a young woman named Lisa.

My wife and daughter and I had reached the river after driving from Denver to Colorado Springs the previous day. While in Denver, I had practiced for an hour on the city's downtown slalom course. Situated at Confluence Park, the man-made course flowed for 50 yards over a series of two-foot ledges. There were about 15 closely-spaced gates. The water itself was somewhat less than pristine. But I enjoyed myself, running the course five or six times. After each run, I carried back up over a strategically-placed rock garden in mid-river. Those who constructed the course knew what they were doing.

We had encountered pouring rain in Denver, and the storm, which had subsided long enough to let me enjoy the slalom course, caught up with us in Colorado Springs. Between showers, Lee and Heather went horseback riding in Garden of the Gods. The rain returned in the evening, but when we awakened the next morning, it was clear and clean, and we continued our journey to the Arkansas River. We arrived at Echo Canyon right on schedule, at 8:15 a.m., and we were greeted by a smiling Dave Burch and his wife Kim.

"Glad to see you."

"Glad to be here."

Dave showed us a map of the river, which flows for nearly 100 miles and offers rapids ranging from Class II to V in difficulty. "We're here," he said, pointing a finger at the map, "and this morning we'll be running a 10-mile stretch between Pinnacle Rock and Parkdale."

I squinted at the section of the map on which his finger was resting and saw a number of rapids rated as Class IIIs and IVs and even a V. I must have blanched a bit, because he smiled and said, "Those are the ratings for high water levels in the spring. It won't be as hard today. Even with the rain we've had, the rapids will undoubtedly be easier at this time of the year."

In a leisurely manner, we loaded everything onto a van and trailer. Dave and Lisa and I would be kayaking. My wife and daughter would be rafting along with a young married couple from Texas. They would be accompanied by a raft guide, who introduced himself. "Hi. I'm Craig. From North Carolina."

"That's where we're from," my wife declared.

"Where?"

"Asheville. Where are you from?"

"Greensboro."

Craig, we learned, had worked previously for the Nantahala Outdoor Center and was now in his second summer with Echo Canyon. He kept us entertained with wild rafting tales as we drove to the put-in. The highway paralleled the river on one side, offering easy access. On the opposite side, rocky hills arose. I was surprised at the river's narrowness. Nowhere was it more than 40' across, and often it constricted to 20', creating the rapids.

A short time later, as Dave and Lisa and I pushed off, I discovered the current to be swift and the water temperature to be cool. But with the sun blazing above, it felt good. The river rushed us along at a swirling Class II pace. Wake-up Rapid was a twisty II+, with a nice surfing wave at the bottom. Lisa, from California, had attended Dartmouth College in New England, where she'd learned to kayak with the well-known Ledyard Club. It was easy to see she had learned her lessons well.

Three Rock Falls was a III, consisting of a two-foot drop into froth and foam, followed by a five-foot drop into more of the same. Five Points was a different type of III, with three-foot waves hurrying us down into a maze of small boulders which we skirted successfully. I was puffing now in the 6,500' altitude, and the adrenaline started pumping harder as Dave said, "Spike Buck Falls is next. It's probably the toughest rapid we'll tackle today."

We coasted along, chatting, and after a while he turned again and said, "This is it. Let's start on the right side and cut back to the left to avoid the falls at the bottom right. Follow me."

He was propelled by rushing three-foot waves into a lengthy rapid, and I bounced along behind him, trailing by 25 yards, with Lisa the same distance behind me. It was indeed a tough one, a Class IV, I felt, as I began losing control. Halfway down, Dave cut back to the left, but I was too slow. The quick current caught me and pushed me to the right, toward the small falls below. I struggled, braced, paddled, prayed, as I careened around big boulders. Luckily, at mid-summer level, the falls didn't amount to much, mostly a short plunge into a curler, which I punched HARD and successfully. As I eddied out, I was soaking wet but smiling.

We surfed at the curler, then joined the rafters for a 20-minute rest on the river bank, where my wife sat on a cactus and jumped up, shouting in dismay. Everyone laughed. "You Eastern greenhorns!" Craig chortled.

We made arrangements for Kim Burch, who was driving shuttle, to photograph us running Shark's Tooth, the next rapid. It was a III, requiring some maneuvering on top and then a seesaw ride down the middle into a five-foot stopper wave, which obviously was "the tooth." I blasted into it, was thrown to the left, braced, and paddled on. Double Dip also was a III, and I roller-coasted through it. Puppy was an easier II+. And that was it.

Three hours after starting, we reached the take-out, where we were interviewed by a young man from the Bureau of Land Management who was engaged in a river-user research project. "We'll hafta hustle," Dave told us, "because we have a group of 15 coming in for our afternoon rafting trip."

Thus it was that an hour later, as Lee and Heather and I stood above the river, studying the section we had just completed, Echo Canyon's van and trailer came whizzing past us with their load of rafts and afternoon customers. And we heard Craig shouting, "Eat water!"

We moved up Highway 50 through Salida to Buena Vista, where we ate an enjoyable mid-afternoon meal at Delaney's Depot. Then it was up, Up, UP and over 12,000' Independence Pass to Aspen, and later to Glenwood Springs, where, as the sun vanished behind western peaks, we basked in the 101 degree water of a huge hot springs pool.

The Arkansas River had been left behind, but it had provided us with an exciting whitewater trip, and we still had two more Colorado rivers to run before heading to Wyoming. Westward ho!

*****

Morning comes late to Jackson Hole in northwestern Wyoming. In mid-summer, it's practically mid-morning before the sun has gathered enough strength to sneak above the Gros Ventre Mountains. Slowly the previous night's chill disappears.

The name "hole" was used by early explorers and trappers to identify high valleys situated between even higher mountains. Thus Jackson Hole is a 6,400' valley nestled between the Gros Ventre Range to the east and the famed Teton Mountains to the west. The Gros Ventre are soft, rounded, forested, much like the Smokies in the eastern U.S. The Tetons are well, starkly spectacular. They cover only 40 miles from north to south, less than 15 from east to west, but at least eight or nine peaks exceed 10,000', and one, Grand Teton itself, reaches skyward to 13,700'. Snow-capped even in July, they completely dominate the landscape. On our visit to Yellowstone National Park, my eyes were drawn constantly back to the Tetons.

I had been to Yellowstone once before in mid-winter, when it was almost deserted. Now Lee and Heather and I were there in mid-summer, along with a zillion others, most of whom kept slowing us down in their huge RVs. We viewed Old Faithful and the Upper and Lower Falls on the Yellowstone River and a few other sites, but frankly, we were glad to escape from the overcrowded park and return to our cabin in Hoback Junction. Looking back, that's a sad commentary. But true.

After a week in Colorado, during which I'd practiced briefly on Denver's downtown slalom course and paddled three rivers for fun, we were now spending a week in Wyoming. The day after our visit to Yellowstone, I waited in mid-morning at Hoback Junction for Linda Hibbard to pick me up. Linda, who said she preferred to be called by her nickname, Link, was the owner of the Snake River Kayak School. She drove up in her "new" van, which actually was a four-year-old model that she'd outfitted for her own particular needs. She chattered at length about the van, pride shining in her face, and it took me a while to get her talking about the river we'd be running, the Hoback.

Most of us as paddlers have a faraway dream river dwelling in the hidden corners of our minds. The Hoback was mine. I had dreamed about it ever since seeing a photo of the river that showed a kayak coming down a narrow passageway through small, sparkling waves, with mountains in the background and a bright sun above. I learned that the photo had been taken at the 1976 National Slalom Championships, conducted on the Hoback, and this increased my interest even more. My vision was magnified when a guidebook described it thusly: "It's about Class III and is more difficult near the mouth than upstream. This handsome river is white and fast. Don't run it alone. When high, it can have heavy water and assorted ledges and rollers. The biggest rapid, near the mouth, is beneath black cliffs and cannot be seen from the road."

With the sun finally starting to provide some warmth, Link parked her van at the take-out, where the Hoback flows into the larger Snake River, and my wife, in our car, drove us up the highway to the put-in. From the highway, we could look down at some sections of the river, although other stretches remained hidden from us. Named for a hunter and trapper, John Hoback, who guided groups into Jackson Hole from 1811 to 1815, the river appeared to be extremely attractive, just as I had imagined in my dreams.

"As is often the case, the best rapids can't be seen from the road," Link warned me, "but they won't be too hard at this time of the year."

Thirty minutes later, from the University of Michigan's Field Station bordering the river, we pushed off into the quick current, and Link indicated it would be a six-mile run to the take-out. The water was ICY cold even in mid-summer, comparable to the Nantahala, and for an hour we kayaked through patches of choppy one-foot waves. The river was shallow, narrow, rocky, with shrubs and trees lining both banks. The sun was bright above, and the mountains surrounded us. During the second hour, we began seeing signs of civilization: houses and people, ranches and horses. But still we had the river to ourselves.

"Where's everyone else?" I asked.

"Over on the Snake River Canyon," Link explained. "The locals paddle the Hoback in the spring, when it's a Class III, sometimes a IV, but in the summer, when it's lower, like this, with Class II and II+ rapids, they all move over to the Snake."

"I think this is a pretty nice river right here, just the way it is."

"So do I. In fact, this is where I teach most of my kayak classes."

Now in her 30s, Link told me she grew up in New England, graduated from Northwestern University in Illinois, and had spent the past dozen years paddling. She was one of the founders of Phoenix, Inc., a company in Kentucky that built some of the world's first fiberglass kayaks. In 1973, she became the U.S. K-1W champion in slalom. At present, she said, she was spending her winters in Boulder, Colorado, and her summers in Jackson Hole, operating her kayak school.

The rapids on the Hoback were increasing in size. The fast, cold current was pushing us through two-foot waves now, and we stopped frequently to do some surfing. We also stopped for lunch atop a big boulder overlooking a deep eddy, and as we ate, I peered down into the crystal-clear water at the trout swimming far below. I sighed, relaxed, and relished the gorgeous scenery, spoiled only by a bunch of ornery black flies.

"The best rapids are yet to come," Link stated. "Let's hit 'em."

During our third and final hour, we ran a number of Class II and II+ rapids, one of which required a nifty swerve over a four-foot drop. A bit later, while surfing in a swift-moving three-foot hole, I was rudely overturned. The freezing water took my breath away, but I rolled up, gasping and wheezing after the current had carried me 40 yards downstream.

As we neared the confluence with the Snake and our take-out spot, we ran one downhill rapid into a long field of three-foot haystacks. "Wow! What a nice one!" I shouted. "Does it have a name?"

"Not that I know of," Link answered, "but let's call it Ambrosia Rapid."

"Ambrosia?"

"Sure. It's nothing but sweet."

Eventually our trip came to an end. The Hoback had been everything I'd hoped it would be: swift and scenic, cold and clear, with rocky rapids that were Class I at the beginning and then Class II and II+, just enough to make it exciting, even in July.

Link interrupted my reverie. "Ready for tomorrow?" she flung at me.

"I guess so."

We were scheduled to kayak the Snake River Canyon the next day. BIG water. ROUGH rapids. Was I ready? With the trip down my dream river completed, I'd now be testing myself on the tough stuff. Hey, bring it on.

*****

"I believe it's an osprey," said Link Hibbard.

"No, I don't think so," I replied. "I think it's an omen of the year to come."

With my paddle lying across my spray-skirt, I remained motionless, letting the current carry me gently down the shoreline. My eyes were focused on the large white-headed bird in the tree ahead. Slowly, cautiously, I pulled back the spray-skirt and fumbled inside the cockpit, easing out my antiquated 8mm camera. As I drifted closer to the bird, I saw that it was indeed what I had hoped, an American bald eagle. The current kept pushing me along, beneath the nesting bird, and I shot about 30 seconds of film as I passed by.

"It's an eagle," I told Link.

"And a beauty, at that," she agreed.

We were on the Snake River Canyon in northwestern Wyoming, and seeing the eagle reminded me that Congress would soon be considering a bill to make the next year, 1982, into "the year of the American bald eagle." This would be in recognition of the fact that 200 years previously, in 1782, the bird was adopted as our national symbol. Now an endangered species, the American bald eagle was in need of protection, and I was thrilled to see one nesting on the Snake.

I had come to the Snake to test my kayaking competence on one of the country's premier whitewater rivers. A quartet of my paddling pals back in Asheville – Sean Devereux, Jim Goldsmith, Ed Krause, Jim Maynor – had done the Snake River Canyon the preceding summer. "Lots of Class IIIs," they told me, "and a few IVs."

As this was to be the most difficult challenge on my four-week western trip with wife Lee and daughter Heather, I had done some extra reading about the Snake, which meanders out of Yellowstone as a calm Class I, snaking its way on a southward course beneath the majestic Tetons. Eventually it enters the canyon section. There, in the spring, the Snake storms through with 10-foot waves and Class V rapids, attracting only whitewater experts. By mid-summer, it has subsided a bit and can be attempted by ordinary mortals like me.

So with Link, I was on the Snake, the nesting eagle behind us, and I tucked away the camera as we became engulfed in two-foot waves. We were being escorted down the river by a covey of rafts from a variety of companies that take thousands of tourists down the Snake Canyon annually. It was a bright and sunny day. The river was fairly warm, and though wide, contained a large volume of rushing water. We moved along quickly, roller-coasting through two-foot and three-foot waves.

"The first real rapid is just ahead," Link said. "It's called Station Creek, and it's not too tough."

She was right. It wasn't too tough. The size of the waves increased a little, to perhaps four feet, and swirled around, buffeting my boat from side to side, but I had no trouble. The next two rapids, Blue Slide and Blue Bell, were similar, with medium-sized waves but no rocks.

Unlike eastern rivers, where the primary problem is not the waves but the many menacing rocks and boulders, the Snake offered larger waves and trickier currents but practically no battering, boat-busting boulders.

"Show us a roll!" shouted some of the rafters drifting past, and Link obliged, deftly turning over and up again with a single swift sweep of her paddle. The rafters applauded. I did a practice roll myself, and we continued downriver.

"The rapids we've done are IIIs," stated Link. "The next two are harder. Big Kahuna is rather unpredictable. We'd better scout it."

Moments later we eddied out on the left side of the river, hopped out, and walked to a large boulder formation overlooking the river. Here the river narrowed, pouring over a ledge and creating a nasty six-foot hole. Link pointed at it. "You don't want to get stuck in that," she shouted over the rapid's roar. "It's a mean one, a keeper for sure. You should sneak it on this side."

I nodded and returned to my boat, with Link remaining on the boulder, a throw-rope in her hand just in case I had difficulty. As always, the landmarks that seemed so obvious from shore vanished as I was caught by the pulsating current and pushed toward the ledge. I back-paddled in the three-foot waves, ferrying slightly, straining my neck to catch a glimpse of the narrow chute which would carry me safely past the deep hole. Then I was in the chute, sucking air into my lungs, pounding down past the ledge into a field of bouncing five-foot waves, eventually eddying out.

Link followed, and though it was a Class IV, she made it look easy. As she paddled up to me, she smiled and said, "There's a harder one ahead. Longer. Bigger waves. Lunch Counter Rapid. Should we scout it?"

"Let's not. I'll follow you down."

We rode Lunch Counter right down the middle. Right through four- and five-foot waves that came at us from every conceivable angle. I was pummeled by the water. My boat was lifted, shoved to the left, submerged, pushed to the right, thrown back, punished, as we hurtled down a 90- to 100-yard torrent of whitewater. The eddy below was swirling, whirlpooling, laughing, taunting as if to say, You survived the tough stuff, but can you handle me? I laughed back, but not until I had carefully climbed ashore.

Link did some playing in Lunch Counter. I filmed her ferrying, rolling, endering. Then we sat and enjoyed a picnic lunch, watching as a dozen rafts from as many different companies came through, their occupants squealing and shouting. Then came two kayakers, obviously familiar with the river and the rapid, displaying strong, solid techniques.

Link talked about Walt Blackadar, maybe the country's best-known kayaker of the 1970s, a close friend of hers, who lost his life in an unfortunate accident on a river in Idaho. He was getting old, she said, and was having shoulder problems. His roll wasn't as good. His eyesight wasn't as good. His confidence wasn't as good. Still, he shouldn't have died when he did, where he did.

"How old was he?" I asked.

"I believe he was 55, maybe 56. How old are you, Chuck?"

"I'm 48."

"I guess you have a few more years to go."

Yes, I thought. I hope I do.

Rope Rapid was next, nestled between canyon walls and the tree-covered mountains farther above. We rode three- and four-foot waves down a long, l-o-n-g 200-yard corridor. Pure pleasure. Champagne Rapid was trickier. Bubbles oozing up from submerged rocks created a foamy surface. Our paddles slid uselessly through the aerated water. It was a helpless feeling. "Isn't this a unique one," Link grinned. Then she added, "The next rapids, Little Cottonwood and Cottonwood, will remind you of eastern rivers. Rocky. Good maneuvering is essential. In my opinion, these are the most dangerous rapids on the Snake, so be careful."

I felt right at home in the Cottonwoods. They reminded me of Quarter-mile Rapid on the Nolichucky, an hour's drive from Asheville. In the Cottonwoods, the waves were smaller, but there were rocks and boulders and ledges scattered across the entire width of the river. Link, knowing the best path to take, hurried on ahead, challenging me to find my own route. I was sweating beneath the warm summer sun. And alone. Link had disappeared around a bend. There were no rafts in sight. I moved slowly, winding my way through the maze with a stroke here, a draw there, another stroke, a brace, another stroke, a bounce off a big boulder, a plunge over a short drop, yet another brace.

Rounding the bend, I saw Link ahead. The rapid continued. So did I, finally reaching the bottom. Sighing with relief. Smiling to myself.

Another mile of two- and three-foot waves brought us to the take-out. As we dragged our boats ashore, Link turned and said, "You're in pretty good shape for an old guy."

"Well, I'm testing myself on this trip. So far I've done all right in Colorado and Wyoming. In two days, we'll drive into Montana, and I'll try the Madison River. We'll stop off in South Dakota to show our daughter the Bad Lands and Mount Rushmore. After that, we'll visit our relatives and some friends in Minnesota, and I hope to paddle a river or two there. Then we'll head back to North Carolina."

Link caught a ride back to the put-in to retrieve her car. As I awaited her return, I watched the unbelievable number of commercial rafts finishing their runs. A teenaged boy, soaking wet, turned to his raft guide and blurted, "That's the most fun I've ever had."

It HAD been fun. What can be better than good companionship, a beautiful day, scenic mountains, and a challenging river to run? It had brought out the best in me. I lowered my head and said a silent prayer of thanks to the Giver of All Good Gifts. Surely our rivers were treasures to be cherished, enjoyed, preserved. How, I wondered, could we get that message across to our national leaders? How can we speak for the American bald eagle? How do we repay God for what He (or She) has given us?

The Snake River Canyon had provided me not only with a day of delight but also with some important questions to ponder.

*****

Even more than I remembered from having grown up in Minnesota, the mosquitoes were in control. They succeeded in chasing me off the Kettle River, located about 90 miles north of St. Paul. Returning home from our western vacation, we stopped in St. Paul to visit my wife's family members and a few old friends.

Lee had grown up in the small town of Forest Lake, which isn't too far from St. Paul. After graduating from high school, she attended Gustavus-Adolphus College on a nursing scholarship. I was there on a swimming scholarship. One day while eating at the college cafeteria, I saw her standing in line, and it was love at first sight. Literally. I turned to my swimming teammates who were seated at the table with me and said, "See that girl over there? She's the one I'm going to marry."

I didn't even know her name, but as I write this book, Lee and I have been married for 53 years. That's another story.

My hometown was Rochester, Minnesota, where my father was a Mayo Clinic physician. He and my mother were initially from South Carolina – he from Seneca, she from Charleston – but dad was called to serve at the Clinic, where he became head of the Internal Medicine Dept. and Vice-President of the Clinic staff. Our family vacations when I was young usually involved going to the Carolinas to visit relatives. So I've had a Southern heritage and a Northern upbringing.

After I returned from duty in Korea with the U.S. Army, Lee and I were married. That was in 1955. By then, she had become a full-fledged Registered Nurse, and I ended up graduating from the University of Minnesota with a degree in Recreation Administration. I wish I could have been a physician like my dad. That's not what the Good Lord called me to do. I was not a healer. But from my dad, I learned about the importance of Cooperation. He was very good at working with others. From my mom, who was sports-minded, I learned about being Competitive when it was necessary. From my mom's sister, my aunt Mary, an educator, I learned about Competence and striving for excellence. From my younger brother Harvey, who had a severe learning disability, I learned about Compassion. From my wife Lee, I learned about Commitment and sticking with a job until it was finished. These were (are) the family members who shaped my character.

Because of my athletic abilities, especially when it came to water sports, I ended up having and enjoying a 40-year career with the YMCA that took me from Minnesota to Iowa to Illinois and in 1969 to Asheville, North Carolina, where I have resided ever since. No regrets. I think my character qualities, as listed in the preceding paragraph, enabled me to have a good Y career.

The YMCA is a wonderful organization, and as I have explained previously in this book, it was through the Y that I became involved with whitewater kayaking and racing. It was my participation in kayaking that took Lee and me and daughter Heather on our western trip, and thus we ended up in St. Paul while en route home.

One day I drove to the Kettle River, reputed to have some of the best whitewater in Minnesota. When I arrived, I discovered that I had the place to myself. So I put my beat-up Perception Spirit into the river at Banning State Park, just 50 yards upriver from famed Blueberry Slide. It was a rapid that reminded me somewhat of Patton's Run on the Nantahala, but was harder.

It had rained heavily in central Minnesota, and the water level was up. I judged Blueberry to be a solid Class III. There were several good ledges at the top of the rapid which I surfed, followed by a 30-yard zip down the left side through three- and four-foot waves, then a cut-back to the right around an assortment of rocks and ledges, and finally another 15-yard zip through two- and three-foot waves. Sort of an S-turn type of rapid.

With my boat on my shoulder, I walked back up the foot path on the right side of the river, and it was there that I met my match. The mosquitoes owned this area and were unwilling to share their space with any visitors. Regardless, I ran Blueberry a second time, catching an eddy on the left side where a five-foot waterfall cascaded into the flow. I sat for a while in the eddy, listening to the sounds of summer. This, I realized for the umpteenth time, was the reason I loved whitewater kayaking so much. I liked teaching and coaching others. I liked racing. I liked winning an occasional race. I appreciated my paddling pals. But this – harmonizing with Mother Nature – was the best part of it.

I wasn't about to let the mosquitoes spoil my party. They were relentless as I walked up the pathway after my second run. But I was determined to paddle Blueberry one more time. I had to slap several dozen mosquitoes away from inside my boat as I fastened my spray-skirt. On my third run, I played all the way down, and I became a bit concerned about the water quality, as the river was the color of iron rust or copper, quite unlike most of Minnesota's clear lakes and rivers.

After dressing and packing up, just as I was preparing to leave, two vans pulled up with Blue Hole canoes and Perception kayaks on top. I chatted for 20 minutes with the paddlers who were from Minneapolis. We batted away mosquitoes the whole time, and that night, when I changed into my 'jamas, my wife counted 30 mosquito bites all over my body.

Mother Nature doesn't always get it right.

*****

Where, I wondered, gulping another mouthful of river water, are Wahoo's Wild Whitewater Wrafters when you need them?

No one answered. But I hadn't expected a reply, since I was up to my chest in the rushing rapids of the Nolichucky River Gorge. I was swimming, not kayaking, and it was deliberately, not accidentally. Scrambling for a toehold, grasping desperately to avoid being swept away, I stretched out and touched the twin-bladed paddle that was impaled on the rocks. As I did so, the circumstances which had led to this bizarre situation flashed through my mind.

It was a month after our family trip out west, and with eight members of the Asheville YMCA Kayak Club, I'd come to the Nolichucky Gorge, which is generally regarded as one of Western North Carolina's most difficult runs. On numerous occasions, we had done an easier section of the river, with its Class II rapids, as part of the concluding river trips for our Y classes. The Gorge was something else. It was a lengthy Class III-IV challenge, at least when water levels were sufficient. I'd done the Gorge twice before, and on this third trip we were being led by calm, cool, collected Chuck Baker.

In addition to the two Chucks – Baker and Hines – we had Mike Harper, Jim Maynor, Murray Parker, Charles White, plus three of our Y teenagers – Chase Ambler, Doug Baker, John Sherman – who'd be on the Noli Gorge for the first time.

At the put-in near the diminutive hamlet of Poplar, we chatted amongst ourselves and with the rafting guides from Nolichucky Expeditions and Cherokee Outdoor Adventures. We laughed as a third outfitter pulled up: Wahoo's Wild Whitewater Wrafters! "That's a new one," someone said, as we watched them unloading half-a-dozen orange inflatables. Then, beneath overcast skies, we were off, stroking the 200 yards that led into the Gorge, from which there would be no exit until we emerged nine miles downriver.

"We'd better scout On-the-Rocks," said Chuck Baker. "That's the first significant rapid, and it's tricky." Eddying out on the left bank, we spent 10 minutes scouting. The approach to this Class IV was straight-forward down a five-foot chute and directly into a pile of rocks. To survive, a quick, hard swerve to the right was necessary. Jim demonstrated as the rest of us watched. He strained as the chute blasted him into the rocks, sweeping hard and leaning, leaning, and he barely managed to squeeze through the narrow opening on the right. I was next, and I banged into the rocks. I balanced precariously, then luckily pushed myself backwards through the narrow opening into calmer water. "I suppose you backed through on purpose, just to show off," Jim chuckled. "Of course," I smiled.

We also stopped and scouted Quarter-Mile. This very challenging Class IV was difficult at any level, but as I watched, most of our guys ran the first 200 or 250 yards with skill and success. Even Murray, who flipped at the first of the two five-foot drops at the beginning, rolled up quickly and continued, cutting back to the right at exactly the right moment, catching the small eddy, and slipping through the big boulder patch.

I was next to last and, like Murray, I overturned at the first drop quite unexpectedly, rolled hurriedly and just in time to plunge over the second drop, skirted the mid-river hydraulic, and eddied out to wait for Charles, who was bringing up the rear. His boat preceded him down the river. He came a minute later, tumbling wildly in the three- and four-foot waves. His paddle trailed, and as I watched, it became trapped in the mid-river madness, one end caught beneath a rock and the other end waving in the air. He made it to the opposite bank about 60 yards farther downriver. His kayak became pinned between two gigantic boulders.

Charles was all right, and his boat could be extricated, but how about his paddle? I could see nowhere to eddy out near the wobbling paddle, so I parked my boat on the right bank, took a deep breath, and waded out into the churning water. It was wavy, slippery, rocky, and hazardous. Had I not been a strong swimmer, I wouldn't have tried it. Even so, I struggled against the overpowering forces of the roaring rapid.

As I reached out for the bobbing blade of the paddle, about 25 yards from shore, it dawned on me that one of Wahoo's orange inflatables would have made an excellent rescue vehicle. It could have bounced right over the offending rocks without any problems, enabling the rider to reach out and grab the trapped kayak paddle. But Wahoo & Co. hadn't shown up, so with a final lunge, I tipped the paddle's blade just enough to dislodge it and send it spinning downriver. Now I had to make it back to shore myself, and by the time I did, I was completely exhausted, my heart pounding furiously and my breath coming in quick gasps. I'm too old for this, I murmured.

Eventually I ferried across to the opposite side, where I worked with Jim and Charles to free the latter's kayak, putting our throw ropes to good use. Then, wearily, I had to face the prospect of paddling the final 200 yards of Quarter-Mile Rapid. I did so with less difficulty than I anticipated and uttered a sigh of relief as I squeezed down the extreme right side of Murphy's Ledge, a boulder-infested six-foot drop at the rapid's end. There I discovered that both Chase and John had flipped and swum as they negotiated Quarter-Mile's final stretches, but both had recovered nicely.

We were now ready to tackle Loner, a Class III, and Roostertail, a IV. Chuck Baker led us through Roostertail, starting at the right side and angling sharply to the left down a steep decline. The riverwide hydraulic, halfway down, threw Doug sky-high. He did an involuntary ender and crashed back into the water. Roll, Doug. Roll. Then I became too busy myself to see if he was rolling. The hydraulic, or hole, captured me, battered me, and I braced, leaned, braced, leaned, and was shoved through into a field of standing waves, eddying out below.

We had been on the river for two hours, but we had traveled only three miles, during which we had encountered eight Class III and IV rapids. "Let's take a break," the trip leader suggested, so we relaxed and ate lunch on a big boulder. We were alone, yet together, beneath the Unaka Mountain peaks that towered 2,000' above us. "It's beautiful here," someone said. "Awesome," came the reply.

But we still had six miles to go. We paddled through a bunch of Class IIIs – Roly-Poly, Upper Rollercoaster, Lower Rollercoaster, No-Name, Eat 'Em Alive – without incident. "Rock Garden is next," Charles warned me. "Yes," I responded, recalling Rock Garden as being 200 yards of, well, rocks. Halfway down, I became lodged between two of the rocks. It became obvious I wasn't going any farther. Reluctantly, I hopped out and carried my boat about 100 yards in ankle- to knee-deep water, slipping and sliding and fuming. While the others in our group – the lighter ones maybe? or the better paddlers perhaps? – eased through Rock Garden, I huffed and puffed and carried. At the bottom, as I plunked down my kayak, Mike cruised up. He smiled slyly and asked, "Problems?" I snorted in disgust. At myself.

Sycamore Shoals was an exciting Class III, with good-sized waves, a large eddy halfway down on the left, and a five-foot plunge into a convergent whirlpool at the bottom. We rounded the bend, riding three-foot waves toward Sousehole, which I skirted on the left side. This was followed by Railroad Rapid, Big Eddy Drop, and Stateline Shoals as we entered Tennessee. Somewhere along Shoo-fly Shoals, a mile-long section of small waves and rock-dodging, I neglected to make a sharp right turn over a drop and plowed into a wall of rocks. Sitting there, I heard the jeers of my paddling pals. I jumped out and took a bow. With Charles' assistance, I backed my boat up, re-entered, and ran the drop the right way, feeling embarrassed.

Finally we reached the calm stretch near Nolichucky Expeditions' wilderness headquarters indicating that the take-out was less than a mile away. We had now been on the river for five hours. At the end were three simple Class IIs, and sure enough, one of them snagged John, who went swimming. "How could I bomb out on that little ledge?" he wondered.

"You're just tired," Murray told him, and I knew it to be true. All of us were tired. My shoulders were sore, my legs stiff, and I had a number of scratches and bruises on my right leg, some still bleeding lightly as a result of "rescuing" the errant paddle back at Quarter-Mile.

Loading up and shuttling back to the put-in to retrieve one of our vehicles took a long time. Nearly two hours. It was slow going through the mountain wilderness. "I guess the inconvenience of the shuttle is one reason we don't do the Noli Gorge more often," Jim surmised, maneuvering his van around a curve on the unpaved road. I nodded in agreement. A mile or so down the road, we drove into a downpour. "I sure am glad we didn't have to paddle in this," Jim said. Again I nodded. "Still and all," he continued, "I had a good time today, didn't you?" Once more I nodded and then, like all good paddlers at the end of an exciting day of whitewater adventure, I dozed off, dreaming of other rivers and rapids yet to come.

*****

"YMCA Kayakers" was the headline in the Citizen-Times. That was all. But the article on September 16, 1981, was long, long, and contained a review of what we had accomplished in our YMCA program. "Recognized as the leader in the sport of kayaking locally is the Asheville YMCA, whose kayakers earlier this year swept the Southeastern Championships of the United States Canoe Association, winning the men's, women's and junior kayak races…

"The Y's involvement started in 1976 when Chuck Hines, the YMCA's Vice-President of Aquatics, was asked by the National Physical Education Management Team to develop a curriculum that could be used by Ys across the country for teaching whitewater kayaking…

"Hines, an occasional canoeist, was somewhat less than enthused, but after a couple of brief lessons in a kayak, he headed to the Nantahala River, whose none-too-gentle rapids spilled him repeatedly. He returned home convinced that lessons given in a warm, calm pool, supplemented by safety instruction given in a comfortable classroom, would be a better way to learn kayaking. He agreed to develop the curriculum and contracted with the whitewater experts at the Nantahala Outdoor Center to assist with creating an experimental course at the Asheville YMCA...

"The first such course was conducted during the winter of 1977, and even with snow on the ground, more people registered than could be handled. So a second course was added, followed by a third, and then a special course just for youngsters...

"It wasn't long before graduates of the Y's kayaking courses were distinguishing themselves in local whitewater races. Hines himself improved so much that he returned to the Nantahala in 1979 and placed first in the Masters slalom competition ...

"Jim Maynor has been the most productive racer, though. He has twice won the Carolina Cup, and he won the men's wildwater race at the Southeastern Championships earlier this year. Perhaps the most versatile racer has been Will Pruett, a consistent challenger and frequent champion in kayak and canoe, slalom and wildwater. Not to be outdone, the Y's women have held their own in whitewater racing. Kathy Koon has been a winner on the Dan, Mayo, and French Broad Rivers. Anne Terrell and Kathy McLaughlin have been winners also...

"Hines said he is proudest of the Y's youth kayakers, listing Brent Lawson, Doug Baker, John Sherman, Chase Ambler, and Rick Hensley as being the race leaders on the boys' team. He also mentioned 11-year-old Mark Mathews, who already can roll his kayak and is pushing the older fellows...

"Amy Pruett, Deanna Davis, Heather Hines, and Karen Miller are the girls who have been winners...

"Curtis Bull of Miami, Florida, and Becky Weis of Lafayette, Indiana, are two 13-year-olds who have won races after training with the Asheville YMCA club…

"With such successful competitive performers on the roster, it's surprising to hear Hines say that the Y doesn't really emphasize racing that much. He said some of the best Y kayakers don't compete at all. They are satisfied running the rapids on treacherous rivers around the country, which Hines said takes just as much skill as racing, perhaps more. He lists Chuck Baker, Kent and Mary Ann Davidson, Sean Devereux, Jim and Carol Goodrum, Ed Hay, Rich Isaac, Rob Kern, Rocky Meadows, Jerry Mills, Ed Scott, and Charles White, all of Asheville, plus Jim and Susan Goldsmith of Marion, Ed Krause of Mars Hill, and John Bayless, Preston Brown, Rich Maggi, Jim and Mark Sheppard, and Clyde Stahl, all of Hendersonville, as being prominent big water paddlers who have successfully kayaked all over the country on various Class IV and V rivers…

"This fall the Asheville YMCA is conducting an adult intermediate course, and as is usually the case, the class is full. No longer does the Y depend on outside instructors. Hines and the other locals have become certified themselves to teach the curriculum they've developed here, which is now being adopted by the National Physical Education Management Team for use by Ys nationally."

That was a wonderful summary of our efforts. In fact, it sounded like something that could have been written by our media department at the YMCA. Hmmmm.

*****

We concluded the year with a number of recreational river cruises. My notebook shows that the water levels were rather low throughout the Southeast, with the Chattooga gauge registering a mere 0.4. As a result, everyone went to a handful of dam-fed rivers, such as the Nantahala, Green, and Broad. A list of those who went on these YMCA-sponsored trips would include Jerry and Linda Ariail, Lorri Cameron, Mike Hill,

Rex Hoffman, Jodi Jackson, Rob Kern, John Lawrance, Harold Mathews and son Mark, Jim Maynor, Les and Joe McGuire, Rocky Meadows, Will Pruett and daughter Amy, Mike Sherrill, Brian Smith, Anne Terrell, and the Hines Kayak Team of Chuck and daughter Heather.

At the Broad, also called the Rocky Broad for good reasons, a few miles east of Asheville, the toughest rapid, nicknamed Rocky Drop, was easy at the top due to the low level but was practically impassable below, with the normal left-side route unrunnable. Jim Maynor banged down the right side, careening crazily, as everybody else watched. Then Will Pruett tried a more direct route down the middle, which required a sharp 90 degree turn around a boulder and a five-foot plunge into the pool below, followed by a quick draw past another menacing boulder. How can a Class II be so annoying? What should we do?

Jim and Will jumped out of their boats and stood in mid-river at the sharp drop and rocky plunge, and they assisted those who needed it, while I stood by with my throw-rope. With their help, everyone eased through, with one flipping and rolling and another swimming into the pool. Others went sideways or backwards. One lost his paddle. It was pretty funny. But we made sure it was safe.

*****

"Dear Chuck," said a letter I received from John Lawrance, a YMCA member and one of our four national champions in Masters swimming, "I've been trying to write this letter to express my feelings about the kayaking course and the various river trips, but haven't found the time until now. First and foremost, I want to thank you and Jim, Will, Rocky, and Anne for one of the most enjoyable and pleasant experiences of my life. But especially you, because you're the one who planted the spirit of adventure in my head back in January and February on several Saturday mornings…

"At one time or another, I suppose all of us are reluctant to change or try something that's different. But you made kayaking seem so enjoyable and rewarding that I felt I would be missing out on something if I didn't take advantage of the opportunity. Meeting new challenges must be the elixir of life! It keeps you young and your senses fine-tuned. At any rate, I have had a great time kayaking with the YMCA this year. Thanks again for a wonderful experience."

The newspaper article about our program was nice, but positively influencing others' lives is what the Y is all about, and this letter has stayed with me ever since I received it. But it wasn't just for me. It was a tribute to ALL those who'd worked so diligently to develop our YMCA kayaking curriculum.

✦Photos✦

Author Chuck Hines started canoeing at age 12 and is seen here with his wife Lee shortly after their marriage in 1955, canoeing down the St. Croix River on the Minnesota-Wisconsin border.

Will Pruett, left, and Chuck, right, were the prime movers in the Asheville YMCA's kayaking curriculum, which was started in 1977 and became a national YMCA program in 1982.

Becky Weis came to the Asheville YMCA to train as a 13-year-old and won U.S. K-1W junior slalom championships in 1983 and 1985. Later she taught beginners in the Y pool and won an international Gold medal in kayak freestyle competition.

Kevin Drury and Mark Mathews, 1985 U.S. K-1 junior champions in wildwater and slalom, prepare for a practice at the Asheville YMCA's French Broad River slalom course with Wayne Dickert, who went on to compete in the 1996 Olympic Games in C-2.

Hundreds of Asheville youngsters learned to kayak in the YMCA pool and then went on river cruises, including this group led by Chuck, seated left, and Jim Maynor, standing right.

For coaching champions in swimming, whitewater racing, water polo, and triathlon, Chuck, seen here surrounded by family members, was inducted into the Western North Carolina Sports Hall of Fame.

Adam Clawson, left, of the Nantahala Racing Club, competed in the 1992 Olympic Games in C-1. Then he qualified for the 1996 Olympics. He also was an Olympic Torchbearer, as was the author, right.

Some of the Nantahala Racing Club's Olympians take a break from practicing at the Ocoee River. Front: Scott Shipley and Lecky Haller. Rear: Scott Strausbaugh, Horace Holden, Wayne Dickert, and Joe Jacobi.

"That way to the Ocoee," points out Horace Holden, as he and Wayne Dickert practice in the Asheville YMCA pool.

Here's Horace and Wayne churning through the waves on the Ocoee River as they win the C-2 race at the U.S. Team Trials and qualify for the 1996 Olympic Games.

After two years of planning, we started a Junior Olympic Program in 1996, and two of the best young stars were the Johnson twins, Russell and Jeffrey, who won numerous national Junior/Junior Olympic titles while representing the Nantahala Racing Club.

An effort was made to enroll more girls in the Junior Olympic Program. Here are some of the K-1W winners at the Southeast regional competition including, kneeling in front, NRC's Becca Red and Gwen Greeley, both national winners who competed internationally.

After playing second fiddle to the famed Bethesda Center of Excellence for many years, the Nantahala Racing Club WON the U.S. Senior Slalom Championships in 1997 and celebrated with an end-of-the-year Christmas party. The Rhinos remained national champions in 1998, 1999, and 2000.

Not even a blizzard that hit Western North Carolina in the spring of 1998 could keep the NRC board of directors from its monthly meeting. Left to right: David Jacobson, president Chuck Hines, Steve Zarnowski, Bob Red, Lee Sanders, Lecky Haller, Mark Singleton, and Allen Mayers.

Bunny Johns, left, president of the Nantahala Outdoor Center, and Steve Zarnowski, who followed Chuck as president of the Racin' Rhinos, celebrated the opening of The Ledges Slalom Course in Asheville, which Steve himself designed and constructed.

The youth program at the Asheville YMCA, a joint venture of the Nantahala Racing Club and the Y, continued to bring in a diverse group of youngsters for pool paddling instruction as the new millennium arrived.

The Nantahala Racing Club won the 2001 Junior Olympics, and the team, seen here, received the first Chuck Hines Cup for their excellence in slalom. The Rhinos won again in 2003, 2004, and 2005.

The author, left, with the 2004 U.S. Olympic C-2 duo of Joe Jacobi and Matt Taylor. As this book goes to press, Joe has accepted an assignment from NBC to cover the 2008 Beijing Olympics, and Matt has been appointed as director of the Adventure Sports Center International.

While enjoying his kayaking days, the author also worked for the YMCA in aquatics and international programming, part of which was the Asheville-Montserrat exchange. Chuck and Lee taught swimming to the island youngsters.

Of course, nothing is more important than Family, and here's daughter Heather and grandchildren Crystal and Charlie at a young age enjoying a rafting trip. Where? Why, on the Nantahala River, of course.

Chapter Nine

As we started another year of whitewater adventure, I received a lengthy report from one of our best Y paddlers, Sean Devereux. It was entitled "The Ups and Downs of C-2 Cruising," and it went like this: "Jim and Carol Goodrum, Nancy Alexander, Paula Dawson, and I met Jim Goldsmith near the little village of Hot Springs, about 30 miles from Asheville, with the intention of running our Secret Creek. But it was so high that after exercising the democratic process of voting, we decided instead to do Big Laurel Creek. Everybody survived. In the Narrows, we instructed Carol, who had never done Big Laurel before, to stay a tad to the left. She chose to err on the side of literalness and stayed so far left that she included part of the old railroad bed in her run. Good thing we didn't tell her to stay FAR left!

"As you know, Jim Goodrum and I have been working to develop as a C-2 team. Our improvement above the surface has been steady, but our somewhat erratic rolling has left us less than satisfied. With two people in a decked canoe, rolling becomes difficult. Kent Davidson and I swam seven times on the Ocoee last August, trying to roll our C-2 upstream, when weeks before we'd rolled downstream with ease in a bad spot at Fayette Station Rapid on the New River Gorge in West Virginia...

"So far this year I am doing better with Jim Goodrum as my new partner. Over the winter, our roll attempts in the YMCA pool were suspenseful, but on our run down Big Laurel, we rolled very snappily in the Narrows. We flushed out of Big Laurel into the French Broad River, which was running over 12,000 cfs or cubic feet per second. That's six times its normal level. BIG water. One in our group compared it to the Grand Canyon run out west...

"Just for the record, we did NOT swim at Class IV (or V) Frank Bell Rapid. It was after we ran this rapid successfully and beached our boat that the trouble began. A mild earthquake – no fooling! – caused part of the beach to collapse, hurling our boat into the rushing river. Happily, the departure of our unmanned C-2 provided the opportunity for a biathlon with the two Jims and Paula and Nancy chasing the C-2 in their kayaks while Carol and I ran a foot race down opposite banks in hot pursuit. If it all sounds a bit confusing, it was...

"The C-2 passed beneath the bridge at Hot Springs, and I followed on foot with two paddles in hand. Eventually we were reunited with our boat and made it home before dusk...

"A day later, kayakers Rich Isaac and Rocky Meadows joined with the two Jims and me to tackle our Secret Creek. This is a beautiful, twisting, narrow stream through a gorge, and though it's just 30 miles from Asheville, it's known to only a few paddlers. We were lucky to find it running at a moderate level. Even so, it seemed to me to be more challenging than Big Laurel in that it is not as open, the drops are blind, and there are fewer pools. Jim Goodrum and I experienced two failed rolls in our C-2. I attribute this to the fact that the water was so cold I began my roll in mid-air before we were underwater. You can get away with this in a C-1 but not (ask Jim) in a C-2. Showing his skill, Jim actually rolled the boat himself both times after I bailed out...

"The following week, Jim and I tempted fate once more with a C-2 run down the Nolichucky Gorge which was running high. We did it with friends from Greensboro. On the river, we encountered a group from Wisconsin. The biggest problem was the wind, which we estimated was at 30 knots per hour. Three of the Wisconsin boaters swam at Quarter-Mile Rapid, which must have been extremely unpleasant. They were in over their heads (literally), but I guess if you've come all the way from the Midwest, you're going to try regardless. They commented that it was our good fortune to be living here. We agreed but didn't encourage them to move here, as it's becoming too crowded...

Author's Note: This was in 1982, and the situation has definitely worsened since then.

"Jim and I flipped our C-2 just below Dave's Hole. We set up calmly and perfectly, but without knowing it, we had drifted upsidedown into a large hydraulic. Thus when we rolled, we were flushed out and twice went a full 360 degree turn into the current. Like being on a merry-go-round. Just another strange incident in the wild and wacky world of decked canoe paddling."

*****

It was back in 1964 that I first joined the American Whitewater Affiliation. I was working for the Des Moines, Iowa, YMCA, and serving as player-coach of the Y's men's water polo team. One of my teammates was attorney Bob Helmick, and one day we started talking about canoeing since a river flowed past the Y facility. "That would be a good new program for us," Bob observed.

"I've done some canoeing in the past on various lakes," I said, "but I'd really like to try the whitewater stuff one of these days."

"That sounds exciting. Why don't you get some info."

I wrote a fellow named Bart Hauthaway in New England who sent a package of materials, and he suggested that I contact the American Whitewater Affiliation, which I did, becoming an AWA member. It was all wishful thinking at that time, however, as Bob and I became busy with our water polo activities. A dozen years later, as you know from reading this text, after I'd come to Asheville, I put aside water polo and journeyed to the Nantahala for my initial attempt at whitewater kayaking, where I ended up swimming more than paddling.

Bob Helmick never did get into the whitewater stuff. Instead, he became president of the Amateur Athletic Union and then president of the United States Olympic Committee, plus becoming a member of the International Olympic Committee. I recall sitting in front of the TV and watching him lead the U.S. delegation into the stadium at the start of the 1988 Games at Seoul, Korea. I kept in touch with Bob over the years and shared my newfound enthusiasm for whitewater kayaking and racing with him, and I know he played an important behind-the-scenes role in getting whitewater slalom reinstated in the Olympic program at Barcelona, Spain, in 1992.

After I started kayaking in the mid 1970s, I renewed my membership in the American Whitewater Affiliation, which nowadays is called just plain American Whitewater, and in 1982 I wrote an article that appeared in their national magazine. The magazine editor prefaced my article by saying, "To run or not to run is the decision facing every whitewater boater. It is a simple point and oft ignored that paddling whitewater holds danger – dangers which are never totally negated by skills, guts, and the right stuff. Chuck Hines, a leader of the Asheville YMCA Kayak Club in North Carolina, shows from his own experiences that the choice of running or not running depends on a lot more than the water level."

My article, entitled "Tale of the Tellico: A Lesson in Judgment," went like this:

"Wha'dya think?" I asked my bearded friend Will Pruett...

"I think we'd better find a shorter, safer stretch farther on downriver."

"Okay."

"We sat in his van, listening to the steady drumming of the rain on the roof and looking out the water-streaked windows at the upper section of the Tellico River, its usually clear surface now an angry brown, pouring over large boulders and cascading down sharp chutes...

"It was early spring, and we'd come to the Tellico in the remote mountains of eastern Tennessee after spending the previous day on the easier Oconaluftee River in Western North Carolina. The Oconaluftee had been a scheduled Asheville YMCA Kayak Club outing, with Will as the trip leader, and a dozen of us had thoroughly enjoyed kayaking its Class II and occasional III rapids ...

"Such scheduled trips include a built-in element of safety. The group gathers at a pre-determined spot, usually the YMCA. The river to be run is known in advance, the water level carefully checked. Several cars are available, making the shuttle relatively simply, and sometimes a non-paddler comes along just to handle the driving. There's a designated trip leader who is familiar with the river and the capabilities of the participants. The leader, at least in our Y club, conducts an equipment check, then appoints one or two sweep paddlers. These are competent people who bring up the rear while running the river. If anyone encounters trouble, they perform the rescue ...

"Fortunately on such a well-organized club trip, a rescue is seldom needed. Everything falls into its proper place like a musical performance that's been rehearsed. So it was on the Oconaluftee, even though we found it running higher than expected. The weather was cloudy, cool, and the water temperature was icy, as we picked our way down this narrow stream which flows through the Cherokee Indian Reservation and requires a special permit ...

"After the run, most of our group headed back home, but Will and I drove in his van to the Nantahala Outdoor Center, where we planned to spend the night before tackling the Tellico. At NOC, we chatted with Dave Mason, the energetic young commodore of the American Canoe Association; waved at Bunny Johns, the defending world champion in C-2M racing; discovered that our waitress at the restaurant was Kathy Gilpin of Indiana, with whom I'd paddled previously on the Conasauga in Georgia; and had a long conversation with Ray McLain from Wisconsin, who'd come to Asheville two years before to help with the development of our YMCA kayaking curriculum. We looked at license plates from Minnesota to Mississippi and from Connecticut to Colorado...

"Where y'all paddling tomorrow?" someone asked ...

"The Tellico," Will replied …

"The races scheduled to be held there have been postponed, y'know."

"How come?"

"High water."

"What's it running?"

"Over 400 cfs and goin' higher."

"We went to sleep early at the NOC motel. It was still dark the next morning when I was awakened by thunder and huge flashes of lightning. Then came the rain. A downpour. I smiled. When a storm hits the Nantahala Gorge, it really lets loose. More than once in the past I'd been plastered and pelted by a Nantahala deluge. I drifted back to sleep and was awakened two hours later by Will's clatter. The rain was still falling, and I could hear the rumbling of the creek adjacent to the motel. "Whazit?" I mumbled …

"Seven o'clock."

"Two hours later, after a big breakfast and with the windshield wipers slapping furiously back and forth, we headed toward Tennessee and the Tellico. The Tellico is a run-off river that usually can be paddled only in the spring, when it becomes fierce and fun. Well, sometimes very fierce and not much fun. When we arrived, we found that we had the river to ourselves. We learned why when we drove up the road alongside the river. The water was pulsating. Dirty. Dangerous. Especially in the upper section. The guidebook I'd read said: 'This is not a trip for beginners, nor is it for those who overrate their abilities or have to depend on luck.' And that was at its normal level…

"A car pulled up beside us with kayaks on top. The driver lowered his window but didn't say a word. He just stared at the river in astonishment. Will asked, 'Do you know what it's running?'"

"Over 600 the last I heard. Maybe 800 by now. Too much for me to handle." He drove away...

"Will and I looked at each other. Wha'dya think? I asked ...

"I think we'd better find a shorter, safer section farther on downriver."

"Okay."

"Unlike the Oconaluftee, this was not a scheduled club trip. There were just the two of us in a single vehicle. Conditions were questionable, at best. We weren't about to do anything foolish. As Will put it, 'If being cautious makes me a whitewater wimp, so be it.' We headed back down the road, looking for an easier stretch to run. Finding it, we dumped our boats and paddles at riverside and drove the van even farther down to the Ranger Station Bridge, our anticipated take-out spot ...

"As if approving of our decision, the rain stopped as we changed into our paddling apparel. Our good luck continued as another car approached, someone who lived in the area. I flagged it down, and we hitched a ride upriver again to our kayaks and the put-in we had selected. I was the first one in. The water temperature wasn't as cold as I'd expected, but the river was flowing extremely fast. It was a solid brown. Yukky, but exciting ...

"I surfed and ferried for 10 minutes, until Will joined me, and wordlessly we turned and rode with the current. Rounding a bend and keeping to the inside, we began bouncing through three- and four-foot waves. The two of us, alone on the river, were carried swiftly through the rapids. Some quick, decisive maneuvering was demanded, but mostly it was a matter of reading the river in advance and then catching the proper chute or tongue. It was, I judged, a wavy Class III whitewater run, somewhat similar to western rivers. Almost before we realized it, we'd reached the take-out bridge. We had been on the river no more than 30 minutes ...

"That's the fastest ride I've had in a long time!" Will laughed as he hopped out …

"I remained in a while longer, surfing and ferrying at the last rapid, concluding finally with a couple of practice rolls. Exhausted, I climbed ashore as the rain resumed…

"An hour later, dressed and warm, we were driving homeward, passing through the village of Tellico Plains, where the river was running well above the foot bridge. It was obviously at flood stage. 'I believe we did the right thing,' said Will. I looked at my boating buddy, who doesn't mind calling himself a whitewater wimp when it comes to displaying good judgment and exhibiting caution when conditions require it. I realized how lucky I was to paddle with a friend like that, one who had the wisdom not to run anything on the river foolishly. Every boater should be so lucky. Are you?"

*****

When it came to our kayaking program at the Asheville YMCA, we were now doing it ALL, or so it seemed to me. We had adult beginner courses with classroom and pool instruction and concluding river trips; a growing club that was conducting frequent river cruises and other social events; a youth program that was drawing national recognition; and a racing component that included operating a 12-gate slalom course on the French Broad River. I was spending 8 to 10 hours weekly of "Y time" on the sport, for which I was being paid, and another 8 to 10 hours weekly of "my time" pursuing it as an avocation or hobby.

Not content, we decided to add intermediate instruction to our efforts. With this, we provided those enrolled with a few more pool lessons, focusing on improving Eskimo rolling techniques, and a couple of river trips, with instruction included. Most of our intermediate trips went to the Nantahala River, as we were continuing to work closely with NOC. On several occasions, we arranged for regular members of the YMCA to raft with NOC while we Y kayakers accompanied the group down the river.

Because of our ever-expanding program, we needed more instructors, but these were hard to find. Paddling proficiently is one thing. Having the ability, patience, and willingness to teach others is something else, a very special skill possessed by few. It was my calling, my profession, and I was fortunate to have Will, Jim, Rocky, and Anne assisting me. We then recruited Charles Creech as our sixth instructor. Like me, he was a YMCA professional and an excellent athlete – a black belt in karate, for one thing – and after enrolling in one of our kayaking courses, he demonstrated amazing river-running competence.

Charles happened to be black, and in a sport that had very little diversity, his participation became extra-important.

In racing, our results remained gratifying. Jim won the K-1 wildwater race at the Southeasterns, this time held on the Nantahala, and Curtis Bull, the youngster from Florida who came to train with us every summer, won the Southeastern K-1 junior wildwater event. Chase Ambler and Mark Mathews finished first in the Southeastern K-1 junior and cadet slalom competition, respectively. Young Becky Weis came from Indiana to practice with us again and then, at my suggestion, began working with the experts at NOC. We had an increasing number of excellent paddlers, both young and older, in our program, and it was time for me to relax, wasn't it?

*****

Well, no. I was still an avid kayaker myself, and I was looking for more whitewater thrills. Finally I found what I was seeking. Various rivers such as the Chattooga and Nolichucky may have been slightly more scenic, while others such as the New in West Virginia and the Snake Canyon out in Wyoming might have been a bit more difficult. There were others including the Nantahala that offered more in the way of good lodging and fine food. But I found the Youghiogheny River in Pennsylvania to be the best of them all, the most enjoyable river I ever paddled.

The Youghiogheny, called the Yough (rhymes with clock) by river enthusiasts, was no secret. It was – and still is – one of the most popular whitewater rivers in the country. A number of our YMCA paddlers including Debbie Angel, Rich Isaac, Rob Kern, Jim Maynor, Rick McGinnis, Rocky Meadows, Jerry Mills, Ed Scott, Charles White, and Dana Worley, to mention a few, had done it before. I'd contacted John Lichter of Riversport in Ohiopyle about running the Yough in May, but it didn't work out for me, so I re-scheduled my visit for July.

Ohiopyle was the small town that served as headquarters for the companies that took rafters, kayakers, and canoeists down what was called the lower Yough. There was also the upper Yough, with a plethora of Class V rapids, which in those days of breakable fiberglass boats was attempted very infrequently. The middle Yough was a good Class II warm-up, ending in Youghiogheny Falls, which was the start of the lower Yough, which contained seven miles of thrilling Class III and IV whitewater.

The chalkboard at Ohiopyle when I arrived indicated that the air temperature was 82 degrees, the water temperature (in the river) 60 degrees, and the water level a somewhat high but still comfortable 2.7. Chatting with amiable John Lichter, I learned that I'd be running the river with two other kayakers and that our trip leader would be Paul Grabow, a bronze medalist in C-2 at the 1981 World Whitewater Championships. John himself and two other instructors would be working with a group of beginners at a local lake.

Early the next morning, after spending the night at a not-very-nice motel, I was back at Riversport, where I met Paul Grabow and the two others in our small group. One was Dan, an irrepressible young man in his 20s. The other was Megan, a shy young woman also in her 20s. We spent the morning practicing on the middle Yough, using both the Riversport slalom course and Z rapid, both located just above the Falls. The beginners joined us for lunch, after which Paul, Megan, Dan, and I carried around the Falls and hopped into our kayaks in preparation for running The Loop.

I was rather nervous, which is normal when running a new section of challenging whitewater. My apprehension was increased by the fact that my aging Perception Spirit was leaking worse than ever and that I was the only one paddling the Yough for the first time. What would I find? Would my old clunker withstand the rapids?

Entrance Rapid was similar to Patton's Run on the Nantahala but about twice as long. We passed two open canoeists sitting high and dry on a boulder, their battered and beaten canoe bobbing up and down in the water as a result of smashing into the rocks. There were three- and four-foot waves, boulders and rocks, ledges and hydraulics.

Just around the bend was Cucumber Falls. We approached from the left side, running through 100 yards of choppy current, squeezing between a big boulder on the left and a keeper hole on the right, then over a sudden drop into a series of waves. Megan flipped in the drop and took a swim. While she recovered, Paul and Dan and I ferried back and forth across the river. Then Dan flipped and swam. He returned to action and flipped again, but this time he executed a nice roll.

We played at easier Turkey Falls for a few minutes, then moved on to Camel and Walrus Rapid and Eddy Turn Rapid, both difficult. I struggled with Dartmouth Rapid but remained upright. This brought us to Railroad, the last rapid of The Loop and the sixth Class III to IV within this short section. There was a trestle above. Paul took Megan down a sneak route on the right, while I followed Dan down the middle. He dropped over a wide ledge into a pulsating hole, flipped, failed to roll, and exited his boat. As I plunged over the ledge behind him, I quickly eddied out on the right, and there I sat for several minutes, trying to locate the path through. Down below, Dan was recovering his kayak. Hmmmm. Where to go?

I ferried across to the opposite side of the river and to an eddy there, peeled out into a chute, and ran smoothly through Railroad to the rapid's bottom. Piece of cake. Having completed The Loop successfully, I spent a long time surfing in Railroad's chutes and ledges and holes, thoroughly enjoying myself beneath the bright summer sun.

Later the four of us climbed up a hill and started walking the quarter-mile back to Ohiopyle. The Loop, you see, was (is) a circle, and we ended up almost where we started. Tired but satisfied with my performance, I felt the only dismal spot of the day's effort was my boat's constant leaking. I was continually using a sponge I kept in my cockpit to remove the 2" of water that collected in the boat's bottom every few minutes. Back at Riversport, I spent an hour re-taping my kayak with duct tape. Hopefully it would do better tomorrow, when we were scheduled to run the entire lower Yough.

While waiting to eat, I hiked along one of Ohiopyle State Park's many trails, one called the Great Gorge Trail, and then I ambled through the Ferncliff National Forest. The watery world is nice, where I feel most at home, but I also enjoy walking and hiking in the outdoors.

Later that night, we gathered at Riversport for a sumptuous steak dinner. From the beginners class we heard of their trials and tribulations during the day. Bronze medalist Paul Grabow and I spent an hour talking, and I learned that he, like I, had been born and raised in Minnesota, with his family moving to the Washington DC area. A senior in college and majoring in kinesiology, he had been an active paddler for nine years, and despite being the U.S. champion in C-2 and C-2M slalom, he said he grew weary of racing and training. "That's why I'm here this summer," he confided in me, "so I can paddle just for fun."

We had fun the next day. The four of us reached the put-in at mid-morning, planning to run the entire lower Yough. Megan spilled and swam right away at Entrance Rapid. I eddied out momentarily and was attacked by a big black raft which was totally out of control. It ran over me (almost) and became pinned on a rock, slowly filling up with water. The guides were unable to free it, transferring the occupants to another raft from the same company.

We plunged through Cucumber and made it down Turkey Falls, Camel and Walrus, Eddy Turn, and Dartmouth. After struggling but surviving in Railroad, we found that we'd completed The Loop in slightly more than an hour. Good going!

There was a churning Class II beneath the railroad trestle, some flat water, and several more IIs, bringing us to Dimple Rapid. "This," said Paul, "is the most dangerous rapid. I'm taking Megan down the sneak route on the right. Chuck, you can follow Dan down the left side. Be careful." On the left, the water piled straight-forward into undercut Dimple Rock, a possible pinning situation where I knew some river-runners had died in the past. As I watched, Dan tried to eddy out above Dimple Rock, behind Pinball, but the whirlpooling water capsized him, and he vanished from view. I took a deep breath, asked for a little heavenly help, and headed toward Dimple, angling to the right, sweeping and drawing, passing Pinball in a flash, and letting the swift current and three-foot curlers carry me safely past Dimple. I discovered this wasn't the end, that there were other rapids immediately ahead, and I maneuvered through three- and four-foot waves into famous Swimmers Rapid.

What's in a name? Swimmers Rapid says it all. It's where many paddlers end up swimming. I didn't, fortunately. Joined by Paul, Megan, and Dan, who only shook his head in disgust when I asked how he'd done coming through Dimple, I ate lunch atop a boulder, and we watched the experts surfing at Swimmers. It was quite a show. They surfed sideways, backwards, pin-wheeling, tandem, and hands-only, and the two ladies there were every bit as good as the guys.

An hour later, we headed downriver. Bottle of Wine Rapid and Double Hydraulic were Class IIIs which we all navigated well, and Paul said, "River's End Rapid, a definite IV, is next. The river is seemingly clogged by giant boulders and appears impassable, but there's a route to the left. It's not easy 'cuz the current tends to throw you into the boulders, so be sharp. If you make it, there are a couple of drops into holes, and you will have to paddle hard and brace … so good luck!"

It was indeed a IV, or more, I thought. Harder than Dimple. I was swept toward the big mid-river boulders, evaded them, plunged downward to the left into a hole, did a brace, bounced up over a pillowed rock into another hole, did another brace, and washed through into an eddy, from which I peeled out and rode three-foot waves another 30 yards to the bottom. Whew.

School House was the last major rapid, not easy, with sizeable waves and a dynamic eddy on the left side, making for a sharp eddy turn and a whizzing peel-out.

Killer Falls was a neat little two-foot chute which we all ran backwards, and there were more Class IIs – Stairstep, Rocky Road, Bruner's Run – that took us to the take-out.

At the take-out, there was a required shuttle service costing $1.25 per person, which transported each paddler and all equipment up a two-mile hill to the parking lot. Tags for this service were purchased at the information booth near the put-in at Ohiopyle and carried down the river to the take-out.

To summarize, the lower section of the Youghiogheny River in Pennsylvania offered me a wonderful opportunity for the very best in whitewater action. Super. Outstanding. A "must" for all serious river-runners. When I kayaked it at a level of 2.7 or perhaps slightly higher, the seven-mile stretch contained more than half-a-dozen Class IIs, 10 Class IIIs, and four Class IVs. Twenty rapids. At least that was my count. Looking back at the 300 river trips I took in the past on 60 different rivers, streams, and creeks – plus the 300 or more slalom practices and races – I would classify the two days I spent at the Yough as being among the most enjoyable.

*****

It takes plenty of proficiency from a physical standpoint to become a good kayaker. But to succeed in whitewater, it takes even more than that. It's an emotional and mental game, as well. We humans have an inherent fear of the unknown, the unexpected, and there's a lot of that when you're paddling through the rapids. It can cause indecision, hesitancy, heart-throbbing fearfulness. For some, it's too much. They try whitewater paddling once or twice, and that's enough. No more. For others, they are able to find the courage that's required. And perhaps the courage comes from faith … faith in yourself… the kind of faith that can produce enough courage to carry you through tight situations on the river.

There's an even deeper faith that's needed if we're to have enough courage to triumph over life's more serious problems, those life-and-death dilemmas affecting our families, our friends, and ourselves sooner or later. No one escapes these situations. This deeper faith is acquired, interestingly, only when we learn to rely less on ourselves and more on the God who created us. For me, that's an even better trip than the Youghiogheny.

*****

The two competent canoeists, Burt Butler and Harold Mathews, looked at me with curiosity as they paddled past. There I stood, knee-deep in the middle of the river, a lonely and pathetic figure, amidst a rushing rapid, grasping my water-filled kayak. The rain continued. It was a bona fide gully-washer. Thunder rumbled overhead. Again I tugged at my kayak, trying somehow to empty out the water and cussing my carelessness at not having prepared my equipment properly for this three-hour jaunt down a river we'd never done before.

We had come, six of us, to Mount Mitchell in Western North Carolina, the highest mountain east of the Mississippi. While it cannot compare to the peaks out west, it is nonetheless an imposing sight at the junction of the Blue Ridge and Smoky Mountains. For three days, Mount Mitchell had drawn a steady rainfall, and we were anxious to paddle the South Fork of the Toe River, which starts its steep descent on the slopes of this illustrious mountain. Twenty miles downstream, it merges with the North Fork, and the two eventually become the Toe Gorge, a section we had run on numerous occasions. But we'd never done the South Fork, about which the guidebook said: "A delightful stream winding down the mountain that generally can be run following periods of wet weather. It cuts through a narrow, rocky gorge that has some ledges and drops which will require scouting."

Armed with this information, Burt and Harold and I headed for Mount Mitchell, accompanied by YMCA kayakers Jodi Jackson, Diane Butler, and Chase Ambler. It was a weekday, a working day, so we couldn't sneak away until mid-afternoon, and perhaps that's why I failed to properly prepare my equipment, an oversight that I came to regret.

The sunny sky vanished as we started driving up the mountain. It became cloudy as we searched for the put-in and ran the shuttle. The sun peaked through again as we squeezed into our boats and headed downstream. At first, I led the way, followed by the other kayakers and with canoeists Harold and Burt bringing up the rear. Within 20 minutes, we'd left behind all signs of civilization. The river was 50' wide, bordered by trees, shrubs, and colorful flowers. The water level was high and lapping into the banks, and flowed gently over gravel bars and shoals. Gradually the Class I turned into Class II, with small drops and rock gardens.

Then, as we rounded a bend, the river disappeared over a narrow ledge. We eddied out and scouted from a large, flat rock overlooking the ledge on the left side. It was a III, maybe a III+ at this level. The water cascaded over the ledge and curved down a tricky waterfall, bouncing off the converging walls on both sides into a pool below, rushing onward into a short chute that ended in another pool.

"Nothing easy about this one," I surmised, and all heads nodded in agreement. While the kayakers studied the situation, the two canoeists returned to their boats. Burt was the first to try it. He plunged down the sluice, trying to stay to the right, but the eight-foot falls pushed him to the left. He careened off the wall and nose-dived into the pool, where he stopped and smiled up at us. Harold was next. He also bounced off the converging walls on both sides into the pool below, where he needed a strong brace to stay upright.

"You're next," Jodi told me. "Show the rest of us kayakers how to do it." In my aging fiberglass kayak, I too bounced off both walls but made it safely into the pool. No problem … except that my boat was leaking and had accumulated several inches of water. As I emptied out, Jodi came whizzing down and overturned. She exited her kayak and, before anyone could reach her, was swept through the pool into the following chute, exhibiting the correct technique for swimming a rapid by lying on her back with her feet raised, hanging onto her paddle with one hand and her kayak's grab-loop with the other hand. Burt helped her make it to the riverbank.

Diane, witnessing Jodi's imperfection, shook her head and carried around. Chase, with typical teenage bravado, came plunging down the falls. Like Jodi, he flipped, but he remained loose and rolled up. Way to go, kid!

For the next hour, we paddled through an increasing number of Class IIs until, once again, the river disappeared down a steep drop. Once again, we scouted from a large, flat rock on the left. "Another III?" Chase asked. I nodded. Burt and Harold ran it in their canoes, both looking professional as they went down the first five-foot drop into smooth water, paddled a few yards forward, and then eased down another five-foot drop into the pool at the bottom. Chase, Diane, Jodi, and I all made it down without any problems, although once again I was forced to empty a surprising amount of water from my leaking kayak.

Soon thereafter, as happens so often in the mountains, storm clouds gathered above. Thunder ricocheted around us. Suddenly we were engulfed in a downpour. It became cooler … downright cold. I wished I'd remembered to pack my paddle jacket. It became harder to see. Jodi removed her dark glasses and inserted her contacts. But I had only my dark glasses with me, and I squinted into the mist ahead. The deluge continued.

Groping, I broadsided into a small mid-stream boulder. I leaned against its cushion, preparing to push around it, and in so doing, I inadvertently exposed the bottom of my boat to the rushing brown current. Somehow and somewhere, a patch popped, and river water roared through a crack, depressing the dilapidated, half-filled-with-air flotation bag. I sank, then flipped, and was unable to roll. For five seconds, 10, 20, maybe 30, I was trapped upsidedown in my kayak, struggling to break free. Thoughts of death crept into my mind before I wrenched free and stood up gasping, holding onto my water-filled boat as Harold and Burt paddled past. It had been a close call, and it had happened on a simple Class II section of the river. I breathed a sigh of relief and thanks.

The rain continued. The current pushed me and my kayak along as I tried to dump out the water. I shivered. If ever there was a forlorn kayaker on any river anywhere, I was it! Why hadn't I brought a jacket or sweater? Why hadn't I sense enough to have the cracks in my old boat repaired? Why hadn't I used some newer duct tape? Why hadn't I replaced my old flotation bag? Why was I still paddling this old clunker?

Suddenly, Harold was in the water beside me. He had eddied out, no small feat in the rushing rapids, and had come to my assistance. He grabbed one end of my boat, and I grabbed the other, and we see-sawed it up and down. Even with his help, it wasn't easy draining out all the water. But we managed, and a few minutes later, I was again paddling down the river.

After a while the rain subsided, and we marveled as we watched water from the surrounding banks filling the river even more. One inch. Two. Three. Four. We maneuvered through unending chutes and rock gardens, with the river pushing us along at a brisk pace. Weariness overtook us, and we were a subdued bunch by the time we reached the take-out. I surfed the last ledge and dragged my boat ashore, where Diane helped me lift and empty it. Gallons of water kept pouring out. "I don't see how you managed to paddle it!" she exclaimed.

Well, I HAD managed, luckily, with the aid of my friends, and I'd even enjoyed the exploration of an exciting new – for us – river. "We need to come back and paddle the South Fork again, and next time I'll be properly prepared," I promised Harold. He smiled.

Author's Note: Shortly after this debacle, I sadly set aside my dependable, long-time friend, my orange Perception Spirit, and invested in a new kayak. After consulting with several others, I was led by Fletcher Anderson of

Colorado to purchase a Prijon model. Like me, Fletcher – who recently passed away in an air accident while flying his own plane – was a whitewater writer, and I respected his judgment. I used my new, bright blue cruising boat for nearly a decade, and it never let me down. Of course, I had two smaller slalom racing kayaks, one of which I purchased new and the second of which I bought second-hand from Max Wellhouse of Arkansas. They too stood me in good stead for many years.

*****

Marge Cline didn't approve of our new Y whitewater kayaking instructional curriculum, and she said so. We were gathered in a room at the YMCA of the USA's national headquarters in Chicago to decide how best to promote the program, which had been approved and sanctioned by the National Physical Education Management Team. "This is a really great new program," said an enthusiastic Marjorie Murphy, the YMCA's national director of aquatics.

"I don't like it," replied a disparaging Marge Cline, as outspoken as ever. "I don't like being told what to do."

Marge and her Chicago Whitewater Association constituency had been using YMCA pools to teach kayaking for a number of years. Their efforts were highly successful and nationally publicized. "I visited Asheville and saw what you're doing," she continued, turning to me. "It's okay. But here in Chicago, we want to do our own thing."

"Nobody's telling you what to do, Marge," I replied. "For one thing, each YMCA is autonomous and generally can do what it wants to do when it comes to programming. The YMCA of the USA sends out guidelines and information and suggestions, which local Ys can accept or not. Furthermore, while the CWA is using Y pools, it's really your program taught by your instructors and not a YMCA program in the truest sense."

"Most Ys have no idea how to use their pools to teach kayaking," Mike King said. "I believe this new program will enable them to become involved with our sport, if they wish."

"I'd like to see 100 Ys around the country using this program," stated Tommy Parham.

Mike, from Georgia, and Tommy, from Tennessee, were on the YMCA's national kayak committee, which I was chairing. Ray McLain, also on the committee, had been unable to attend our meeting at the Y's headquarters in Chicago, but had sent his blessing from Wisconsin.

As I sat there, I remembered something I'd been told by Bob Lindberg, the CEO of the Des Moines YMCA. "Chuck," he said, "whatever you do in life and no matter how altruistic your motives, there will be those who oppose you. They won't like you, or they won't like your proposals. So you will encounter unexpected setbacks, and it will take you longer than anticipated to achieve your goals. You will become discouraged. It is at this time that most people, maybe 90%, quit. They lose patience. They walk away. But the world belongs to the 10% who don't quit, who keep on keeping on. Only you can decide which you'll be."

Despite Marge Cline's dissenting voice, which I respected because of her devotion to a sport that I also loved, we ended the meeting on a positive note, and I flew back to Asheville feeling confident that various YMCAs around the country would indeed be using the new curriculum and program that I and others had labored so long to develop.

*****

"Dear Chuck," began another letter I received, this one from Jack Stewart, a YMCA member and one of our former water polo players, "this is just a brief note of gratitude for your supervision of the recent beginners kayaking course at the YMCA. For years, I have rocked unsteadily and bailed unmercifully along in a canoe, always vowing to one day make the big leap into kayaking. Now, at the completion of your course, I am comforted (and humbled) to know that I have made more of a splash into the sport than a mere leap…

"I sincerely appreciated your thoughtful instruction and kind encouragement over these past seven weeks. Likewise, I was especially thankful for your assistance (a modest way of saying "rescue") on the Little Tennessee River where I first discovered that the single most critical technique to learn in the sport of kayaking is the inevitable wet exit, a technique I am now proud to say I have mastered…

"Thanks again for a memorable and pleasurable experience, and I trust we can continue to renew our friendship as the years pass by. Until then, know that I appreciate your efforts and remain your favorite whitewater kayaker (and swimmer)."

*****

Frankly, I don't remember "rescuing" Jack Stewart. It must not have amounted to much. Jack was a strong swimmer, a water poloist, a competent canoeist, and on his way to becoming an avid kayaker – along with being one of Asheville's best defense attorneys – and obviously he was a man of good humor. I do recall another incident that happened on one of our YMCA class trips. It involved another attorney who had been struggling all afternoon.

A tall fellow in his 30s, he'd been unable to do a roll in our pool, although he'd learned to perform the various strokes and some other skills while attending the six lessons at the Y. Now, after a flat-water session on the French Broad, he was with the class on its concluding river trip. It wasn't going well for him. Twice while practicing at Class II rapids, he'd dumped and swum. Nothing serious. But we, the instructors, noted that he was shaky and shivering as we approached the last rapid of the day. It was a Class II+. We had scouted it with the class, and we'd decided to let everyone give it a try.

Anne Terrell was to lead the first two students down the rapid. I would follow with the struggling gentleman right behind me and with Rocky Meadows closely behind him, thus insuring that he had an instructor in front and back. Three more students were to trail behind Rocky, with reliable Will Pruett bringing up the rear as the sweep. Had we planned it less thoughtfully, it's possible a disaster could have occurred.

The other students, fore and aft, all made it through the rapid without any difficulty, as Anne kept an eye on them. However, our cold and troubled gent, following me, though running the three-foot drop successfully, somehow lost control a few yards farther and capsized. Glancing over my shoulder, I saw what was happening and immediately eddied out. I watched as he bailed out, lost contact with his boat, then his paddle, and was swept over to the bank, where he grabbed a tree limb. Close behind, Rocky picked up the paddle and eddied out where the gentleman was floundering to assist him.

The man's kayak, meanwhile, had broadsided onto a mid-stream boulder and was stuck there. With difficulty, I parked amidst strainer-type limbs, waded out into the current (hadn't I done this before somewhere?), slid over the rocks to the captured kayak, and worked five minutes to push it free. Rocky reached out and grabbed it, thereby reuniting the boat with our exhausted and struggling student.

I was struggling myself to return to my own boat, but I made it just in time to watch our student shove off into the current again. All he had to do was follow Rocky down, but it couldn't do it. Unaccountably he swerved sideways and broadsided precariously into a gigantic boulder. Pinned there, he remembered to lean downstream, but I held my breath, waiting for the waves to flip him upstream and upsidedown against the boulder. Suddenly, from out of nowhere, came Will who, seeing the situation, had eddied out to assist if needed. Whizzing across the current and placing himself in a dangerous position, he reached out and grabbed the front-end grab loop on our student's kayak, gave it a hard tug, and succeeded in pulling the boat off the big boulder and back into the waves. Our flustered gentleman, looking pale and scared, managed finally to paddle into calmer water.

Will and I exchanged glances of relief. Rocky shook his head. Anne smiled. It had been just another simple beginners class on an easy Class II river, but luckily:

* We had four instructors accompanying six students, a better than normal ratio, and this enabled three of us to take turns assisting the one struggling student while our fourth instructor remained apart and watched the remaining students.

* We had scouted the rapid at which the trouble occurred in advance, so everyone knew the correct route to take.

* We recognized the difficulty being experienced by one student, and we were prepared to rescue him not only once but twice.

* We were able to improvise the rescue of the student's boat, paddle, and him personally.

* The student twice helped himself, despite feeling flustered, initially by exhibiting correct swimming techniques to reach shore after capsizing, and then by leaning properly against the boulder's cushion after broadsiding into it.

For me, this demonstrated the importance of what we were doing in our YMCA kayaking program. And by the way, the student in this story is now a well-known judge in Asheville.

Author's Note: There were several unsung heroes in our YMCA kayaking program. Instructors Rocky Meadows and Anne Terrell were two of them. They both spent half-a-dozen years teaching others without ever receiving a penny in return. Anne was a Class III kayaker who also did some racing. She went on a NOC-sponsored two-week-long kayaking and rafting trip to the Grand Canyon, about which she wrote an excellent article that was published locally. Rocky was a Class IV kayaker who wasn't into racing, but he cruised a lot of the country's best rivers. He went on a NOC-sponsored week-long sea kayaking trip to Mexico's Baja Peninsula. We at the YMCA are indebted to the volunteers like Anne and Rocky who make our programs possible.

*****

As the year came to an end, an article appeared in the November issue of the American Whitewater Affiliation magazine under the heading of Club Profile. It was about our Asheville YMCA Kayak Club, and it was written by – of all people – Marge Cline of Chicago. She'd called me and said she was sorry she hadn't been more supportive of our Y kayaking curriculum and that she'd like to make up for it by writing an article about our club. Without hesitation, I consented. This is what Marge wrote:

"FELLOWSHIP. FITNESS. FUN. These are the objectives of the Asheville YMCA Kayak Club located in the mountains of North Carolina. Now in its fifth year, the club follows the Y's guidelines and procedures...

"The club has a spot and a vote on the YMCA board of directors, according to Will Pruett, and works diligently to fit in with the Y's programming philosophies, rather than operating on its own...

"Pruett, 45, who has been running rivers for more than a decade, is currently the club's representative on the board of directors. He is also one of five volunteer kayaking instructors. The Y conducts five or six kayaking courses annually. Beginning and intermediate courses, racing instruction, river safety seminars, even kayak instructor clinics, are all available. One such clinic, held in 1980, attracted instructors from eight states...

"We were aided by the experts from the nearby Nantahala Outdoor Center when we put our paddling program together in 1977 and 1978," says Chuck Hines, 50, the YMCA's Vice-President for Aquatics, "and we still work with the NOC professionals occasionally. They've been very helpful to us."

"Since 1977, the Asheville YMCA has taught over 500 people, ages 11 to 55, how to kayak. The Asheville curriculum includes pool and classroom instruction as well as river cruising. It is a program that is being adopted by many other Ys across the country. The club cruises have been to the Nantahala, Nolichucky, Chattooga, Tuckaseigee, Little Tennessee, Toe, Oconaluftee, Raven Fork, Big Laurel, French Broad, Pigeon, Green, and Snowbird, all within a two-hour drive, and the Ocoee, a four-hour drive from Asheville. Longer trips have been taken to the New and Cheat in West Virginia, the Youghiogheny in Pennsylvania, and to the Arkansas, Snake, Salmon, and Colorado (Grand Canyon) out west...

"We have plenty of big water boaters on our roster," states Pruett, "such as Nancy and Ellis Alexander, Chuck Baker, Mary Ann and Kent Davidson, Sean Devereux, Jim Goldsmith, Ed Hay, Rich Isaac, Rob Kern, Kathy Koon, Ed Krause, Jim Maynor, Rocky Meadows, Jerry Mills, Ed Scott, Anne Terrell, and Charles White, all capable of Class IV kayaking. But we have at least twice as many Class II-III cruisers, and we make a real effort to schedule trips that the majority can enjoy. We also conduct cruises for our younger paddlers...

"While teaching and cruising occupy most of the club's time, some members also have been successful at river racing. Jim Maynor, 37, is a good example. He graduated from one of the Y's first kayak courses and has since won the Carolina Cup men's wildwater championship twice and the Southeastern championship twice, plus many lesser races. Another Y graduate, Kathy Koon, wears the Southeastern women's wildwater crown. Pruett and Hines, the club's oldest competitors, have been Southeastern Masters champions in wildwater and slalom, respectively...

"Many of the Y's younger paddlers have been consistent race winners. Brent Lawson, 17, has won slalom races on the Nantahala and Chattahoochee. Doug Baker, 17, and Amy Pruett, 17, have won downriver and wildwater races on the French Broad, Mayo, and elsewhere. Curtis Bull, as a 13-year-old, won a Nantahala novice slalom race. Ten other Y youngsters have pulled off a first or second somewhere along the line in river racing...

"We don't spend much time sitting around and talking," chuckles Maynor. In fact, the club used to meet monthly but now meets just quarterly, enjoying a spring, summer, autumn, and winter family potluck supper. Guests are welcomed, films and slides are shown, cruises are planned, races are announced, and a good time is had by all, even the canoeists in attendance...

"*Canoeists?* Yes indeed. The club contains many good open boaters. 'Actually,' explains Hines, 'we call it a kayak club only because the YMCA teaches kayaking. We leave the canoeing instruction to the local Red Cross. We feel we want to identify with what the Y teaches.' The YMCA helps underwrite a bimonthly newsletter, 'The Whitewater Paddler,' edited by Hines, which goes out to the 80 Ashevilleans who are club participants and to another 100 or more paddlers from coast to coast...

"The Asheville YMCA Kayak Club is a member of the American Whitewater Affiliation, the American Canoe Association, the American Rivers Conservation Council, and the United States Canoe Association, and can be contacted c/o Asheville YMCA, 30 Woodfin Street, Asheville, NC, 28801."

Author's Note: We are thankful to Marge Cline for writing this nice article. In the 25 years following 1982, Marge became one of our sport's finest national leaders. Known affectionately as "River Mom" for introducing hundreds of Chicago-area residents to whitewater kayaking and canoeing, she was honored by the American Canoe Association and several other organizations. Unfortunately, Marge died in 2007, just as I was collecting material to write this book. We love you, Marge, and we miss you.

Chapter Ten

Although we'd had a fair amount of success with whitewater racing, local interest seemed to be declining. So in 1983 we set about to upgrade our efforts. We publicized our twice-weekly practices at the slalom course we were operating at the Firefighters Camp and doubled the number of paddlers who went to practice there, from 20 to about 40. Not all were eager racers, but we convinced them that (a) one slalom practice weekly with Will Pruett would undoubtedly improve their strokes and (b) one downriver practice weekly with Jim Maynor would certainly improve their speed and stamina.

We purchased a video camera with which to view and critique each paddler's performances, and we offered a free one-day clinic at our slalom site on the French Broad for anyone interested. In the morning of the clinic, we taught the latest rescue techniques. In the afternoon, we taught slalom skills.

Finally, we put 10 spring and summer races on our schedule. These were being held in Alabama, Georgia, Tennessee, and of course North Carolina, and we were represented at each one. Mark Mathews, 13, won the Ramone Eaton Cup, which consisted of a series of slalom races for youngsters held on rivers in the aforementioned states.

Becky Weis, 15, who had started in our Asheville YMCA program, came and spent the summer training on the Nantahala, and she won the U.S. K-1W junior slalom championship.

I had turned 50, which proved to be somewhat of a traumatic experience. I injured my back severely when lifting a 50-gallon drum of liquid chlorine at the YMCA pool. After being sidelined (from the river) for several months, I couldn't stand it any longer and went on a trip with one of our YMCA classes. My wife Lee drove, just in case I had to get off the river because of pain. I remember her asking, "Why are you doing this?" as we stood on the banks of the lower Green.

Our group of 15 included five beginning and five intermediate students from the Y, plus four instructors, and me. Yes, I was normally an instructor, but not on this day. My goal was simply to get down the river in one piece and enjoy myself, if at all possible.

We waited patiently at the put-in pond for the river level to rise, practicing some ferrying and peel-outs as the water, released from the dam at Lake Summit, gradually filled the river bed. "It's colder than usual," one of the instructors said.

"Yes," I agreed.

"As cold as the Nantahala, I believe."

"Well, almost."

The water was definitely colder than we'd anticipated, and the sun kept vanishing behind a skyful of clouds, keeping the air temperature in the low 60s. We gathered around Will Pruett, who was serving as the trip leader. He gave directions, then led the way through the first rapid, a Class II like all the others we would be encountering. When it was my turn, my glasses fogged up, and I paddled more by memory than by sight, aiming down the middle of the rapid, evading a rock garden on the left and an outstretched tree limb on the right. We waited in an eddy for everyone to join us.

Gosh, I thought, this must be boring for John Bayless, whom I'd recruited to work with our intermediates on this trip. John had paddled some of the toughest Class IV-V rivers in the country – the Gauley, upper

Yough, Grand Canyon out west – yet here he was, helping teach our YMCA class. Murray Parker, another big-water boater, demonstrated hands-only paddling through one rather tricky channel.

Will Pruett and Anne Terrell helped the beginners with their strokes, braces, ferrying and, for a couple of them, their wet exits, as they toppled over into the cold but forgiving Green. It took us the better part of an hour to reach the first bridge and its rapid, above which a tree had fallen, creating a strainer and necessitating an unusual approach which everyone managed successfully. There we disembarked, stretched our legs, and relaxed.

"How are you feeling?" asked my wife, who was driving down the dusty road next to the river.

"I'm a little stiff, but not bad," I replied. The ruptured disc in my back WAS painful, though, and because I couldn't lift anything heavy or twist from side to side, I was running the river in my little 19-pound slalom racer. It had proven to be a mixed blessing. The racer was light and maneuverable, but it was too cramped and uncomfortable for a lengthy river trip.

The gnats pestered us as Lee continued, "I still don't understand why you're doing this. It's not a particularly pleasant day. The water's cold. Your boat is so small it's pinching you. I know your back is hurting. The shuttle is a drag. The insects are driving us batty. It's a river you've paddled dozens of times already. You're here with a bunch of beginners. I don't understand."

Before I could conjure up an answer, Will was calling us back to our boats and to the river. Ah, yes, the river. As we negotiated the second section of the lower Green, heading toward Big Corky Rapid, I wondered how I could explain the river's appeal to anyone who's never run the rapids in a small kayak or canoe. "When you discover what a river does," someone has said, "your life will never be the same." How true. But what is it a river does? It babbles. Bubbles. Frolics. Cries. Whirls. Waits. Rushes. Smashes. Smiles. Changes its mind. Complains. Challenges. Throbs with the pulse of life.

"The river is not your friend," somebody else has said. True. The river will show you no favoritism. It will chart its own course, go its own way, fulfill its own destiny, with no regard for you whatsoever. You may come along for the ride, but only at the river's pace and at your own risk. When you and I are gone – from the river, from life itself – the rushing waters will still be there, trickling and splashing and plunging and promenading over rocks, around corners, beneath the tree-shaded banks.

Riding the river in a little boat is like dancing, singing, harmonizing with Nature, even with eternity. It's communicating, concentrating, celebrating. It's stepping away from the sharp clashes of civilization into a simpler time. Peering into the past, paddling in the present, getting a glimpse of the future.

Best of all, it's an excitement, an enchantment that can be enjoyed in the company of others. We are, after all, social creatures. From a Biblical perspective, the earth has been given to us for our benefit, for our appreciation, for our stewardship. We modern-day humans are discovering that we cannot feel satisfactorily at home in the concrete jungles we call cities any more than our ancient ancestors felt safe and secure in the real jungles from which Mankind emerged. Is it possible that we are happiest with a foot in each, stepping forward with one foot into our own creativity while keeping one foot behind, anchored in God's original and incomparable Creation?

Such thoughts filtered through my mind as we kayaked downstream, approaching one of the hardest Class IIs. As I found myself near the rear of the pack, I paddled briskly to the front, shouting, "Killer Corky ahead! Beware, you beginners!" The beginners laughed, but not without a touch of anxiety in their voices.

Will led the way, followed by two of the beginners. I was next. This was a 60 yard slope through one-foot waves and around a scattering of rocks and boulders, ending with a couple of two-foot waves and gently swirling eddies on both sides. Reaching the bottom, I glanced back over my shoulder just enough to throw me slightly sideways, and I slammed into a hidden rock. In my somewhat larger cruising kayak, I would have bounced off the rock into calmer water, but my tiny, tippy racing boat, with its sharp edges, caught the current and did a quick flip. Wow. It WAS cold. I felt another boat on top of mine, so I waited, tucking tightly, as I scraped over an underwater boulder whose acquaintance I had made before on a few occasions. Then I flicked out with my paddle and popped up.

"What a roll!" one of the beginners exclaimed.

It hadn't been all that difficult, but I felt the disc in my back snapping out of place and cursed my carelessness. The river and its "Killer Corky" had chastised me for making fun of it, allowing the others to pass through unimpeded but letting me know it was still the boss. The beginners, who had done their share of swimming during the day, were delighted to see me upended, although one declared later, "I can see that rolling makes kayaking a lot more pleasant."

Yes, whitewater kayaking can be pleasant … and unpleasant … often at the same time. There's something mystical about it, something exhilarating, something unexplainable, that makes me want to "go with the flow," even with a bad back and aging reflexes. So hopefully I'll be out there again and again, paddling and philosophizing, riding the waves and chasing dreams. Will I see YOU there?

*****

I had learned the basics of river-running on the Green, Nantahala, Tuckaseigee, Little Tennessee, Chattooga, and Nolichucky. But gradually, over half-a-dozen years, while traveling to other popular rivers from West Virginia to Wyoming, from Canada to Colorado, I'd grown to appreciate the river that flowed through Asheville, which was almost in my own front yard, just four miles from where I lived. The French Broad.

In the past, I'd practiced frequently at our slalom course, but now, as my back healed, I started going to another section, where I could paddle more for fun. One day, I took off from working at the YMCA on a weekday afternoon and, with an out-of-town friend, went to the river, arriving at 4:30 p.m. The level was 2.9 on the local gauge, which was 6" above average. The section in front of us had fast water and small waves and mid-river swirls and whirls and neat ledges for surfing. My friend and I played for about 30 minutes. Then I made a mistake. I paddled downriver through a narrow channel between the river bank and a lengthy island. At a lower level, the channel would have been impassable, but at this higher level, it was shallow but runnable. The current was swift, and I was swept along beneath a canopy of trees and chirping birds. It was scenic and satisfying. But the island was l-o-n-g-e-r than I anticipated, and I was well downriver before I was able to rejoin the main flow.

Now I faced a 500-yard jaunt UPRIVER, against the quick current. Paddling as hard as my bad back allowed, I made it, but it wasn't easy. I was sweating profusely. It had taken me five minutes to coast down through the channel but 25 minutes to battle my way back upriver to the put-in, where my car was parked. It had been a real workout, and I was hurting.

On the way home, my friend and I spotted two cars that were pulled up at another section. Parking, we hiked down to the river. Rich Isaac and Jerry Mills were playing at a beautiful, exciting surfing hole, better than those found on other well-publicized rivers, and within a 15-minute drive of downtown Asheville. They had it to themselves and were hands-only surfing and rolling in the hole, time after time. Impressive.

The French Broad isn't the cleanest river in the world, but it's not bad. Most of its discoloration comes from silt that washes down from its dozens of tributaries. It offers everything from slow Class I to heart-pounding Class IV or even V, when the water is sky-high.

Because of its large size, the French Broad can be paddled year 'round. I resolved to help protect this hometown gem by joining the French Broad River Foundation. I was urged to do so by the organization's president, a guy I knew by the name of Will Pruett.

A week after paddling with my out-of-town friend, I read in the Citizen-Times that a university professor from Illinois had drowned during an open canoeing trip on the French Broad. He was not wearing a life-jacket, although he was paddling through Class III rapids. I wondered if he was a strong swimmer. Two-thirds of all paddling fatalities occur when a canoeist or kayaker or rafter flips and becomes, for all practical purposes, a swimmer.

A week later, I was back on the French Broad with Karl Byas, one of our YMCA youngsters. Karl WAS a good swimmer – he had an advanced lifesaving certificate – and he WAS wearing a life-jacket. When he overturned while surfing a two-foot ledge, he snapped out a hands-only roll.

"That was super," I shouted.

"I learned it at the YMCA," he smiled.

*****

Since 1979, when national champ Linda Harrison visited us, we'd been conducting pool slalom practices and races as part of our Asheville YMCA program. The concept of using pools for slalom originated with the Ledyard Canoe Club of New Hampshire in 1962. When we picked it up, there were perhaps a dozen communities or clubs around the U.S. that were offering this indoor activity during the winter months.

With our new kayaking curriculum now officially sanctioned by the YMCA of the USA, we decided it was time to sponsor a "national" pool slalom competition in the winter of 1983-1984. The idea was simple. Kayakers and canoeists would be timed on a designated course in their local pools, and then we would compare times from all of the participating programs. What could be easier?

First of all, we had to publicize what we were doing, and gradually we signed up seven or eight pools or clubs to take part. This included two Chicago YMCAs, where Marge Cline and her cohorts from the Chicago Whitewater Association were teaching classes, and the Green Bay YMCA, where Ray McLain was teaching, plus a YMCA in Indiana and one in … was it Ohio? A couple of non-YMCA pool programs wanted in on the action, so we included them, too. It wasn't a large number, but it was a start.

Second, we had to agree on age divisions and boat categories. We decided on having every possible age group to encourage participation, but limiting the event to decked boats only. No open canoes.

Third, we had to come up with a slalom course. Somebody suggested the English Gate. That was okay with almost everyone. I suggested the English Gate for beginners and the Double English Gate for the more advanced. There was hesitancy, but finally this was accepted.

Fourth, the participating pools and clubs could conduct their local slalom races at any time during the month of February, with the results then sent to us at the Asheville YMCA for compilation. The complete results are no longer available, having been lost over the past 25 years, but I can tell you that Asheville's 14-year-old, Mark Mathews, was the fastest in the junior boys division. His time for the Double English Gate was 2:18. We had two other boys, Karl Byas, 17, and Heath White, 15, who were entered, and they placed fairly high.

One woman from Asheville took part, Barb Schlee, and she finished 12th in her category of competition.

Will Pruett and I participated, of course. Will was fourth or fifth among men ages 40 to 49, and I, at the age of 51, was fastest in the men's 50 and older Double English Gate with a time of 2:27. Yea. But I must admit: it's not hard being the fastest when you're the only one entered in your age group!

Our "national" pool slalom competition was reasonably successful, and those who participated from Chicago and Green Bay and the other clubs gave it a favorable evaluation. But when we tried to find another YMCA to pick it up and sponsor it the next year, we had no takers. Thus it ended up being a one-year wonder. It was more than a decade later that pool slalom racing was recognized "nationally" again under the direction of Wayne Dickert from the Nantahala Outdoor Center. More about this later.

*****

Our renewed emphasis on racing was paying dividends. Young Mark Mathews opened the new outdoor season by traveling with his dad, Harold, to Alabama. A report in the Citizen-Times said: "Mark Mathews of the Asheville YMCA Kayak Club, competing last weekend in the Dixie Division racing championships of the American Canoe Association, finished first in the K-1 junior slalom and third in the men's slalom. The event attracted several dozen competitors from the South and East. Mathews, 14, was the youngest entry in the men's slalom."

Two months later, there was a huge headline in our newspaper stating that "Champions Will Compete in River Races Here," and the following article said that "at least six current or former Southeastern champions, all from the Asheville area, will be competing Saturday and Sunday in the sixth annual French Broad River Races, along with several dozen other kayakers and canoeists…

"The downriver races, sponsored by the Buncombe County Parks and Recreation Department, will be held Saturday at 9:00 a.m. The starting point is Glenn Bridge Park, with the finish line five miles downriver near Sandy Bottoms. Three of the top competitors will be Jim Maynor, Chase Ambler, and Will Pruett of the Asheville YMCA Kayak Team...

"The slalom races, sponsored by the Asheville YMCA and the Western Carolina Paddlers Club, will be conducted Sunday at 1:00 p.m. The top-ranked canoeist is Steve Epps of Arden, who has been a two-time Southeastern champion. Asheville entrants Chuck Hines and Mark Mathews will be among the favorites in the kayak races...

"The YMCA's expanded 15-gate slalom course is located at the Firefighters Camp on Clayton Road."

There were 70 athletes entered in the downriver race and 57 in the slalom, totaling about 100 different individuals altogether. They came from five states. The Georgia Canoeing Association sent a large delegation, and while they performed well, it was our YMCA racers who led the way. Chase Ambler, 18, was probably the star of the show. He was the fastest in the downriver race, edging Jim Maynor, and then won his division of the slalom.

But young Mark Mathews was the fastest of ALL the slalom entrants, winning the K-1 junior kayak event. Other winners in the various kayak and canoe categories were Tom Blue from the Nantahala Outdoor Center; Julia Gaskin, Mildred Neville, and Dan and Nick Meyers from the Georgia Canoeing Assocation; Steve and Laurie Epps from Arden, North Carolina; and Nathan Brown, Rebecca Clemenzi, Kevin Drury, Harold Mathews, Molly McMillan, and Will Pruett from the Asheville YMCA Kayak Club. Oh, yeah, a guy named Hines.

I also became somewhat involved – from a distance – with the Los Angeles Olympic Games. Prior to the start of the Games, the Asheville YMCA had taken part in the Torch Relay as it came through town. Four of our Y athletes – Doug Miller, Debbie Robinson, Karl Straus, Jim Taylor – carried the flame. Then we were asked to host a weekend

Olympic Development Water Polo Clinic. We flew in Joe Vargas, a Californian who was a member of the U.S. silver medalist men's team. He stayed two nights at what is now the Renaissance Hotel across the street from the YMCA and did a terrific job of conducting the clinic in our small YMCA pool. Over 40 attended, from ages 10 to about 50.

The Torch Relay and the Olympic Development Clinic took a lot of my time, and we even revived our defunct YMCA water polo program as a recreational activity, but my main interest now was whitewater kayaking and racing. In November, I unexpectedly received an award. It was from the Dixie Division of the American Canoe Association, proclaiming that I was its Coach or Instructor of the Year "for working with youth kayaking at the YMCA of Asheville, North Carolina." Very nice.

In December, I unexpectedly received another award. A letter came that said, "Dear Chuck, on behalf of the Physical Education Society of the YMCA of the USA, it is with a great deal of pleasure that I present you with the Distinguished Director of Physical Education Award…

"This award is given in recognition of the outstanding kayaking program you have developed and implemented. This program will serve as a model for other YMCAs. It is our hope that it will be replicated throughout the country…

"The Distinguished Director of Physical Education Award is presented to persons who commit a great deal of time and creativity to the development of administrative and program models that can be used by their peers…

"Since the first award was presented in 1930, only 137 other YMCA professionals have earned this recognition. You join this list of dedicated leaders. Thank you and congratulations."

In those days, we YMCA professionals were expected to start out with a college degree in almost any field of endeavor. Mine was in Recreation Administration from the University of Minnesota. Then we were asked to earn what was called the Senior Director's certificate. This was similar to a Masters degree, except that instead of being in a single specialty, it required a variety of grad school courses in such subjects as Accounting, Christian Education, Philosophy, and Psychology. There was even a course in YMCA History. I'd received my certificate in 1968, one year before leaving the Midwest and coming to Asheville.

The Distinguished Director of Physical Education Award was the Y's equivalent of a Ph.D. It's not the same, obviously, but it's comparable. For me to earn this honor for my efforts in KAYAKING was, well, almost beyond comprehension. But I wasn't complaining. It was a wonderful way to end the year.

Chapter Eleven

It was freezing cold at the Nantahala, but there we were, in mid-January of 1985, for NOC's mid-winter races. The air temperature was 30, the water temp was 42, a brisk wind was blowing, and then it started snowing. Were we crazy?

An article in the Citizen-Times – yes, the paper was giving us plenty of publicity – told the story. It said: "Mark Mathews doesn't look like an athlete. Having just turned 15, the Asheville High School student is too light at 111 pounds for football and too short at 5-5½ for basketball. He could be a budding wrestler, except that he's slightly-built and seemingly non-aggressive. That is, until he hops into one of his kayaks and attacks the rapids on such whitewater rivers as the Nantahala, Nolichucky, Ocoee, Chattooga, and French Broad. Then, suddenly, the ninth-grader is transformed into an athlete who could become a national champion…

"For the past two years, Mark has been the best junior kayak racer in the South, winning the Ramone Eaton Cup for his proficiency at slicing through waves and sliding his sleek racing kayak through slalom gates with speed and skill. This summer, he should finish in the top four or five at the U.S. Junior Whitewater Championships to be hosted by the Nantahala Outdoor Center near Bryson City. The junior category is for youngsters ages 17 and under…

"Mathews' coach, Chuck Hines, the Vice-President for Aquatics at the Asheville YMCA, thinks that Mark could become *the* national champion. Hines, who introduced Mathews to kayaking four years ago, has been teaching youngsters since 1978 and has helped develop a number of junior titlists. The list of Hines' champs includes Chase

Ambler, Doug Baker, Curtis Bull, Deanna Davis, Rick Hensley, Heather Hines, Brent Lawson, Karen Miller, and Amy Pruett, all winners at various races around the South...

"One youngster, Becky Weis of Lafayette, Indiana, came to train with the YMCA team in 1981 and 1982 and ended up winning the U.S. junior girls slalom championship in 1983. She competed in Europe with the U.S. Junior Team in 1984...

"Hines, who has coached national champions in swimming and water polo, said that whitewater racing is a tougher sport. Once a beginning swimmer gets over his initial fear of the water and learns the basic crawl stroke, he indicated, it's fairly easy. At the YMCA, he said, they had swimmers as young as eight who could swim 10, 20, even 40 laps of the pool...

"Water polo, Hines said, adds an element of body contact and roughness, plus the necessity of having teamwork and team tactics. But both swimming and water polo are normally conducted in warm and comfortable pools, in a controlled environment, which makes them safe...

"That's not true of whitewater racing, Hines said. He and assistant coach Will Pruett watched with alarm last weekend as their newest junior racer, Whitt Mills, 14, tipped over into the rushing rapids. Mills had been trying to negotiate a slalom gate on the Nantahala River, and he leaned the wrong way, causing the current to upend his 20-pound kayak. However, the youngster performed a quick Eskimo roll maneuver which turned his boat upright, and he completed the race...

"As expected, the fastest junior kayaker at the Nantahala event was Mark Mathews, whose clocking of 1:20 plus a penalty of five seconds for touching one of the 22 slalom gates not only won the junior category but tied him with Mike Larimer, winner of the men's competition, for fastest-of-the-day honors. Larimer, from Atlanta, represented the U.S.

at the 1983 Pan-American Games, so tying him was no small feat for the up-and-coming son of Mr. and Mrs. Harold Mathews of West Asheville...

"Tied for second in the junior boys kayak race were the YMCA's Heath White, 15, and Kevin Drury, 14. Whitt Mills finished fifth. Their toughest opponents, aside from the swirling water, were from Atlanta and the Nantahala Outdoor Center. Adam Clawson, 15, of NOC, was the winner of the junior boys decked canoe competition...

"Most of the youngsters who have participated in the Asheville YMCA kayak curriculum have had parents who are whitewater paddlers. Hines said the Y couldn't conduct the program without parents like Tom Drury, Harold Mathews, Jerry Mills, and Charles White...

"The young racers from Asheville will again be heading to the river this coming weekend, when the Atlanta Whitewater Club plays host to its annual Snowball Slalom. Yes, Hines said, it will be cold and uncomfortable, and that's the reason his young athletes are so special."

*****

The U.S. Championships were held six months later, in mid-summer, on the Nantahala River. The junior races were on a Wednesday, and as much as I wanted to attend, I couldn't. I was busy with our YMCA swimming program. That was my real job, the one for which the Y was paying me not-so-big bucks. It was swimming and other instructional programs that financed our overall aquatic operation, just as it was rafting that kept NOC open and operational. Such programs provided the foundation, the broad base, the monetary stability, for what we were doing, with the racing being just a small part. Racing was important, yes, but still small. The tip of the iceberg.

On the day that the Whitewater Championships were held, we had almost 300 youngsters taking swim lessons in the YMCA pool. This included our four regular learn-to-swim classes and our three day camp groups. I had to be there. As I was preparing to go home in the early evening, I received a phone call from one of our kayakers. "Did you hear? Mark Mathews won first place at the Nationals!"

It was true. Mark, who was seeded fourth out of 14 competitors from across the country in the K-1 junior slalom, had two fast runs down the course to take top honors. In addition, Becky Weis had won again in the K-1W junior slalom. There weren't enough 17-and-unders entered in the wildwater races to have a separate junior category, but our Kevin Drury participated in the men's competition and proved to be the fastest youngster, so he was declared the K-1 junior wildwater champion. We had three winners, three national champions, all reaching the top without their coaches being there. I resolved to stay away from their other races in the future.

*****

My good friend Tom Thrailkill was the Director of Physical Education at the Asheville YMCA. He was an expert. Tom also directed the YMCA's Blue Ridge Leaders School held each summer in Black Mountain, a suburb of Asheville. This was (still is) the No. 1 school in the world for training teenagers. Over 600 teens and young adults from dozens of American YMCAs and usually several other countries attended the week-long school annually. All had received extensive training in leadership skills back home at their local YMCAs, and the summer school enabled them to intermingle and share stories and ideas.

The teens also received instruction at BRLS in two dozen different activities from a team of 60 adult advisors and instructors. The adults volunteered their time, receiving room and board but no money. This kept the cost of the school low for the teen participants. It was only $185.00 for the full week, everything included – housing, meals, outstanding instruction with a spiritual emphasis – in 1985.

Author's Note: *It's now about twice that amount, which is still very reasonable.*

I'd taught water polo at BRLS in the 1970s, and now, in the 1980s, we were teaching pool kayaking. Actually, Charles Creech and Will Pruett were doing the teaching. They were using our equipment from the Asheville YMCA. Charles, who was black, had moved from Asheville to Harrisburg, Pennsylvania, where he was the CEO of a YMCA there. He had become an outstanding big-water paddler, running the Gauley, upper Youghiogheny, and other Class IV-V rivers. But he came back to Asheville for several summers to teach kayaking at BRLS. He and Will worked together extremely well. They taught about 40 youngsters each year, the most we could handle in the beautiful 25-yard by 25-meter outdoor pool.

While it was nice to have had three junior national champions from our program in 1985, it probably was more important for us at the YMCA to be teaching basic swimming, lifesaving, and kayaking skills to hundreds of children and adults. Our Y activities continued to try and improve each participant physically, mentally, emotionally, and spiritually. I was proud of what we were doing, what we were accomplishing.

*****

Nonetheless it was time to move on. I didn't want to start a completely new chapter of my life, but it was time to turn the page. We were still teaching kayaking at the Asheville YMCA and promoting whitewater racing, but we'd stopped doing the weekend river cruises. It was more than we could handle. Thus the YMCA Kayak Club morphed into a new organization, the Western Carolina Paddlers. Will Pruett and Charles White were the first two WCP presidents.

I needed some time off for contemplation, so in November, during Thanksgiving Week, I set out on my own personal Week of Rivers. I envisioned spending the week of my 53rd birthday visiting five old friends. These "old friends" were challenging rapids on five different rivers, rapids that had provided me with a lot of fun in the past. I wanted to rely only on myself, and I planned to visit each river, each rapid, alone. My back was still giving me trouble, and it would have been easier to spend the week at home, reading and relaxing. I didn't want this to happen. I wanted to see if I could drum up the courage, the determination, the self-motivation to grow older without growing OLD. And in the process, to follow Jesus' advice. He said, "Seek ye first the kingdom of God," to which he added, "The kingdom of God is within you."

I kept a daily journal of my Week of Rivers, and here's what I wrote:

* Sunday, November 24. The Nolichucky. Driving through the village of Flag Pond, I notice that the creek running alongside the highway is full. It's South Indian Creek. Usually it's just what the name implies, a shallow creek. Today it's high and hoppin'. A few miles farther, after being joined by the flow from Rocky Creek, it's almost runnable in a kayak. But I'm not interested. I'm heading to the Nolichucky, and if the creek is jumpin' and pumpin', it's likely the larger Nolichucky will be even better.

It's a 55-mile drive from my house in suburban Asheville to the 'chucky. I guess that's one reason I prefer this river to the Ocoee. It's closer. It's longer. It's prettier, being nestled in a deep gorge with lush mountain scenery on both sides. It's a lot less crowded. And any river that's nicknamed the 'Chuck(y) is bound to be the best.

I'm so lost in my thoughts that I fail to turn off the highway at the proper exit to reach the Nolichucky. I drive another mile, turn around, and miss the exit again. The third time turns out to be the lucky charm. I'm soon driving alongside the Nolichucky, and it's HIGH. As with all my trips this week, I'm making a special effort to be careful. I've chosen one spot on each river where I'll be paddling. At the Nolichucky, it's at Chestoa, below the dangerous gorge, where there's a small park and ample parking space and a nice put-in. The water here is normally Class II, but with the higher level, it's at least II+.

It takes me 10 minutes to don my gear, and then I'm getting into my kayak. It's a dreary afternoon, and although there's no wind, it's typically late-November weather. The river water is cold, and it's moving at a brisk clip. Faster than I realized. It takes me several minutes of uncoordinated paddling to reach the waves above the put-in. There I discover a nifty surfing ledge. Two ledges, actually. The first one is two feet deep, the second a bit less. I am cautious, not yet warmed up, so I ferry to the opposite side of the river, doing a poor job, losing my angle, out-of-control. I shake my head in disgust. Get with it, Chuck!

I work the rapid for a while, regaining some semblance of paddling proficiency. Ah, that's better. I drop into the two ledges, surfing sideways, spinning, and then riding the two- and three-foot waves down to another couple of ledges. Not as good. I keep playing, then decide to rest in a mid-river eddy. Sitting there, I see a young boy accompanied by his father watching from riverside. They wave. I wave back. Then they depart.

Time to get moving again. I'm getting chilly, and it's becoming dark. I didn't start this trip until after church and lunch, so I'm running late. The sun already has vanished behind the mountain peaks. I paddle upriver and spend time playing at the two best ledges, sticking my bow into the deeper dip and riding it confidently. My ferrying is better, and I move cross-current and do a duffek and slide into another eddy. I unzip my cuff and look at my wristwatch. Gosh, I've been on the river for an hour, more than intended. I peel out and bounce my way one more time through the waves down to the park. At the take-out, I compose a little poem:

All alone on the river. No one else in sight.
In my kayak. Darting. Dancing. November night.

I change into dry clothes. Then, before leaving, I walk down to the river for one final look at it. On the other side, a steep mountain goes up, Up, UP almost vertically from the river's bank. The trees there are bare. Not a single leaf to be seen. Not a bird. Not a living soul anywhere in the area, except for me. And, of course, the river. A living river? Sure, why not? Not human, maybe, but still alive. Small drops of rain are falling, and I return to my car, start it, and head back home. 55 miles. After an hour on the 'Chucky.

* Monday, November 25. The Little Tennessee. Is there a name for this rapid? We've been calling it "Nevermore" for the past decade. It's the culmination of our YMCA trips for beginners on the Little Tennessee, a Class II+. The Little Tennessee was the first river I ran with my daughter Heather, when she was 12. That was eight years ago. Seems like yesterday. After graduating from high school and being away from home for a couple of years, she's now back in Asheville, and she's even back in her kayak, performing hands-only rolls in the YMCA pool and winning the K-1W downriver race in the recent French Broad River competition.

Coming through Balsam Gap, the sun peeks out momentarily, but it soon vanishes, and now, as I stand here surveying "Nevermore," it's cool and cloudy. The drive from home to the Little Tennessee has been 72 miles. I've parked at riverside and stand looking and listening. The river's a bit shallow, but the rapid emits the usual roar of excitement and enticement. There's a gentleman standing on the bank, fishing. Otherwise it's deserted. We're well off the highway at this point, out in the wilderness.

I walk up and down, stretching my legs, squinting across the river, which is 125' to 150' wide, to the toughest part of the rapid, where the water plunges past a couple of abrupt boulders. At higher levels, the water flows right over the boulders and so do the paddlers, sinking chest-deep into the frothy holes behind each boulder before being spit out. But the water level on this day is lower, and I can't see the exact situation on the opposite side. Guess I'll find out when I get there. It's the unknown that makes river-running so much fun.

As I don my equipment, the fisherman departs, and I am alone. Good. I deposit my boat into the water at the top of the rapid and squeeze into the cockpit. Before I can adjust my spray-skirt, I'm swept away. Wow. I'm nervous about the unknown boulder route on the other side, so I ferry across the river, finding the water to be alternately slow and swift. Above the field of boulders, I am unable to see the path to take. There's just a thin stream easing over the boulders, which means I can't wash over them – I'll have to maneuver around. I select the left side, bump over the first three-foot drop, and eddy out. I'm glad I didn't choose the right side, as I can see it's blocked. I swing around and sweep past several of the boulders and into the backwash below. It's Class II+ that burps and bounces and bubbles and brings me a sense of satisfaction as I feel my body loosening up, relaxing, harmonizing with the flow.

I peel out and am carried through a handful of small waves into a bigger boulder that blocks my path. Here, not so long ago, we rescued one of our YMCA beginners who had more than his share of problems during the day. In fact, it took three of us – Rocky and Will and I – to pull him to safety. The water was higher then and I remember wading out into two-foot waves … but let's not dwell on the past. Today there's a nice eddy below the boulder, and I spend 15 minutes practicing eddy turns.

Crossing the current, I find a nice surfing wave. It's *very* nice. I'm wired, psyched, enthralled. After all, today's my 53rd birthday. Is this the proper way to spend it, kayaking on a river? You bet. The water splashes up across my spray-skirt and hits my chest, washes my eye-glasses. I dig in deeper and sink lower, connecting with the pulse of the river, feeling its power. Ride 'em, cowboy. May the force be with you! But time's up. My wristwatch shows I've been out 57 minutes. Doesn't seem possible. Except for an infrequent vehicle on the riverside road, I've been alone on the river and in the wilderness and amongst the splendor and grandeur of God's Great Outdoors. What exquisite pleasure.

* Tuesday, November 26. Back to work. Although I'm on vacation this week, I still have job obligations. That's the way it is when employed by the YMCA. In the morning, I attend a meeting about outdoor activities, which have become a big part of our Y programming. In the afternoon, I sneak into the pool and swim 40 laps. I'm a strong swimmer, but teaching others, especially youngsters, is what I do best. It's a low-profile and low-paying job. Oh, I earn enough to get by, but that's about all. The reward is in the doing, and I'm lucky to receive a birthday bonus this week, a small raise in pay, plus a letter from a YMCA member that says, "You do so much for everyone at the Y. I see the results every day." No amount of money can replace such (undeserved?) praise. Before leaving, I adjust the chlorine content in the pool. The YMCA is a good place, but I need to get away from it, from the facility, more and more often as I grow older. Away from the clatter. The chatter. The city. The crowds. The confusion. Back to the *real* world. To the river, the rapids.

* Wednesday, November 27. The Chattooga River. It's sprinkling as I drive west, and by the time I reach Balsam Gap, it's pouring. I am dismayed at the prospect of picnicking in the rain. Today I'm hoping to have an afternoon picnic on the banks of the Chattooga. My initial plan was to hike into Section Three, but because of the wet weather, I've decided on Plan B.

I turn south, driving over the Tuckaseigee at Dillsboro, and then it's up the mountain to the charming town of Franklin, turning there toward Clayton, Georgia, and then onward to the Route 76 Bridge just below famous Bull Sluice Rapid on the Chattooga. As I pull into the parking lot, I check my odometer and see that it's been exactly 100 miles from my driveway to Bull Sluice.

Plan B calls for me to spend an hour playing in the Class II rapid below the Bull. It's running low, but I'm not too disheartened, as the rain has disappeared. There are several park employees hanging around, but I'm the only boater. Signing in, I carry my kayak down the long paved trail to the river, climbing over an abundance of rocks to the put-in. Quickly I glide out into the current, which even at this low level is swift. Below Bull Sluice are a bevy of two-foot waves, and I stick the pointed nose of my kayak into the trough. Whoa! Look out! That's tricky. The water is boiling and squirrely. I throw out a brace to keep from flipping. Then I eddy out on the near side to catch my breath, and I feel myself being pulled back into the hydraulic at the bottom of Bull Sluice's double drop.

I backpaddle, then ferry across the narrow width of the river, and I park there, climbing ashore and rock-hopping to the top of the big boulder beside Bull Sluice. I spend 10 minutes looking and listening. The rapid looks hard, like the Class IV (or V) it is. I glance upstream and down.

I'm totally alone. Not a person in sight. Not an animal. Not even a bird. Silence, except for the roar of the rapid. The water below is clear, but I don't see any fishes there, either.

I clamber down the maze of slippery rocks, watching my every step. This is no place to suffer a sprained or broken ankle. Back in my boat, I spend more time surfing and let myself be drawn into the hydraulic, maneuvering to stay out of danger. I glance at my wristwatch. I've been out 40 minutes. There's a neat little chute on the near side, and I peel out and am drawn through it into two-foot waves. Eddying out, I see another surf spot on the far side, and I paddle over to it. But it's not so hot, keeps kicking me out. I reach an eddy and sit there studying the river, the boulder formations, the pines and other trees, the small sandy beach at riverside, the Route 76 Bridge above.

My hour is up. But hey, the hardest part remains. It's carrying my boat and accessories back up the paved trail to the parking lot. Not easy for an ol' guy with a bad back. It's an uphill struggle, but I manage it. Now the reward: a picnic at riverside.

Back down the trail. A short hike. A flat rock just a yard from the river. Cheese and summer sausage. Root beer. Silence, except for the thrashing of the river against the rocks and ridges. I have a book with me, "The Soul of the Night." It's part astronomy, part philosophy. I read a chapter while munching on the goodies. The author quotes Emerson, the famous American essayist: "He who knows what sweets and virtues are in the ground, the water, the plants, the heavens, and how to come at these enchantments, is the rich and royal man." What more needs to be said?

* Thursday, November 28. Thanksgiving Day. My wife, a Registered Nurse, is working the day shift, so my daughter and I join my 89-year-old mother, several elderly aunts and uncles, and a visiting cousin from Boulder, Colorado, for a delightful turkey dinner at noon. A bit later, my daughter and I do maintenance work on the YMCA pool, which is

closed for the day. We vacuum the pool bottom and clean up around the sides. In the evening, my wife joins us and we attend an inspirational movie at one of the local theaters. It's been a Family day.

Teach me, Father, when I pray, not to ask for more, but rather let me give my thanks for what is at my door. For food and drink, for gentle rain, for sunny skies above, for home and friends, for peace and joy, but most of all, for love.

* Friday, November 29. The Nantahala. The rain that started Wednesday is continuing. It's been raining for 48 hours. The mountains are shrouded in clouds. Still pouring, as I drive into the Nantahala River Gorge. But there's a pause in the downpour as I stretch my legs at the Nantahala Outdoor Center, taking time to chat with junior racers Adam Clawson and Dan Meyers and national champions Kent Ford, Bunny Johns and Mike Larimer, and canoe designer Bob Lantz. There's a race today, the annual Thanksgiving Weekend Slalom, which I've entered in the past. But it's not on my agenda, so I hop back into my Buick and drive upriver. Once again I've planned for an hour of riverplay as a certain site. But it's crowded when I get there. A group of rafters are eating lunch, and several canoeists are milling around. I'm irritated.

I drive up and down the river, seeking an alternate spot. How about that one? No. How about this one? No. The drizzle returns. Now I'm annoyed at myself for procrastinating. Did you come to paddle, Chuck, or to drive around?

I head back to my original site, and lo and behold, it's deserted. Most likely the rain motivated everyone to get moving. I dump my paddle and boat at an easy, convenient put-in, drive a few hundred yards farther down, park, don my equipment, and walk back up to the put-in. This stretch of the river is Class II or maybe II+ today, as the water level is an inch or two higher than normal. Nothing too tough, but as I ferry out, I feel the river's speed and strength. I paddle 100 yards upriver, trying to relax, to loosen up, but I'm tight, tense. Eventually I swing around and ride some one-foot waves downriver, coasting along in the current, performing a sweep to the left and a stiff brace on the right, skipping into an eddy, a calm spot of water behind a rock. I sit there a while, feeling my body beginning to soften, to adjust, to catch the rhythm of the river.

I peel out, and 50 yards farther down, I find in mid-river a lovely series of surfing waves, three of them, two-foot-high rollers, and I drop into their midst, leaning, bracing, enjoying. I could stay here forever. I surf and surf and surf until my arms grow tired. It's the perfect spot for me on this day. A small group of four or five kayakers comes paddling past. One shouts, "Hey, Chuck, what are you doing here?" It's Jack Stewart, one of our former YMCA students. "Where else would I be?" I reply.

Eventually I let myself be swept away, and I play in several other waves before taking a breather. The rain is continuing, but I don't mind. I'm alone, believe it or not, on the Nantahala. I shove off from the bank where I've been resting for five minutes, and I permit the current to carry me across the river, where the water is gathered to form sort of a chute with a three-foot wave at the lip and a series of two-foot waves below. I coast sideways down the chute, eddy out on the near side, and ferry to a micro-eddy on the far side, barely squeezing into it. Not very smooth, Chuck. So I repeat the process four times, trying to maintain the control needed to hit the micro-eddy right on target. Only once do I perform to my satisfaction. Ah, well.

Time's flying, and I want to finish today's adventure at the nice surfing waves I've found earlier. It's a chore to paddle back upriver, but I do it, moving eddy to eddy to eddy, against the churning current. I'm puffing, panting, but I make it and spend the last few minutes of my riverplay in the rollicking two-foot rollers, leaning and bracing and enjoying. I could stay here forever, or have I already said that?

There's now no one around me at this particular spot on the Nantahala. Unbelievable for a holiday weekend. They must all be at the slalom competition. I climb out of my boat and drag it uphill to my car. It's still raining slightly, and this becomes the least pleasant task of the day, lifting my kayak onto the top of my car, tying it down, and then changing into warm, dry clothes. As I conclude, a fleet of seven or eight kayakers paddles into view, stopping to play at the same site I was enjoying so much. Have a good time, I wish them silently, and thanks for waiting until I was done.

Back at NOC, which is one of my favorite places in all the world, I can't resist stopping for a meal at River's End Restaurant, joining several racers I know, including Snow White and the two dwarfs. While eating, I think up a little Haiku, a Japanese version of poetry that has five syllables in the first line, seven in the second, five in the third.

>   *The river runs fast*
>   *through the Nantahala Gorge.*
>   *Fun for everyone.*

* Saturday, November 30. The Green River. There's good news and bad news. First, the bad. It's still raining. There's bumper to bumper traffic. It's the start of the Christmas shopping season. The YMCA pool is jammed. Everyone's working off the Thanksgiving turkey. My back is stiff, sore.

Now, the good news. It's still raining, and as a result, the Duke Power Company has opened both flumes at its dam which feeds the Green River. The Duke spokesman says they've had 3½" of rain in the past 72 hours and have had both flumes open for the past 24 hours. At noon, I head out from the Y in a heavy rainstorm on Route 26 South, and my back is killing me. On one hand, I'm reluctant to be doing this. On the other hand, I'm determined to complete my Week of Rivers.

I know it's 38 miles to the put-in at the lower Green, and frankly, I'm more worried about the road to the river than the river itself. In fact, I'm quite anxious about it. The rain continues and I drive into fog as I turn off at the Saluda Exit and head DOWN, Down, down the gravel road which drops 600' into the Green River Gorge. As I expected, it's a sea of mud, and although I'm driving in low gear, it's hair-raising. There are 17 curves on this road. Slowly, carefully, I maneuver down and around and down and around and … finally I've reached the bottom. I realize I've used up my day's supply of adrenaline.

Stopping at the put-in parking lot, I walk 30 yards to the river. The brook that adjoins the river, usually just a trickle, is high enough to be runnable. The river itself is sky high. The highest I've seen it since I paddled it at flood stage back in … was it 1979? I'd planned to spend an hour playing farther downstream at Big Corky, but as I stand here at the put-in, the rain stops. An omen, perhaps. Why not play here, I ask myself. This is supposed to be a week of visiting "old friends," and the put-in pond is certainly an "old friend." I've come here 30 times. More than that, 40 times, and have introduced 300 beginners to river-running at this spot. Let's do it.

Shortly thereafter, with no one else in sight, I'm easing out into the wide pond, on which the water level is extremely high. It's brownish, with stumps and limbs floating past. The two feeder streams, one on the left and the other on the right, are churning, and the rock formations usually so evident are totally inundated. I stick my boat into the surfing waves on the left side. There are two-foot-high waves and a hole that's one-foot deep, and the eddy in the middle has a swirling movement that sucks the rear end of my kayak downward. The waves coming from the other feeder stream across the pond are one-foot high and reach all the way to my surfing spot, and where the different sets of waves collide, there's a huge eddy wall.

I enjoy playing for a long time, making dynamic peel-outs, faster than anything I've done earlier in the week, and quick ferries and eddy turns. I surf and surf and surf. But my back is still hurting. Badly. I decide to stop after 40 minutes. After drying off, I drive down the river. The road is muddy, slippery, with water-filled pot-holes. The Class II rapid at the first bridge is a complete washout. Big Corky has two- and three-foot waves which would make for a thrilling ride, but the usual surf sports are gone. The neat surfing waves above Little Corky are completely changed due to the high water. There's one superb wave in mid-river. I'm tempted to park and give it a try. My back says NO. Little Corky itself is submerged. But the river level hasn't yet reached up to the road on which I'm driving, which it did on that trip on the flooded Green back in … yes, it was 1979.

As I return home, I'm a tad disappointed that I didn't stay in the water longer. I was alone on the Green, on a Saturday afternoon, with the river bursting and rapids surging. But with my unending back problems, I believe I've exercised good judgment. As if in agreement, the sun peeks out briefly as I drive into Asheville at 4:00 p.m. My Week of Rivers has been completed.

* Summary. There's a place in whitewater paddling for Class IV and V thrill-seeking. That's not what I've been doing this week. Not what I ever do, in fact. I'm not good enough, for one thing. It's not my style, for another.

On this Week of Rivers, I wanted to challenge myself by going alone to five "old friends," five Class II or II+ rapids. It was just the right amount of "danger" for me, requiring a certain degree of self-discipline both mentally and physically. For too many of us as we grow older, there's a widening chasm between what we'd like to do and what we actually do. We talk, but we seldom walk. I hope other paddlers turning 50 will keep on going to the rivers, as I'm doing.

Furthermore, I found time on my trips to be contemplative. Often our river trips are just as crowded and noisy as the other facets of our lives. If you're like me, you need to find time for yourself. To seek peace and quiet. To explore "the God who dwells within." Few places are better for doing this than our rivers. I can't share all my thoughts from this past week with you. But it was a very satisfactory experience for me.

Author's Note: This was the era before cell phones and other means of instant communication. When you went out into the wilderness, onto the wild rivers, alone, you were really by yourself. It was indeed a time to reflect and, if necessary in the Biblical sense, to repent. But it could be dangerous. For paddlers, the boats we used were still made of easily-breakable fiberglass, and the accessories were less reliable than what is available nowadays, in 2008, as I write this. So solo paddling could be quite an adventure.

*****

Becky Weis had traveled to Europe with the U.S. Junior Slalom Team. Now it was Mark Mathew's turn to go with the Junior Slalom Team. An article in the West Asheville Neighbors newspaper, accompanied by a large photo of Mark and his boat, said, "He's a typical teenager, except for the fact that on any given morning around 6:00 a.m., you can find Mark Mathews out on a lake or in the French Broad River, paddling his kayak around…

"He said he spends 40 minutes there, then comes back home for breakfast before heading to school. Each day after school, he spends another hour practicing…

"His determination and hard work are paying off. Mark, the 16-year-old son of Harold and Diane Mathews of the Wilshire Park area in West Asheville, has won a place on the U.S. Junior Slalom Team. He will soon be on his way to Spittal, Austria, for the 1986 Junior World Championships. He won his placement during a two-day event held recently in Pennsylvania…

"Competition is nothing new to Mathews, who started paddling a kayak when he was 11, working with Chuck Hines at the YMCA. He already has won the Dixie and Southeastern Championships twice, and last year he won the National Junior Slalom Championship. Mathews said he gets into about 15 races every year. This involves a lot of traveling and an organizing of his time, but he said it's fun…

"He is proud of the fact that he and his father designed and built his kayak. To hear Mark tell it, it's an easy process of applying layer after layer of Kevlar and S-glass into a mold that he and his father made out of fiberglass. The whole process was accomplished in one month's time, and the kayak is the one young Mathews will be taking along for his competition in Austria. Once the European trip is over, he'll be back home, in training once again for an upcoming trip to South Bend, Indiana, where he will defend his national slalom title."

This initial article was followed a week later by an even longer article and an additional photo in the Asheville Citizen-Times. The headline was "Asheville's Kayak Kids to Paddle in World Competition." The second article told us to "call them the kayak kids. Kevin Drury is a slender, smiling freshman at Asheville Country Day School. Mark Mathews is a lean, serious sophomore at Asheville High School. At first glance, neither looks like an athlete. But both have been junior national champions in whitewater kayak racing, and both will be representing the U.S. in Europe this summer…

"Drury, 15, the son of Mr. and Mrs. Tom Drury of the Erwin Hills area, began canoeing in the Asheville YMCA program as an 11-year-old. A year later, he took up kayaking, and a year after that, he started winning races. Last summer, he was the fastest junior contestant at the National Wildwater Championships, in which the competitors raced as swiftly as possible down the eight-mile length of the Nantahala River near Bryson City. Earlier this year, at another wildwater race on the Nantahala, he easily won the junior category, confirming his trip to Europe this summer…

"Mathews, 16, the son of Mr. and Mrs. Harold Mathews of West Asheville, also began participating in the Asheville YMCA program as an 11-year-old, and he too started winning races when he was 13. Last summer, he was the fastest junior entrant at the National Slalom Championships, in which the competitors maneuvered through two dozen gates hanging at Nantahala Falls…

"This should have qualified Mathews for the European trip this summer, but the slalom racing rules were changed for 1986, and he was required to attend a recent race in Pennsylvania to re-qualify. This he did, although he lost the top spot on the U.S. Junior Team to Eric Martin, a youngster he defeated at the Nationals last year…

"Both Drury and Mathews possess unique athletic ability, according to the Asheville YMCA's Vice-President for Aquatics, Chuck Hines, who has taught and coached both boys. A kayaker himself and two-time Southeastern Masters champion at slalom racing, Hines said it was apparent from the start that the two boys felt comfortable in their kayaks. They possessed skill at controlling their boats and maneuvering through the waves and around the rocks and boulders...

"Hines said he and assistant coach Will Pruett then detected the boys' tough-mindedness, a hidden quality that most top athletes have...

"The Asheville YMCA has helped develop a number of Southern and Southeastern champion kayak racers over the past decade. One is Chase Ambler, Jr., of West Asheville and currently a student at Appalachian State University. He also will be competing in Europe this summer as a member of the U.S. Senior Wildwater Team...

"As wildwater racers, Ambler and Drury will be leaving for Europe on June 14, while Mathews, a slalom racer, will be leaving later in the month. Each Ashevillean has a special home-made racing boat which he will be taking with him, plus such personalized items as paddles, helmets, and life-jackets...

"Hines points out that Mathews, Drury, and Ambler all have had outstanding parental support. The YMCA also has helped, Hines said, and so has the American Canoe Association, which is working hard to develop a strong junior racing program."

Author's Note: Although none of our YMCA kayakers returned home from Europe with a medal, all three learned a lot and had a great time, and we were very proud of their efforts.

*****

I was still in a contemplative mood and wrote an essay for "The Whitewater Paddler" newsletter, of which I was the editor, which was picked up and re-published in the American Whitewater Affiliation magazine. Here's what I wrote:

"It's quite peaceful here at the top of the rapid, the 10th Class II or II+ of the 11 rapids that are encountered when paddling the lower Nolichucky. I'm sitting in my bright blue cruising kayak, waiting for the others to catch up. It's late August. Jim Maynor and Will Pruett and I are guiding a bunch of YMCA students down this stretch of river. There are eight others in our intermediate group, all on their fifth or sixth river trip with us...

"There's nothing harsh or intimidating about the lower Nolichucky, which starts below the well-known Noli Gorge. I've paddled the Gorge, with its Class III and IV rapids, several times in the past. But I'm more familiar with the lower Nolichucky, having done it on perhaps two dozen occasions with students from our YMCA kayaking classes...

"I've run the lower Noli when the wind is whistling at 30 knots per hour and when a torrential rainstorm is in progress and when a fire is consuming homes along the river bank and when the water is just about at flood stage. But mostly I've run it when it's simply another average Class II or II+ trip. Such is the case today. It's nothing spectacular. Still and all, it's a good way to spend a Sunday afternoon, and as I sit in an eddy above the 10th rapid, listening to the cascading of the water onto the rocks below, I reflect on the fact that only a few other 53-year-olds like myself can be found kayaking down a river on this particular day. Or any day...

"Earlier in August, my wife Lee and I spent several days skin-diving at Key West and Key Largo. We'd enjoyed ourselves, had seen sea urchins and turtles and barracudas and an assortment of colorful fishes and interesting coral formations. Lee and I have been diving together since we went to Hawaii in 1959. I became one of the first 50 certified scuba instructors in the entire country in 1960. Our daughter Heather, who just turned 20, is also a certified diver. It's been one of our Family activities for many years, and it's a recreational activity I thoroughly enjoy...

"Yet when we were recently in the Florida Keys, I noted I was the probably the oldest male out there on the reefs. Sometimes I wonder if I'm doing the right thing for my age. I have friends who are prominent attorneys, powerful businessmen, and successful physicians. My best friend from the 1960s, Bob Helmick, with whom I once played international-level water polo, is now president of the United States Olympic Committee, and I've seen his picture in numerous national publications. Maybe I'm a bit envious of his successes…

"So what am I doing, at my age, sitting in a kayak at the top of this Class II+ rapid? I'm a bit weary. We've been out on the river for three hours, and my endurance isn't what it used to be. My back is hurting, but that's normal. What am I doing here? What was I doing underwater in the Florida Keys and at St. Croix in the Caribbean in recent months? What prompts me to go cavorting around like a kid?

"Ah, maybe that's it. Maybe I'm just trying to recapture my youth. To find a taste of adventure, of excitement. To renew myself in God's Great Outdoors. To drink in the splendor of His Creation. To leave behind the increasing commercialism that pervades our everyday lives. To escape the artificiality of so many places and programs…

"There's nothing artificial about this river, though. Or the rapids I've run. Or the winding path through the rapid that lies just ahead. Nothing artificial about the ocean reefs. Or the ocean creatures. Or the stars circling above. Nothing contrived. No make-believe out here in Nature's Realm. No obnoxious Madison Avenue hype. No haughty Hollywood huckstering. This is Reality. This is Life. This is the Real Thing. And that's why, at 53, I'm here."

Chapter Twelve

There were big changes at the Asheville YMCA. We had decided to build a second pool. It was needed in order to fully serve those enrolled in our ever-expanding aquatic programs. At the same time, I was asked to assume a new position, that of Vice-President for Community Services. I left my office downtown which was adjacent to the pool and moved into an office at another Y facility. I also became more involved with YMCA international work, which from 1985 to 1995 took me and my wife Lee to 22 islands in the Caribbean. Our trips there lasted from two to five weeks. Occasionally there were two trips annually. This had its good and bad points. The new international assignment was very rewarding and enabled Lee and me to do more oceanic skin-diving in the process.

But on two occasions, it kept me from accepting opportunities to go to Europe as an assistant coach with our U.S. Junior Slalom Team. If I remember correctly, I had a chance to serve as an assistant to Peter Kennedy on one occasion, to Ron Lugbill on another. Wow! I was tempted, but my YMCA duties prevailed, especially since Lee could accompany me on our trips to the Caribbean. Family first!

Due to my new YMCA assignments – one locally and one internationally – I had less time for my involvement with whitewater kayaking. We already had dropped the YMCA Kayak Club and passed responsibility for all "social activities" on to the new Western Carolina Paddlers organization, letting WCP, now being led by dynamic Chris Bell, conduct the weekend river cruises. We also decided to eliminate the adult intermediate instruction from our program in the future.

However, we maintained our slalom course on the French Broad River, and for this – our ongoing usage of the site – we received an award from the Land-of-Sky Regional Council, which gave its annual Friend of the River award "to the Asheville YMCA for your efforts to use and enhance the French Broad River and its tributaries." Will Pruett and I attended the ceremony and graciously accepted the award on behalf of the Y.

We increased our youth programming. The YMCA had two very special thrusts that were being operated by its Community Services Branch, of which I was the leader. One of these was with needy inner-city children. The other was with troubled and 'at risk' teenagers. We brought both into our kayaking program. We also reached out to more youngsters from south Asheville, an area we weren't serving very well previously.

As usual, the Citizen-Times gave us good PR. Under the heading of "YMCA Kayak Program Starting," the article said, "The Asheville YMCA kayak program, which has produced three junior national champions in recent years, kicks off its new season with slalom practices on the French Broad River and instructional classes for beginners in the Y pool...

"Since its inception a decade ago, the program has taught kayaking to more than 1,000 youths and adults...

"Chuck Hines, YMCA Vice-President for Community Services, encourages any interested youngster to sign up. Hines says that kayaking is challenging and demands concentration, and is thus a refreshing and revitalizing experience."

To be honest, it was Will Pruett who kept our youth program going in the late 1980s. I was busy elsewhere. Will had served as the first president of the Western Carolina Paddlers, and now he was president of the French Broad River Foundation. He also had "anchored" our YMCA program for many years. He was doing all this as a volunteer while heading up his own business, Blue Ridge Computer Services. Jim Maynor continued to assist Will. I did what I could to help over the warm-weather months, and at a meeting of the Western Carolina Paddlers in September, I was unexpectedly awarded a plaque that said: "Western Carolina Paddlers presents to Chuck Hines a Special Award in appreciation for 10 years of service and contributions to the Western North Carolina paddling community."

In "The Whitewater Paddler" newsletter, I said, "I'd like to express my appreciation to WCP for presenting me with an award at the club's last meeting. I'm not sure I deserve it. So I would like to recognize three others who made it possible for me to receive this award. They are John Bayless, Will Pruett, and Jim Maynor. These men, who are not only fine paddlers but also outstanding leaders, share in the honor I've received. To all of you, many thanks."

I also received a letter from Bill Masters, president of Perception, which at that time was the largest kayak-manufacturing company in the U.S. Located at Liberty, South Carolina, Perception always supplied us with reduced-price kayaks for our YMCA kids whenever we needed them. Bill wrote, "Dear Chuck, you have been a prime mover in building the sport in Asheville and the surrounding area. Your untiring efforts to bring new boaters into the sport and to promote safe boating by paddlers of all skill levels has been a good example for all of us. I wish you the best and trust you will continue to keep in touch."

By the time Thanksgiving Week rolled around, I was ready for another personal adventure. This time, it turned out to be a Week of Creeks, and as before, I kept a daily journal. Here's what I wrote:

* Saturday, November 22. The French Broad. "It's a bit cold, ain't it?" The fisherman is leaning against a big boulder, clad in a heavy parka, gloves, and boots. I hadn't seen him when I carried my kayak to the river on a sunny but COLD and windy day. His voice startles me. I dip my fingers into the water and feel them numbing quickly. I turn to the fisherman and nod.

Leaving the kayak at river's edge, I hike back to my car and return with the other items necessary for whitewater adventure – paddle, helmet, spray-skirt, sweater, and life-jacket. The fisherman has moved upstream, apparently cherishing his privacy as much as I do mine. Today I'm wearing wet boots, a concession to the weather. As I slide out into the swirling one- and two-foot waves at my favorite play spot on the French Broad River, just down the road from my home in suburban Asheville, I laugh aloud. Here I am, preparing to celebrate another birthday, and once again I'm attempting my own Week of whitewater excitement. Crazy? Maybe.

Suddenly life has become more complicated. My wife, a Registered Nurse, has started her own business. Our daughter, now 21, is recovering from surgery. My elderly mother is in a nearby nursing home and not doing well. And I have a couple of new assignments with the YMCA. So here I am, already shivering, as I ferry back and forth in the waves, gradually relaxing and harmonizing with the flow. This play spot on the French Broad normally attracts a dozen or more boaters every day. It's a Class II or II+, depending on the water level. I start out alone, and after surfing for 10 or 15 minutes, I note a C-2M putting in. It's Windy Gordon and one of his partners. Windy has represented the U.S. internationally. He and his female partner in their decked canoe and I in my kayak share the waves, ferrying and surfing and playing. Then they leave. I depart myself a few minutes later. Looking at my wristwatch, I see I've been out on the river for one hour, 10 minutes. It's not a bad way to begin my special, personal week.

* Sunday, November 23. A Snakeskin Sermon. It's still cold. The wind has dissipated, but has been replaced by a steady rainfall. After church, I change into paddling gear, and my wife shakes her head in disbelief as I head out the door. She has her own hobby, singing, and nothing can keep her from attending her scheduled performances. So she should understand my obsession.

Overnight I've had a change of plans. I've decided to visit four local creeks – two of them well-known, the others less familiar – within 30 miles of Asheville. The one I've selected for today is a bit south of town. I've hiked it a couple of times but never paddled it. As the rain continues, I dump my boat and my paddle at a certain spot alongside the stream and drive a quarter-mile downstream and park. Then I walk back up, hop into my kayak, and shove off. The stream is no more than 25' wide, which is the width of our swimming pool at the YMCA. Narrow, with high banks on both sides. I paddle upstream, against the current, maneuvering around rocks and fallen tree limbs. It's not only narrow but also shallow. So I turn around and let the current propel me downriver, er, downcreek. There are a few ledges at which I can surf, but it doesn't amount to much.

Except for the gentle patter of the rain, there's no noise whatsoever. I had hoped to see some wildlife, but there's none except for a couple of squirrels and a family of jays that all spit invectives at me as I pass beneath their tree. At the last of the surfing ledges, I see a long tree limb above my head, and I note that hanging from the tip of the limb is the remnant of a snake's skin. It's still in one piece after being shed by the snake, which must have been at least a yard in length. An hour has passed, and the rain is picking up, and I've reached the take-out. As I hoist my kayak onto my roof rack and toss my wet apparel into the car's trunk, the silence remains.

The snakeskin was interesting, I think, the first I've seen while paddling. Wouldn't it be nice if we could shed our prejudices and excess mental baggage, our old and useless clichés, our worn-out and worthless traditions, as easily as a snake sheds its skin? Why do we cling so relentlessly to the past? Oh, I like history, like to study what's happened, what's been done by others, and learn from it. But then you need to move forward. I'm going through some changes in my life, at home and at my job. It's a little disconcerting, a bit scary, and I'm not sure what awaits me in the future, around the bend or over the horizon line. But like my kayaking, I've gotta put a smile on my face and go with the flow.

* Monday, November 24. Against The Current. Still cold, still raining. The creek I've chosen today is east of Asheville, and as I drive to the put-in, I detect a wet, heavy, hazy fog in the surrounding mountains. There's a gravel road alongside the stream, and I can hear but not see automobile traffic from the nearby highway. I park on the side of the road, lock my car, and carry my boat and my paddle to streamside, having chosen this particular place because I can see a sweet two-foot surfing ledge.

The ledge immediately provides me with 20 minutes of fun as I ride the tumbling waves. Then I catch the current and head downstream. It's narrow, shallow, but I keep going. While rounding a sharp bend, I find that a large oak tree has fallen across the stream, blocking my passage. The fog from the mountains is now gathering around me, here in this little creek. I turn around and paddle against the current, back to the put-in, to where I started. It's taken me 10 minutes of going with the flow to reach the oak tree. Now it takes me 20 minutes, maybe more, to paddle upstream to my starting point. I surf again on the ledge at the top and then decide I've had enough.

I change into dry clothes and sit on a large boulder and munch on a peanut butter sandwich and coconut cookies. Gulping a soda, I feel refreshed. It's still drizzling, but I don't care. Yesterday I thought about the importance of going with the flow. But today I had to paddle upstream, against the current. Maybe the secret to a successful life is knowing when to go with the flow and when to stop, to take a stand, to fight the uphill battle. I'm no philosopher, but I know that life can be confusing, that it takes courage to confront life's twists and turns. Just like whitewater kayaking.

* Tuesday, November 25. What The Road Passes By. It's funny how things turn out. Today is my birthday. I'm 54, no escaping it, and this was to be the day I paddled on a creek west of Asheville. I drive a winding mountain road through a light rain which turns into mist as I reach an altitude of 4,000'. Parking just off the road, I hike downward into a valley toward the creek. Down I go, beneath a canopy of trees and over a carpet of wet, slippery leaves. I keep going on … and on … until finally I reach the creek. It's attractive, about 35' wide, with sparkling clear water, and I can see an abundance of Class II and III rapids as I look upstream and downstream. Very nice.

But it's too far from the road. Hiking back to my car, I count 877 steps, all uphill. I'm gasping, and my heart is pounding. At my age – 54, right? – I don't want to carry my kayak and other equipment all the way down to the creek and then, after paddling, all the way back up. Disappointed, I decide to spend the next few hours scouting, so I head north and drive farther into the country, away from the clashes of so-called civilization. The twisting, turning road takes me past farms and fields and forests, and my dismay turns to delight as I cross a small stream I'd forgotten about. It looks promising, and I quickly add it to my Week of Creeks. I'll come back and do it tomorrow. Eventually, while driving home, where my wife and daughter await me with a birthday cake and gifts, I'm smiling and humming. The day's going to be a good one, after all.

It's surprising what the road passes by. In this era of freeways, we often miss out on viewing Nature's splendors. We rush from one city to another, from one commitment to another. We need to pause more often and think about where we're going, what we're doing. We need to swerve off the congested streets and find the path less taken, that leads to contemplation, to a re-connection with our inner selves. As Dag Hammarskjold once said, "I feel an ache of longing to share in this embrace of Nature, a longing like carnal desire but directed towards earth, water, sky, and returned by the whispers of the trees, the fragrance of the soil, the caress of the wind, water, and light. Content? No, no, no, but refreshed, rested, while waiting."

* Wednesday, November 26. The Joy of Discovery. As the weather forecasters predicted, a tremendous thunderstorm moves into Western North Carolina overnight. I am awakened at 3:00 a.m. by the thunder and flashes of lightning. Six hours later, as I leave home for a morning of family obligations, it's still pouring. Altogether, over a period of 10 hours, we are deluged by more than 3" of rain.

But by early afternoon, the skies have cleared as the storm marches on to the east, and the sun is shining, enabling me to return to the creek, or steam, that I discovered yesterday. I'm sure others have paddled it, but for me, it's a heretofore undiscovered gem lying just 20 miles from my home. Yesterday it was a Class I-II, with a reasonable number of rocks and ledges and chutes, but when I arrive today, it's entirely different. The overnight rainfall has raised the stream's level by two feet or more, and there's not a single rock or boulder in sight. Everything is inundated by a brown and unappetizing torrent of waves, reminding me of two trips I've taken in the past to flooded rivers, one on the Green with Lorri Cameron and Al Preston and the other on the Tellico with Will Pruett.

I park and walk down a streamside path and look at my challenge for this day. It's running high and is filled with dirt and silt and debris, swirling swiftly and unpredictably along, with continuous two- and three-foot waves.

As I prepare to enter this remote creek, which now resembles more of a rumbling river, two teenaged boys walk up and watch my efforts. "A bit high, ain't it?" one asks.

"Is it?" I reply.

"Higher than usual."

"You ever see any other kayakers and canoeists here?"

"A few. Not many. Not when it's flooding like this, anyway. But me and my friends have gone inner-tubing here in the summer when it's warmer and the water's lower."

"What's around the bend down there?" I ask anxiously.

"Guess you'll find out."

I ferry back and forth across the width of the stream, spending 20 minutes warming-up and feeling the water flushing beneath my boat before I turn and head downstream. It's a rush. Fast. Frantic. Fantastic. But smelly. Dirty. Not a good place for a swim. The stream runs to the west, into the larger French Broad River, and directly into the late afternoon sun, which turns the water in front of me into an opaque mirror. I squint and paddle and squint and paddle. Yesterday I couldn't see where I was driving because of rain and fog. Today I can't see where I'm paddling because of the bright sunlight. Typical. Mother Nature always throws you a curve when you least expect it.

It takes me only 20 minutes, maybe 25, to reach the spot when I intend to stop. Twice I've come close to tipping, flipping, after being side-swiped by three-foot diagonal waves that seem to grab at me, but both times I brace my way through. I've had enough. It's been a rapid run, a quick cruise, but it's a bit dangerous, and I don't want to overstay my welcome. Eddying out on the right, I put my paddle across the back of my boat in the time-honored manner, bracing it against the bank, pulling myself up out of my tight-fitting kayak. I lower myself into the water, wriggling my toes in an attempt to touch the bottom of the stream which surely must be just below the muddy surface. Even though I'm within an arm's length of the bank, my feet keep going DOWN…Down…down…pulling my body with it. In an amazing display of athletic inability, I sink completely out of sight. Even with my head submerged, my feet still haven't touched bottom.

Gasping, sputtering, I bob up and shove my kayak over onto the bank where luckily it remains. But the current is carrying me into a submerged bush, and I envision myself being caught there in its leafless branches. I toss my twin-bladed paddle onto the bank and with both hands grab the branches of the bush, pulling myself up, Up, UP onto the bank, where I stand, shaking my head in disbelief at what has just happened so swiftly and surprisingly.

Obviously the water level on this obscure little creek is much higher than I realized, and I probably shouldn't have tackled it by myself. Kayaking can be risky, and disaster can strike when you least expect it, and it never pays to be careless.

Be that as it may, I've had the joy of discovering a new stream for myself and running it at a high and exciting level. That's worth a lot. This is what we need to do with our lives, accept new "challenges." I'm feeling stoked as I return home, and once again I compose a little ditty:

*Days of danger on the river. Raging rapids, frothing foam.
Remembrances of past adventures. Week of creeks. Whitewater poem.
Slender kayak, tossed and turning. Icy water, leafless trees.
Cloudy skies, solo paddling. Excitement in the autumn breeze.*

* Thursday, November 27. Thanksgiving Day. It's a day of family togetherness. I like my job with the YMCA. It's my vocation, my career, my calling. I love kayaking, being on the rivers, weaving through the waves and riding the rapids. It's my avocation, my hobby, my most pleasant pastime. But nothing is more important to me than FAMILY. I shan't elaborate in this book, which is about my whitewater wanderings, except to say that my wife Lee and daughter Heather always have been and always will be No. 1 in my life, and to this short list I'll add son-in-law David and grandchildren Crystal and Charlie.

* Friday, November 28. Am I Having Fun Yet? The rivers are still smokin' after nearly a week of continuing rain. I drive down to the YMCA and swim 60 laps to work off yesterday's sumptuous turkey dinner, procrastinating for an hour about going kayaking. Finally I head out in the early afternoon, driving to the last creek on my schedule. I park at the bridge where the east and west forks meet, change into my paddling apparel, and carry my kayak about 300 yards up the east fork. Entering, I play for 20 minutes in the icy Class I+ water, gradually working my way down toward the bridge, under which there's a Class II rapid that concludes with a III surfing ledge. It turns out to be the best surfing spot during my Week of Creeks, and I play and play and play, riding the crest of the wave, diving into the trough, and sliding from one side of the stream to the other. I peel out from the corner eddy and do spins in the whirlpooling waves. Wheee! It's not hard. It's easy. And fun.

Driving home, the odometer on my "newer" Buick hits 100,000 miles. In this car, I've driven to West Virginia and Pennsylvania and Colorado and Wyoming and Minnesota and other places to go kayaking and to the Florida Keys and elsewhere to go skin-diving. But there's plenty of action right here where I live in the mountains of Western North Carolina. I am an advocate of traveling and broadening one's horizons.

It's a big world out there, worth exploring. But at the same time, there's no place like home. Like friends and especially family. It's a conundrum, a puzzlement. There are times I can't wait to get away, to see what's "out there," and then times I can't wait to return home, to the familiar.

Author's Note: Wasn't it the poet T.S. Eliot who once said that we shall not cease from exploration, and the end of all our exploring will be to arrive where we started, and know the place for the first time.

Yes, it's been a terrific Week of Creeks. I started out on the larger French Broad River last Saturday with a cold warm-up. Then it was Hominy Creek and the snakeskin on Sunday; the Swannanoa and upstream paddling on Monday; bypassed Spring Creek and its too-long hike on Tuesday; overflowing Ivy Creek and my step into its depths on Wednesday; and finally, after a family-style Thanksgiving on Thursday, the upper forks and oh-so-nice surfing ledge at Big Laurel Creek on Friday. Not a bad way to spend the week of my 54th birthday.

*****

"You've gotta be kidding," I laughed.

"No," said the reporter from the Asheville Citizen-Times, "it's the truth."

"Tell me about it."

"We've had several reports from whitewater paddlers about seeing an Otter Boy on a river not too far from here. One group was exploring a river section that no one has paddled very much, and they said they glimpsed a bunch of river otters playing. The otters were sliding down a rain-slickened bank into the river, having a great time, as otters are inclined to do. Then they saw there was a boy, about 12, amongst the otters. He had two arms and two legs, but his body was covered by fur. When the otters and the boy saw the onlooking paddlers, they all submerged and headed across the river, staying underwater. Eventually they disappeared."

I looked at the reporter, my eyebrows raised, but said nothing.

The man continued. "Two other groups of paddlers have told us they also have seen this boy cavorting with otters. What do you think, Chuck?"

"I guess our Otter Boy must be a distant relative of the Big Foot that inhabits the Pacific Northwest."

The reporter knew I was being snide. He didn't know about my own encounter with an all-too-human muskrat. You see, we were out there alone, on the French Broad River, the muskrat and I. It was winter. I'd found a sunny Saturday sandwiched between the usual Southern rainstorms, during a week when the Northern and Western states were being blanketed by snow. The rain had caused the river to rise nearly two feet above normal. Then the storm had vanished and with it the blustery wind, leaving behind a cool but bright day.

Deciding on the spur of the moment to go kayaking, I'd been unable to find a paddling partner, so I went to the river by myself. Not always a wise practice, but it was a stretch of the river with which I was fully familiar, and I was planning to spend my time at a single rapid. Besides, there are times when I, at the age of 55, needed to seek solitude in the wilderness.

I set 45 minutes as my limit on the river and, to assure adherence to this self-imposed restriction, I'd brought my skinny slalom racing boat, a tight-fitting and uncomfortable 19-pound kayak, knowing that well within the allotted time it would be cramping my hips and strangling the circulation in my legs. It was a 50-yard walk from my parked car to the river, and I made two trips, enjoying the quietness, carrying first my boat and paddle and then my helmet, paddling jacket, spray-skirt, and life-jacket.

The trees at riverside had lost their leaves, and they viewed my approach with indifference, with complete silence, with an absence of waving or whispering as was their custom in the summer months. Even the cardinals and blue jays and thrushes in the branches and bushes remained quiet, apparently skeptical of my intent to invade their territory at this time of the year.

Sliding down the bank, I stepped into the water with my sandal-clad feet. It was as cold as I'd expected. Maybe I should have worn my wetsuit. But there was no way I could have squeezed into my tiny slalom racer with neoprene on my legs or feet.

The high water had overrun the usual eddy at the put-in spot near the bottom of the rapid, and I had to grasp a tree limb to steady the kayak as I shoe-horned into it. Then I released the limb and let myself be swept out into the quick current, ferrying across to the opposite side. I ferried back and forth several times, warming up, and then spent five minutes straining my way upstream against the current, struggling to reach the top of the rapid. The big boulders on top, normally exposed, were all completely inundated, and the water pouring over them created a number of Class III ledges. Although my needle-nosed racing kayak was not the ideal boat for surfing, I spent 30 minutes riding the ridges, romping in the froth and foam, maneuvering from one ledge to another, across the entire width of the rushing brown river.

Suddenly, as I coasted down from one ledge, I spotted a furry face staring up at me from the water. We moved along together, about 10 yards apart, being carried down the river, looking at each other. Its black eyes displayed no fear. It submerged, waving a pointed tail at me as it plunged into the dark depths. A beaver? No, not with that tail. A mink? Maybe. Ah, yes, a muskrat!

Along the bank I discovered its habitat, a sloppy array of sticks and mud and roots and leaves. As I sat there, the muskrat resurfaced upriver, again riding the current down to its abode. It repeated the procedure several times. Was it seeking food, or was it merely playing? I wasn't sure, but to me it seemed to be playing. I joined it. For 15 minutes, we played together, side by side, by ourselves in the wilderness, on the river, one of us small, dark, furry, and the other larger and fair-skinned, yet both belonging to the same world, to the same Creator.

In its element – the river – the muskrat was more at home than I, and so glancing at my wristwatch and stretching my aching legs within the confines of my narrow boat, I surfed at the ledges one more time and let the waves propel me backwards to the bottom of the rapid. I squinted into the sun, trying to see the muskrat once more, but it was gone.

At the bottom, I ferried back and forth and finally forced myself to leave the water. Standing on solid ground once again, I was startled when a solitary, brightly-colored duck came flapping down the river, not more than a few feet above the water, honking furiously. Hmmm. What was that all about? Moments later, two canoes came into sight, their occupants speaking to each other so softly that I couldn't make out their words. They passed by, without seeing me, and I watched them disappear around the bend.

Except for the slapping of the water against the bank, all was silent. I stood there alone, listening but not hearing anything and looking but not seeing anything, except for the mighty river flowing past.

Reluctantly, I hoisted the small, sleek kayak onto my shoulder, grabbed the wooden paddle, and began walking to my car. Halfway there, still amidst the silence, I suddenly turned around, casting my thoughts out into the river. "Goodbye, muskrat. It was nice to meet you. Take care of yourself. I'll be back to visit you again soon, and we'll enjoy the river together."

*****

In the late 1980s, concern for the environment was just starting to heat up. At the YMCA, we were striving to include an environmental component in our various outdoor activities – biking and hiking, sailing and boardsailing, backpacking and skiing, skin- and scuba-diving, canoeing and kayaking, plus our high ropes course at the Community Services Branch – and in 1988 we were rewarded for our efforts by being listed as having the second-best all-around outdoor educational program of all the YMCAs and YWCAs in the country. Topping the list was the Frost Valley YMCA of upstate New York.

This was our fourth such national award. In 1976, the Asheville YMCA received recognition from the U.S. Swimming Foundation for having the best water polo program and the second-best all-around aquatic program of all the YMCAs and YWCAs in the country – the Y at Little Rock, Arkansas, finished ahead of us – and in 1985, we were recognized by the American Canoe Association for having the No. 1 youth paddling program in the U.S. That was the year three of our YMCA-trained youngsters won national whitewater racing championships.

I wrote an article for Green Line, a local environmental newspaper, and it went like this: "Although my wife and I love Asheville, having resided here since 1969, we recently began looking around for some other place to retire. We didn't find any place that attracted us. We wrote to Naples, Florida, and their response was typical of what we heard from ALL the cities and communities we contacted. We were told that Naples was the fastest growing metro area in the country, with a population that had exploded from 7,000 in 1967 to 125,000 in 1987, and that Naples' growth rate over the next three years would require 9,000 new housing units. Not a single person who sent us info from Naples bothered to mention Quality of Life...

"I'm not surprised. It's this seeming lack of concern for Quality that over the past decade has kept us away from the Atlantas, the Bostons, the LA's, the Chicagos, and even the Charlottes. When I read that the population of the U.S. is going to increase by 26.6 million by the year 2000, I normally shrug it off. But when the nice, smaller communities like Naples succumb to the bigger is better, therefore biggest is best concept of modern madness, I become aggravated. Growth alone does not make this a better world...

"That brings me to the main point of this article: in the out-of-control expansion of our industrialized society, we're in danger of destroying the world that God has created. We're becoming careless stewards. Let me share my personal experiences with you. Here in Asheville and Buncombe County, I've seen the smog sneaking slowly into our valleys, turning the blue sky brownish at times. I've seen the forests of the Smokies along the Appalachian Trail shredded by acid rain. I've seen the rivers lowered by drought and contaminated by chemical wastes. I've seen fishes by the thousands killed by federal dams that don't work. I've seen the government trying (unsuccessfully, thank heaven) to designate an area just down the road from my home as a nuclear dump. I could go on...

"While we're turning our larger cities into jungles (okay, that's just MY opinion), we are by an ironic twist of fate cutting down the real jungles and forests at the rate of 10,000 acres per day, obliterating animal habitats, destroying prime farm land, sending sludge into the ocean, and even altering the oxygen/carbon dioxide content of the air we breathe...

"In his prize-winning novel, 'Dr. Zhivago,' author Boris Pasternak wrote that it often happened in history that a lofty idea has degenerated into crude materialism. Could that define life in our society nowadays? If so, what can we do about it?

"At the YMCA, we've incorporated environmental awareness into our kayaking and skin-diving courses and are planning to do this in various other activities...

"Individually, it's not too late for you and me to become more involved. We can support organizations such as American Rivers, the Cetacean Society, The Cousteau Society, the Dolphin Research Center, the Environmental Defense Fund, the Florida Keys Land Trust, Friends of the Sea, Greenpeace, the Planetary Society, and Reef Relief, to mention a few with which I'm familiar...

"We can make our voices heard so that Asheville doesn't become just another over-developed and overcrowded city. After looking around, my wife and I have decided to remain here in our retirement. I hope we're making the correct choice."

*****

In addition to our environmental concerns and our international programming, we at the YMCA were working diligently in Asheville's inner-city. We brought a bunch of inner-city boys and girls into our pool for kayaking instruction. One, 13-year-old Ben Baldwin, who lived just four blocks from the Y in downtown Asheville, penned a school report that he shared with us. Ben wrote, "It all started in September of 1988, shortly after I moved here from Los Angeles. The way I found out about kayaking was through Chuck Hines of the YMCA, who helped me get a scholarship to the Y…

"He told me that people were practicing kayaking on Thursday evenings in the pools. I asked him what a kayak was. He said to return the next Thursday to find out. I went back and he told me to go and get a spray-skirt. I asked him was a spray-skirt was. After I got everything together, I got in my first kayak, a yellow Dancer XL. My first instructor was Doug Baker, a college senior who had been the Southeastern junior champion in wildwater racing as a 16-year-old. He started showing me the basic kayak strokes. I wasn't understanding very much until the third or fourth Thursday I attended, when he taught me how to roll. My first Eskimo roll in the Y pool was an experience to remember! I wasn't sure I had done it by myself, but I guess I did. From then on I could do the roll regularly…

"Spring came, and Will Pruett started taking us youth kayakers out to the rivers. I didn't have much money, but luckily Will and the YMCA didn't charge much, just $30.00 for six lessons, and I got it at half price because I was willing to help load and unload the kayaks and other equipment. On Saturday mornings, about eight or nine or maybe 10 of us youngsters went with Will and sometimes Chuck Hines and Heath White to the slalom course at the Firefighters Camp on the French Broad River. We practiced from 9:00 a.m. until noon. The Saturday practices were in March and April, and it was always cold and cloudy, but Will and Chuck and Heath taught us a lot…

"We had to postpone one or two trips to the Nantahala, but one Saturday in May, when I came to the YMCA, Jim Maynor and Virginia Oursland asked me if I wanted to go with them and Virginia's son

Norman, a member of our youth group, to the Nantahala. I said I did. When we arrived there, Jim dropped us off and took the van back to where we'd be getting out of the river. He hitched a ride back to us. We checked all our equipment and then kayaked down the river. Jim told us to go into the various eddies, which we did, and he taught us to do other things. We kayaked all the way down to Nantahala falls, and Norman and I decided to call it a day. Jim and Virginia ran through the Falls. I swam once, but otherwise I didn't have any problems, and I hope to return to the Nantahala soon."

While the Asheville YMCA received an award one year for having the best youth paddling program in the country, we generally played second fiddle to the C-CATS from Bethesda, Maryland, a suburb of Washington, DC. Under the direction of their coach, Bill Endicott, that club was producing young paddlers who were winning world championships. Blazing out of the opposite end of the country, from the State of Washington, came another star. His name was Scott Shipley, and he became the world K-1 junior champion, or Gold medalist, in slalom.

But our Y program was still doing all right, in its own way, and I was asked to write an article for "The American Canoeist" magazine, which I did. It was entitled "Building a Junior Paddling Program," and I said that "their names may not mean anything to you. Chase Ambler, Doug Baker, Curtis Bull, Karl Byas, Deanna Davis, Kevin Drury, Rick Hensley, Heather Hines, Brent Lawson, Mark Mathews, Karen Miller, Amy Pruett, John Sherman, Becky Weis, Heath White...

"These are youngsters from our Asheville YMCA junior paddling program who in recent years have won at least one race in Dixie/Southeastern competition. Three have finished first at the U.S. Junior Championships. Eight have competed internationally. One was a finalist for the U.S. Olympic Team last year...

"What have we done at the Asheville YMCA to enable us to develop one of the best junior paddling programs in the country? Tradition was a factor in the Asheville program. When we started in the 1970s, we were able to build on a strong YMCA competition background. We had been producing champion swimmers and water polo players, and it wasn't hard to switch our emphasis to whitewater paddling. Here's how we did it:

* We borrowed some "bat boats" from the nearby Nantahala Outdoor Center, whose experts have been continually supportive of our efforts, and we encouraged our young water poloists to try their luck at kayak polo. From there we switched to whitewater paddling.

* We solicited a nice $1,000 donation from a local restaurant which enabled us to purchase equipment. Perception also helped us out by making boats and accessories available at less than cost.

* We conducted a number of instructional clinics, bringing in champion racers like Linda Harrison and Dave Mason. This attracted a lot of attention.

* We were very conservative when introducing our juniors to the thrills and spills of the rapids. We started off with several Class I and II cruises, then half-a-dozen Class II to III trips. I believe being cautious is important when working with youngsters, not only for them but also for their parents.

* We constructed a 12-gate slalom course on our local river, the French Broad, and used it for training twice weekly, and we also conducted a number of races there.

* We hung a couple of slalom gates in one of the YMCA's small pools and practiced there during the winter months, using the time to build team spirit and camaraderie.

* We made sure there were always plenty of (inexpensive) prizes as the kids learned to roll, showed improvement in running the English Gate, or completed a dozen river cruises.

* As we progressed, the sports editor of our local newspaper, who happens to be a friend of mine, gave us just enough publicity to motivate the kids into doing better.

* While we practiced rolling and slalom and engaged in timed sprints, we also spent a lot of time running rivers. The kids saw the river trips as a reward for their slalom practices in the pool and at our French Broad River course. Some of our best youngsters moved into wildwater racing and whitewater rodeos and squirt boating. Whatever turns you on, we declared.

"There you have it – nine ideas for developing your own junior paddling program – but the 10th idea is the most important. It's the LEADERSHIP that is provided by a handful of interested, dedicated adults…

"As the YMCA's Vice-President for Aquatics, I was the front man in developing our junior program. I was proficient enough in my boat to win some Masters races and to cruise a variety of Class III-IV rivers from West Virginia to Wyoming. That provided some degree of authenticity in coaching the kids. But it was my assistant coach, Will Pruett, who made our program work. A bearded native of Western North Carolina's mountains, Will recalls cruising down the Nantahala when the only other living things there were a few trout. Since we initiated our junior program a decade ago, Will has contributed thousands of dollars in equipment and hundreds of hours of volunteer time…

"For what it's worth, let me say that Will and I sacrificed a lot of personal paddling in order to supervise slalom practices and take our Y youngsters on cruises. **You need a couple of adults who are willing to do this, to put the kids first, if you hope to make your program work...**

"Parents also have played a key role in our efforts. We found that kids who have the best family support end up being the best paddlers. Either their moms, dads, or siblings paddled, or they were willing to run shuttle or take the youngsters to special clinics and races when Will and I couldn't go...

"But don't think you'll be successful only if every child in your program becomes a national champion, because the sport is much broader than that. While we have coached 15 youngsters who've been winners at major competitive events, we've taught another 300 who've simply enjoyed cruising through Class I, II, and III rapids. Developing a life-long love affair with the river is the best gift you can give your students...

"Working with children is always a tough task, and it's especially challenging when you're on the rivers and tackling the dangers of the rapids. But the rewards are overwhelming."

Chapter Thirteen

In October of 1989, the U.S. Whitewater Slalom Team came to town.

After a lapse of 20 years, whitewater slalom racing had been reinstated in the Olympic Games. The slalom races at the Games of 1972, held in Munich, Germany, had been very successful, but had been dropped thereafter from the Olympic agenda for a variety of reasons. Now the slalom event was scheduled to be held again at the 1992 Games being hosted by Barcelona, Spain.

The U.S. Olympic Committee was suddenly looking for training sites as the four-year 1989-1992 Olympic Quadrennial got under way. One possible site was Asheville's own French Broad River. The newly-selected U.S. Olympic Coach, Bill Endicott from Bethesda, Maryland, came to Asheville with several of his top whitewater athletes, including Fritz Haller, Cathy Hearn, and Ron Lugbill, all of them world champions. The U.S. Team had adopted an interesting motto: No Pain, No Gain, No Spain. On the possibility of the French Broad becoming a training site, Bill Endicott said, "It looks feasible to me."

Asheville had created a Riverfront Planning Committee which was hoping to improve sites along the banks of the French Broad, and racer Windy Gordon was heading up a sub-committee that was looking at the possibility of building a $5 million slalom course. I was not involved, being busy with YMCA responsibilities, but the national and local interest in using the French Broad River more extensively seemed promising.

However, Will Pruett was never one to sit idly around waiting for others to act. In September, with little help from anyone else, he and his daughter Amy conducted two races as part of the 11th annual French Broad Riverfest. Three dozen paddlers entered Saturday's five-mile downriver race, and two dozen competed in Sunday's slalom. It wasn't as large as our past races on the French Broad, but it wasn't bad.

Some of the downriver winners were Windy Gordon, Lee Reading, David Jacklin, Shannon Rose, and Ben Baldwin, the inner-city boy from our YMCA program. Even I participated and won the Masters category, in which I was the only entrant. It turned out to be my last race. I was 56 – wasn't that the age at which famed kayaker Walt Blackadar met his demise on a river out west? – and the others gave me a round of applause as I crossed the finish line. I was no Blackadar, but I was still alive and paddling.

I had hoped to enter the slalom, my best event, the next day, but fate intervened. The small island of Montserrat in the Caribbean, with which the Asheville YMCA had just started an international exchange project and from which my wife Lee and I had just returned, was hit by Hurricane Hugo on the weekend of Will's races. I spent Sunday trying to communicate with our new Montserratian friends.

Slalom winners on Sunday included Tom Asher, Todd Murdock, Windy Gordon, Steve Heiselman, Wes Gattis, and, once again, our budding inner-city star, Ben Baldwin.

Now, almost 20 years later, it's hard to overstate the significance of Will Pruett's past contributions to whitewater kayaking and racing in the Asheville area. In my humble opinion, it was Will more than anyone else who kept us going and who made the difference over a period of about 15 years, from the mid 1970s until the early 1990s. Thanks, my friend.

With whitewater slalom racing back on the Olympic Games menu, the sport's hierarchy chose several sites around the country to be Centers of Excellence, where good coaching and daily training could be found by our top athletes. One site was the Nantahala Outdoor Center, and NOC created a separate non-profit entity called the Nantahala Racing Club to actually conduct the competitive program. We had been working with the Nantahala experts for many years, so it was no surprise that they asked us to serve as a NRC satellite operation.

The plan was for us to continue teaching the basic skills to youngsters and send those boys and girls who might become interested in racing to NOC and NRC. This worked out perfectly for us. We were able to disassemble our YMCA slalom course, which I no longer had time to supervise. Windy Gordon and his gang didn't have anything official going yet insofar as their proposed new $5 million slalom course was concerned. So we at the Asheville YMCA concentrated on teaching the basics. We continued to fill up our youth and adult kayaking classes, using the Y pool for teaching and the French Broad River for training, minus the slalom course, and our trio of coaches – Pruett, Maynor, Hines – remained at the helm.

We began sending a few of our youngsters to the Nantahala for racing instruction, and our relationship with NOC was strengthened. When NOC conducted the 1990 World Rafting Championships, we followed-up by hosting a dozen of the visiting Russians here in Asheville. Steve Heiselman and Monty Wooten, two outstanding local kayakers, were in charge of this endeavor.

Windy Gordon and the Riverfront Planning Committee met with NOC's president, John Burton, to discuss the $5 million French Broad slalom course. As the year came to an end, the Citizen-Times published three very long and positive articles about the creation of this planned course. One article was headlined, "Olympics in Asheville?"

Was it possible? Well, Atlanta had just been awarded the 1996 Summer Olympic Games, and everyone knew they didn't have enough whitewater there to conduct the slalom races. The Olympic sailing races were going to be contested in the ocean at Savannah, Georgia, so why not the whitewater slalom on the French Broad River in Asheville, North Carolina? It made a certain amount of sense.

Meanwhile, our programming for inner-city youngsters was attracting attention. Of the 40 boys and girls on our kaYak kids roster at that time, at least half were from the inner-city. The Citizen-Times and several other publications wrote about what we were doing. The American Canoe Association asked me to submit another article to "The American Canoeist," this one about our work with minority youngsters, and I did. It was entitled "Does Our Sport's Responsibility Extend beyond the River?" Here's what I said:

"Let me tell you about Ben. He moved to Asheville from Los Angeles and came to our YMCA as a husky 13-year-old. I knew other members of his family, and I arranged for him to have a free Y membership…

"Ben lived in the inner-city, just four blocks from our downtown YMCA facility, so it wasn't unusual to see him two or three times weekly. First we taught him to swim reasonably well, and then we taught him such sports as water polo, snorkeling, and yes, kayaking. Two of our former junior champions, Doug Baker and Kevin Drury, worked with Ben in the Y pool, teaching him the paddle strokes and the Eskimo roll. Will Pruett and Heath White and I took Ben and a dozen other inner-city youngsters out to the French Broad River on numerous occasions. Jim Maynor then took Ben to the Nantahala for additional instruction…

"At the 1989 French Broad Riverfest, Ben won both the slalom and downriver races for boys 15 and younger. He was showing such potential that we felt he would eventually become as proficient as some of our former Southeastern and national junior racing champions…

"Wouldn't it be something, I told Will, if we could coach Ben into becoming the first junior national kayak titlist who's a black youth from the inner-city. It wouldn't be easy. Ben had no real family support, no money, no way to purchase his own paddling equipment, and no way to get to the river(s) unless we drove him. But the YMCA is famous for working with such deprived youngsters, so we forged ahead…

"Then our hopes were dashed when family misfortunes caused Ben to return to Los Angeles, to LA's inner-city, to crime and drugs and a school where, according to Ben, the teachers had all given up. No pools in his neighborhood, he told us over the phone, and no opportunities for swimming or water polo or, of course, whitewater kayaking. I'm just trying to survive, Ben said. That was 18 months ago. Since then, we've not heard from Ben. He's moved from the place he was staying, and we have no idea where he might be at the present time…

"Meanwhile, the sport of whitewater kayaking is continuing without Ben. What about all the Ben's of our society? How many black inner-city kids have the opportunity to attend our national training camps around the country? Very, very few, as you know. Other sports such as baseball, basketball, and tennis have started special programs designed to reach inner-city children, providing them with equipment, coaching, encouragement, and even transportation to practices and competitive events…

"Such programs put an emphasis on developing self-esteem and other important values. Wouldn't it be something if our sport decided to do the same."

*****

Our Asheville YMCA international exchange project with the Caribbean island of Montserrat was also a study in diversity, aimed at improving relationships. The YMCA was working with a YWCA on the isle. Our people were mostly male and white. Their people were mostly female and black. But it went well. After my wife and I visited Montserrat for the second time, I wrote another article that was published nationally. It was entitled "Montserrat, the Emerald Isle," and told the following tale:

"My heart skipped a beat. When you're 100 yards offshore, alone in the Caribbean Sea, and you turn and discover a four-foot shark staring in your face, you're bound to feel apprehensive. Yet after a moment of anxiety, my heartbeat returned to normal. I calmly reached behind my back to grab my camera, but before I could take a photo, the shark disappeared into the depths…

"A day later, my friend Joe, who's spending a year working on this island, reported seeing the same small shark at the opposite end of the bay…

"This island is in fact Montserrat, the Emerald Isle of the Caribbean. It's small, just 11 miles in length by seven in width, with 13,000 residents. Mountainous winding roads make driving a challenge, especially because it's done on the left side. This is an island for the working class. Nobody will cater to you just because you're a wealthy American tourist…

"Montserrat was named by Christopher Columbus when he sailed past in 1493. Like most of the Caribbean islands, it was inhabited by Indians at that time. Eventually the English and Irish came and settled the island in the 1600s, importing slaves from Africa to work in the sugar mills and on the tobacco farms. Those who remain nowadays are the black ancestors of the slaves. Economically poor by American standards, they are a proud and well-educated people, following the British system of education…

"My wife Lee and I were there to initiate a partnership between the Asheville YMCA and the Montserrat YWCA and perhaps some other organizations on the small island, and to enjoy skin-diving in our spare time. While I wasn't quick enough to catch the shark in my camera lens, I did on this trip get good photos of thousands of jacks that totally obscured the bottom, two flying gurnards with their wings (fins) widespread, a porcupine fish, two types of eels, an octopus, several reef squid, sea spiders, and an elusive spotted drum that made me dive and literally stand on my head at a depth of 30' before I cornered it under a ledge. We also sighted but did not photograph three dozen other species of fishes ranging from angels to wrasses, and Lee saw a couple of mating turtles that I missed…

"Some of the sunsets were spectacular, and there we'd stand with our face masks, snorkels, and fins, on a black sand beach, with no one else in sight, watching in awe as the sun plunged into the distant ocean…

"I'm sharing this information with you because we're also working with the Montserrat National Trust, which is hoping to attract more visitors by creating a snorkel trail at one of the most popular beaches. We've been asked to spread the word."

A week after our second visit there, which prompted this article, Hurricane Hugo totally demolished the island. That was the same weekend Will and Amy Pruett conducted their races on the French Broad River.

This was followed by the visit of Coach Bill Endicott and the U.S. Slalom Team; the proposal to build a $5 million slalom course on the French Broad; the creation of the Nantahala Racing Club as a Center of Excellence; the establishment of the Asheville YMCA as a satellite operation of NRC; and the visit by the Russian rafters. There was a lot going on. And then on December 31, 1990, I retired from full-time work at the Asheville YMCA.

Chapter Fourteen

Since 1956, I'd been employed by various YMCAs in Minnesota, Iowa, Illinois, and North Carolina. It had proven to be a rewarding career. No regrets. The Citizen-Times announced in a nice article printed in January, 1991, that I would only be "semiretired," that I would continue to work for the Asheville YMCA part-time as director of international programming. Without boring you to tears, let me say that I indeed continued to work part-time, 10 to 12 hours weekly, until mid-1996. This gave me a full 40 years of working for the Y either full-time or part-time.

I remained involved with whitewater kayaking, as our Y program continued to serve as a satellite for the Nantahala Racing Club, nicknamed the Rhinos. Becky Weis was a good example of the Asheville-Nantahala connection. She had come from her home in Indiana when she was younger to train with us at the YMCA. Then she worked with the Nantahala experts, twice winning the U.S. K-1W junior slalom title, after which she spent several years kayaking some of the most challenging whitewater rivers in the country, from east to west. Eventually she returned to Asheville to attend our local university, at which time she helped us teach beginners in the YMCA pool. After completing college, she won a Gold medal in the women's competition at the World Whitewater Freestyle Championships, held in Germany. Freestyle, by the way, was a new discipline in which the participants did stunts and tricks in the rapids.

Looking back at my life as a teacher and coach of athletes in several sports, many of them All-Americans and national champions, I would have to say that Becky Weis was the best. She continues to reside in the Asheville area as I write this.

Returning to our efforts of the 1990s, four Nantahala Racing Club athletes made the U.S. Team for the 1992 Olympic Games in Spain. They were Joe Jacobi and Scott Strausbaugh in C-2, Adam Clawson in C-1, and Scott Shipley in K-1. Joe and Scott won the Gold medal, which resulted in a lot of good publicity for the sport in general and for NRC in particular. Shipley, the former world junior champion from the State of Washington, had moved east and was now training with NRC.

We were still teaching youngsters in Asheville, but very few were moving into slalom racing, despite the successes of the older Rhinos. It was frustrating, and we were debating what to do when I was diagnosed with cancer of the prostate. Surgery was scheduled for December 1, 1992. With my friend Will Pruett, I enjoyed what was to be my final day of FUN on the river – well, in the water, anyway – on November 25, which was my 60th birthday.

It was a cool day, but relatively uncrowded on the Nantahala. I entered the water at the park halfway down the river, waiting for Will to join me, and there I played at a surfing wave for 30 minutes.

Author's Note: Surfing on the river is not quite the same as surfing in the ocean. On the river, the water moves while the wave remains stationary. In the ocean, the wave moves while the water remains stationary. You figure it out. Or ask the Otter Boy.

Eventually my wife Lee shouted at me from the riverbank, "They've turned off the water at the dam."

"Yes, I can feel it going down."

"Will was here, but he decided to put-in down at the Falls where he can paddle a bit longer before the water level drops completely."

"I'll hustle on down and join him there."

As I'd done at least once before, I raced the dwindling water down the river. Hurry, hurry. It seemed familiar. I even remembered the shallow ledge where I'd flipped when this had happened many years previously. I reached Nantahala Falls and plunged over, and there was Will, a smile on his face. "About time," he said.

We played in the waves for 30 minutes until the water level was simply too low. I did one final roll, and that was it.

After my surgery, which required a six-day stay in the hospital and a six-week recovery period at home, I tried kayaking again, but it was too painful. I spent a lot of time supervising the YMCA's international exchange program with the island of Montserrat, which was still recovering from Hurricane Hugo. My wife and I frequently took coaches, camp counselors, and swim instructors to Montserrat and in turn brought back a number of islanders for training in Asheville. This was a terrific project that earned national and international recognition, including a letter of commendation from the president of the World Alliance of YMCAs.

I was unsure of my future in whitewater kayaking and racing until I received several very encouraging letters. One came from Peter Kennedy, the director of AdventureQuest, a unique program for youngsters headquartered in Vermont that combined high academic standards with the world of whitewater. Peter provided mentors and teachers and coaches for the teenagers in his program, who traveled all over the world to study and explore rivers and occasionally race. In his letter to me, Peter wrote, "I am happy to hear that you are recovering from your surgery. Your contribution to the young paddlers of Asheville needs to continue. I have followed your progress with the YMCA kids for many years now. You have been the perfect example of an adult who puts the kids first and believes in LEADERSHIP. I applaud everything you have done in that area of the country. So please keep up the good work in Asheville. You've always been a model for me, and the kids there deserve YOU."

Another letter came from Brian Smith, one of our former kayaking students at the Asheville YMCA. He wrote, "It is too rare that people take the time to express appreciation, and this letter is long overdue. A decade ago, I took two kayaking courses that you taught. Since then, I have benefited so much from your instruction. The YMCA classes combined a lot of special ingredients. Along with the techniques and safety training, there was a lot of enthusiasm, appreciation of rivers, and (most of all) fun. Several other instructors share in the appreciation I feel. Will Pruett, Jim Maynor, Anne Terrell, and Rocky Meadows come to mind. I moved to Maine nine years ago and teach kayaking here, and I have tried to pass on some of what I learned at the Asheville YMCA to other beginning boaters. Thanks to all of you."

Those letters and others I received from Bunny Johns, Payson Kennedy, and Ray McLain were very meaningful to me, and I shall forever be appreciative. It is always surprising what a few words of encouragement can do!

Thus I organized a group called ACES, the Asheville Committee for Excellence in Slalom. Our purpose was (a) to keep the YMCA's youth program moving forward and (b) to work with the Y and NRC to revive racing in Asheville for adults and especially for youngsters. The Mountain Xpress, Asheville's weekly newspaper, published a great article complete with photos. It was entitled "Asheville's Quest for Whitewater Racing Excellence," and it said, "Whitewater racers from Asheville brought home three second-place trophies from the USCKT Slalom Shootout, held recently on the Pigeon River in Tennessee. Competing against members of the 1992 U.S. Olympic Team and other outstanding athletes, Lee Sanders in C-1, Tom Piccirilli in K-1, and Ben Griffith in K-1 cadet all were runners-up in their respective classes…

"The three are members of ACES – the Asheville Committee for Excellence in Slalom – a volunteer group working to promote local whitewater racing…

"From 1978 through 1990, the Asheville YMCA had one of the best whitewater programs in the country, with its racers winning over 20 Southeastern and National championships. The program was discontinued in 1991 when Coach Chuck Hines retired from the Y. But after a two-year lapse, it was revived in 1993 with a lot of volunteer help, including two 1992 Olympians who live in Asheville, Scott Strausbaugh and Corran Addison. They are being assisted by Chris Bell, Gordon Grant, Rocky Meadows, Will Pruett, Shannon Rose, and Steve Zarnowski, among others...

"Working with the YMCA and the Nantahala Racing Club, ACES has taught basic kayaking techniques to 60 youngsters in the past year, many from the inner-city. Fifteen have become racers. ACES' efforts earned recognition this spring as one of the best youth instructional programs in the country...

"Seven ACES racers are nationally-ranked: Lee Sanders in C-1, Windy Gordon and Steve Mattioli in C-2, Andrew Bell in C-1 junior, Mark Mathews and Tom Piccirilli in K-1, and Ben Griffith in K-1 cadet...

"The youth racers, according to Coach Chuck Hines, are Andrew Bell, Wilson Bell, Karen Broach, Josh Burton, Mark deVerges, Ben Griffith, Matt Levine, Aaron Mitchell, Cody Pettry, Anna-Kate Schneider, David Serra, Sarah Smith, Natalie Williams, Jenny Zarnowski, and Steve Zarnowski, Jr...

"For all ACES members, the immediate goal is to qualify for the 1996 U.S. Olympic Team Trials, which will determine who'll represent the U.S. in the Olympic whitewater competition...

"For further information on ACES' instructional program, call Gordon Grant, John Griffith, or Steve Zarnowski. For information on racing, call Chuck Hines, Mark Mathews, or Tom Piccirilli."

Along with ACES, I also sponsored and financed a two-day women's whitewater clinic at the Nantahala Outdoor Center. By golly, I wasn't going to walk away from the sport I loved just because my old back injuries and new prostate surgery problems were keeping me out of my boat. There was still plenty I could do from the sidelines. Over a dozen women and girls from five states attended the clinic, which was taught by Eileen Ash, the K-1W alternate on our 1992 U.S. Olympic Team. It was a resounding success.

*****

On April 1, 1994, the phone rang at our house and a voice asked, "Is this Chuck Hines?"

"Yes."

The caller introduced himself and stated that he was representing the Western North Carolina Sports Hall of Fame and that I was scheduled to be inducted a month later. We chatted a while, and he hung up. I turned to my wife, laughing. "Somebody just played an April Fool's joke on me." I told her about the phone call.

A week later, I received two more phone calls about being inducted, and I suddenly realized it wasn't a joke after all. It was the *REAL* deal. I had been selected because of my "coaching feats." Over the years and generally through the auspices of the YMCA, I'd coached national championship teams and individuals in four sports – swimming, water polo, triathlon, whitewater racing – and earned Coach of the Year awards from the YMCA of the USA (1969), American Swimming Coaches Association (1973), Amateur Athletic Union (1975), and American Canoe Association (1984). Some of the athletes I coached had won Gold, silver, and bronze medals in Olympic, Junior Olympic, Special Olympics, and World competition. Not bad for a small-town boy.

On May 3, I was the 50th person to be inducted into the Hall of Fame, whose selections date back to the 1940s and include a wide variety of pro and amateur athletes and coaches. The induction ceremony was conducted at Asheville's prestigious Grove Park Inn and was attended by about 450. It was a night to remember.

A week later, I received a letter from an executive of the YMCA of the USA, and he wrote, "Congratulations on being named to the Western North Carolina Sports Hall of Fame. You have long been in the YMCA's South Hall of Fame."

*****

In 1994 and 1995, several of us became involved with the Junior Olympic Task Force, a national group that met at NOC to do what we could to promote youth paddling from coast to coast. This resulted in the first-ever Whitewater Junior Olympic Championships, which were held at Wausau, Wisconsin, in 1996, immediately after the Atlanta Olympics were concluded. Those who played a key role in getting the JOs started were Eileen Ash, Karin Baldzer, Gordon Black, John Brennan, Wayne Dickert, Peter Kennedy, Mike Larimer, Tom Long, Risa Shimoda, and this writer. We received advice from Richard Fox of Great Britain, the world K-1 slalom champion who was conducting a clinic for NRC.

While no longer kayaking myself, I was still skin-diving with my wife and daughter on our trips to the Caribbean. Stretching out in the water while swimming or skin-diving seemed to be something my body could tolerate. But when cramped in a tight-fitting kayak, my body rebelled, especially when bouncing over the rapids. In 1994, a major conference was conducted at Nassau, and I was asked to give a talk on the exchange project between Asheville and Montserrat. As always, I wrote about this assignment, and the Citizen-Times picked up my article and published it: "Chuck!" my wife Lee shouted. "There's something huge swimming around here...

"Frankly, I doubted it. We'd been snorkeling for an hour just off the coast of New Providence Island in the Bahamas, not far from Nassau, where we were attending a four-day conference. Lee and I were there with 180 others from around the globe. The main topic was 'Can Small Islands Survive?'

"Lee and I had flown from Asheville to Fort Lauderdale and then to Nassau so I could present a lecture about the small Caribbean island of Montserrat, with which the Asheville YMCA had been doing international programming for several years…

"We'd learned a lot from the other speakers, visited Coral World, attended a musical drama, enjoyed sight-seeing, and found time to don our face masks, snorkels, and fins for a bit of underwater adventuring. The visibility wasn't very good, and we weren't seeing much. For two people who have enjoyed skin- and scuba-diving for nearly 40 years, visiting over 100 different dive sites in the Midwest, the Carolinas, the Florida Keys, the Bahamas, the Hawaiian isles, and throughout the Caribbean, it was disappointing. We were heading back to shore when Lee shouted at me…

"Give me a break, I muttered to myself, as I turned around to face her. And I almost swallowed my mouthpiece. Right there, an arm's length from my wife, was indeed a large creature. It was so big that it took me a moment to identify it as a barracuda. We've seen dozens, perhaps hundreds, of barracudas over the years, from two feet to four feet in length, but this one was larger … longer … than my wife. I figured this guy was at least six feet in length, and there he was, swimming with us in the shallows, just 30 yards offshore, near Nassau …

"I swam as closely as possible and snapped a few photos. With each flash, the giant barracuda became more agitated and aggressive, closing in on us and baring his teeth. It was becoming rather dangerous. Finally Lee and I swam back to shore, and I mentioned what we'd seen to the young man operating the dive concession…

"Yes," he said, "that barracuda visits this area frequently. I've seen him myself for several years and have watched him grow to about *seven* feet. It's probably a record for the Bahamas. We don't publicize him, though, as we don't want to scare away the tourists…

"Which just goes to show: you never can tell what thrills await you underwater. With just our face masks, snorkels, and fins, Lee and I have seen not only barracudas but also dolphins, sharks, sting rays, mating turtles, reef squid, hidden octopuses, eels, and dozens of different varieties of fishes, plus coral gardens so splendid they defy description."

I've been a swimmer since I was nine years old, and I competed in my first swim meet when I was 10. I went canoeing for the first time when I was 12. When I was in my 20s, I became an enthusiastic water polo player. Also in my 20s, I earned national certification as a scuba instructor. At 43, I started whitewater kayaking, which, aside from my family, has become "the love of my life." I've enjoyed ALL the water sports at one time or another, but there's nothing quite like the oceanic underworld, and I wrote a poem that reflected how I felt:

There is a mystic world I know, where silent shadows come and go, Where sunbeams fall in soft delight on coral rainbows, dancing bright, Where finny folk play hide and seek, the stronger searching for the weak, Where friendly fishes shake your hand, and others burrow in the sand. Where weed beds wave majestically, like haughty maidens of the sea, and whisper of the demon men, who come to look, and come again. Where shipwrecks sit in regal grace, their skippers missing, lost ... no trace! It is a weird world far apart from all we hold dear to our hearts, a fluid world where fishes fly like windswept eagles in the sky, and adventurers like you and I, with mask and snorkel come to spy, and stare in disbelief, and sigh, and learn that God Himself is nigh. There is a mystic world I know, where silent shadows come and go. It is God's Creativity, it is the world beneath the sea.

Back home again, I was asked to write a column for the monthly newsletter of the U.S. Canoe and Kayak Team, and in 1994, 1995, and 1996, I wrote over 20 such columns. These reported on all the slalom racing programs being offered by clubs across the width and breadth of our country and also on preparations that were being made for the Olympic Games in 1996. There were half-a-dozen pre-Olympic races held on the Ocoee, some of which attracted the best whitewater athletes from around the world. Many of us helped organize and conduct these events. It was an exciting time, and should I choose to do so, I could fill another chapter or two with all we were doing locally and nationally and internationally. But let's move on to the Olympics.

We'd been hoping that the Olympic slalom races would be held in Asheville, on our own French Broad River, utilizing Windy Gordon's proposed new $5 million course. An article appeared that indicated this might happen. It said, "Olympics Moved to the French Broad River." Wow! I eagerly read what was said: "According to a reputable source within the whitewater racing community, the Atlanta Olympic Organizing Committee is close to moving the slalom competition for the 1996 Olympics from Tennessee's Ocoee River to Asheville's French Broad River...

"This surprising turn of events was made necessary by UNC-Asheville environmental studies professor Richard Maas' discovery of a brand new species – the cockaded copper darter – nesting at the Ocoee site. The need for a change of venue became a foregone conclusion after Maas petitioned the U.S. Fish and Wildlife Service to list the new species as endangered. Known to exist only on the upper Ocoee between TVA dams two and three, the copper-darter is a textbook case of evolutionary mimicry gone wrong. While its colors allow it to blend with the natural habitat, the male of the species has a fatal attraction for such brightly colored objects as kayaks. Maas said he was a big fan of the Olympics, but that allowing all those Olympic racing boats in the world's only-known copper-darter habitat could spell an end to the species...

"Scott Shipley, star U.S. kayak racer, doesn't share Maas' concern. Reached in an exclusive interview, Shipley fumed, saying Maas' proposal to move the Olympics had better be a joke. Shipley said he had moved all the way from the State of Washington to train with the famed Nantahala Racing Club on the Ocoee. He said if the birds could survive the chemical spills and Little Debbie cream-filled cupcakes discarded by boaters on the Ocoee, they could survive 'getting it on' with his kayak...

"Recognizing that the loss of its planned venue had the potential to strike whitewater slalom from the 1996 Olympics, and knowing an opportunity when they see one, the shakers and movers in Asheville's racing community have leapt to fill the void. Just last week, Chuck Hines formed Bring Us North Carolinians Olympic Memories Before Eternity, or BUNCOMBE, explaining that while the name is long, it is a clever triple-entendre evoking thoughts of the proposed venue's location, both state and county (Buncombe), and our deep religious roots…

BUNCOMBE's Windy Gordon and Karen Cragnolin made a closed presentation to the City Council last Thursday, proposing a $5.6 million artificial course required by the IOC for the French Broad River as it flows through West Asheville. Though initially skeptical, the City Council was won over when Gordon disclosed that over $1.1 million would be spent bringing decent sidewalks to historically under-served West Asheville. Action on the change of venue is expected soon. The U.S. Fish and Wildlife Service has proposed listing the copper-darter as endangered, and the Atlanta Olympic Organizing Committee is meeting April 1, at which time a final decision will be made."

Wow again! Imagine, the Olympic slalom races here in Asheville!

Of course, it was all a big joke, as there was no such bird as the cockaded copper-darter. The article, written by Chris Bell, an outstanding Class IV-V kayaker, was strictly tongue-in-cheek.

There was indeed an Olympic Committee here in Asheville, of which I was co-chairman, which was prepared to host the 1996 Olympic slalom races. But it gradually became obvious that the event would be held as scheduled at the Ocoee River in eastern Tennessee. Since U.S. Coach Bill Endicott and some of his athletes had come to visit in 1989 and the Citizen-Times published three articles in 1990 about the Riverfront Planning Committee's proposal for a $5.6 million race course, absolutely nothing had been done by the "development people" to make the French Broad into a suitable site for national and international competition.

Thus we were all trekking monthly, sometimes weekly, to the Nantahala and Ocoee Rivers for practicing. I began working occasionally with Kirsten Brown, a racer from "up north" who'd come to train here in the South in preparation for the Team Trials. I also tried to talk Becky Weis into returning to slalom and trying out for the U.S. Olympic Team, but she wasn't interested.

Coaches and other officials for the Team Trials on the Ocoee had to be nationally approved, and I was relieved when my credentials finally arrived. I was one of just 11 coaches cleared to coach at the Trials, for which Mark Mathews had qualified in K-1, Lee Sanders in C-1, Kirsten Brown in K-1W, and the duo of Windy Gordon and Steve Mattioli in C-2. They were among 100 athletes nationwide who were hoping to make the nine-member U.S. Olympic Slalom Team for the 1996 Games. Sadly, none of the five with whom I was involved made the Team, but afterwards I received a nice note from Kirsten, saying, "Dear Chuck, Thanks for your incredible help and support. You really helped to lift my spirits when things were not going so well."

Unfortunately, Kirsten has passed away since we spent several days together at the 1996 Olympic Team Trials. It's my understanding that she died of breast cancer. She was a lovely young lady, and by the way, she was the only black participant out of the 100 competitors at the Trials.

On a brighter note, four NRC Rhinos made the 1996 U.S. Olympic Team: Scott Shipley in K-1, Adam Clawson in C-1, and the twosome of Wayne Dickert and Horace Holden, Jr., in C-2. Hooray!

*****

As the countdown to the start of the Summer Games in Atlanta (and on the Ocoee River) continued, I ran with the Olympic Torch as it passed through Asheville and Western North Carolina. Well, I didn't actually run. Here's what happened. In one of our ACES meetings at the YMCA, Scott Strausbaugh suggested nominating me for the Torch Relay. I turned it down, believing that I didn't deserve such an honor. A month later, my daughter Heather came to me and said, "Dad, as your birthday present, I've nominated you for the Torch Relay." Well, who can turn down a gift like that?

There were over 300 nominated from around our area, and I was one of 40 chosen. NRC Olympian Adam Clawson, who'd competed at the Games in 1992 and had qualified to compete again in 1996, was selected as our local athlete to carry the Torch. For Adam to be chosen over all the prominent basketball and baseball and football players said a lot about the high visibility of our sport in Western North Carolina. I had known Adam since he was a youngster competing for the Nantahala against our YMCA kaYak kids. Actually, he raced in C-1, or the decked canoe, while we were specializing in the kayak category.

For those interested, I carried the Torch on a day in late June, 1996. A week previously, I had given up my part-time position at the Asheville YMCA as director of international programming, thus concluding 40 years of Y employment. I almost decided against doing the Torch Relay, as my bad back was acting up, but I was told that I could walk, if necessary. That's what I planned to do. But when I was handed the Torch, which was HEAVY, the Assist Runner, a fellow who was accompanying the Torch along the route and providing guidance for each official Torchbearer, said, "Chuck, we're running late. The mayor is scheduled to welcome the Torch at City Square in a few minutes. So whether you have a bad back or not, you've gotta RUN." I didn't exactly run, but I jogged.

My wife Lee and daughter Heather were there, along with my grandchildren, Crystal and Charlie, all urging me on as I hustled down Biltmore Avenue in south Asheville with the Torch. Also on hand was one of our Caribbean friends from the island of Montserrat, Rachel Collis. The day was made complete when my good ol' paddling pal Jim Maynor showed up with his camera and took a bunch of photos. It wasn't the river, and there weren't any rapids, but it was one of the best days of my life.

*****

As a writer/reporter/columnist for the monthly newsletter of the U.S. Canoe and Kayak Team, who had been covering preparations for the big event on the Ocoee, I could have received a "press pass" for the Olympic slalom races. That would have put me in a special section reserved for the media. I decided not to do so, as I preferred to sit with my wife and daughter amidst the 14,000 other spectators who came daily. When it was all over, I wrote another article for the USCKT newsletter that read as follows: "From a spectator's standpoint, the 1996 Olympic slalom races were quite successful. My wife Lee and I attended, accompanied by our daughter Heather, who was a good paddler during her teen days, and our granddaughter Crystal, 5½, who was a mascot of the U.S. Team...

"We sat at varying times with friends from Asheville, from around the country, and from Europe. Our friends from Germany, Helmut Schafer and his wife and daughter, certainly were pleased with the race results...

"Many of us stayed in a motel at Murphy, North Carolina, including Tom Piccirilli of Asheville, Dirk Davidson of Knoxville, and Tom and Debbi Long of Idaho and their family and friends. Each day we drove over to the Ocoee venue, parking at the high school or elementary school, from where we were bused to the race site. Except for a single delay on Saturday morning, when the venue was double-checked for safety following the bombing in Atlanta, everything ran according to schedule, at least for us, and if there were any logistical problems, we escaped them...

"The bleachers on the right side of the river were jammed each of the three days with 14,000 onlookers. The official attendance for Sunday was announced at 14,400. When you add the athletes, coaches, support staff, timers and gate judges and other officials, and media, which included reporters from all over the world, plus a TV crew from Europe that ran "live" coverage of the races – all situated on the left side of the river – you realize that over 15,000 were in attendance daily. Announcers Kent Ford and Lamar Sims and their assistants continually urged spectators to squeeze together to make room for latecomers...

"Visitors from around the country appeared to be amazed at the beauty of the river setting…

"This was truly an international competition, featuring 134 racers from 30 countries, and if one objective of the Olympics is to bring people together, this event succeeded. One example: Max Wellhouse of Arkansas was coaching a racer, Ben Kvanli, who was representing Guatemala. Another example: 1992 gold medalist Joe Jacobi was hosting the Japanese contingent at his home in nearby Copperhill. A third example: the overflow crowd cheered not only the Americans but also the foreign competitors, especially when they overcame adversity on the river…

"I'll leave it to others to dissect the performances of the U.S. Team, except for saying that our athletes continually exhibited the highest standards of good sportsmanship, as always. Although no team scores were kept, the French were undoubtedly the top performers, with the Czech Republic and Germany vying for second and third. The U.S. and Slovakia battled it out for fourth and fifth, and then came Slovenia, Great Britain, Italy, Ireland, Poland, and Canada…

"Whatever the results, this was an outstanding once-in-a-lifetime experience for me and my family, and for our friends, and for the thousands of others who attended. To all who worked so hard to conduct the 1996 Olympic slalom races, many thanks."

I wrote another article for "The Whitewater Paddler," the bimonthly newsletter I'd been editing and sending out nationally for many years: "This was my second direct involvement with the Olympic Games, having served as secretary of the U.S. Olympic Water Polo Committee and Team for the Games of 1972, when our U.S. men brought home the bronze medal from Munich. This time, I helped do some of the planning for the slalom competition on the Ocoee, raised money for the Olympic-UNICEF youth fund, coached at the U.S. Team Trials, carried the Olympic Torch, and covered the Ocoee slalom races as a reporter. You can't bring together 10,788 athletes from 197 countries plus 82,500 volunteers plus 800,000 spectators plus the worldwide media without having at least a few problems, but let me share some of the more positive facets of the Olympics with you:

* The IOC, or International Olympic Committee, funded the participation of athletes from two dozen impoverished third-world nations.

* The Atlanta Olympic Organizing Committee and UNICEF raised $15 million to be used to finance sports programs in 15 war-torn countries.

* Several dozen South Korean families now living in Atlanta hosted visiting families from their enemy, North Korea.

* The families of black athletes from Africa were provided with free accommodations by a number of Atlanta families, many of them white.

* Free tickets valued at $800,000 were distributed to poor Atlanta families and children.

* Over 250,000 pounds of left-over food from various restaurants was used to provide 167,000 free meals for needy Georgians.

* The members of our winning U.S. men's basketball team, most of them well-paid professionals, donated all of their earnings from the USOC, about $165,000, to help in the rebuilding of burned-down Southern churches.

"Asheville's Robert Wooten, after witnessing the Olympic Torch coming through our community, wrote an inspirational piece for our local paper, emphasizing what the Olympic Movement is all about, which is bringing people together in peaceful competition. I'm proud to have played a small role in it."

There was another significant story behind the story, and it involved NRC racer Scott Shipley, resulting in his receiving the USOC's coveted Fair Play award. An article in "The Olympian" magazine, entitled "Whitewater Samaritan," told this extraordinary tale: "Samir Karabasic huddled atop his patched second-hand kayak in a holding area of Atlanta's Hartsfield International Airport. Drowsy from the hot, humid early July afternoon, the veteran of four years of siege in the trenches of Bihac, Bosnia, waited for a bus which would carry him to Tennessee's Ocoee River. There, he would be the lone whitewater athlete to compete for his country in the 1996 Olympic Games…

"Karabasic's ordeal read like something from a movie script. For four years, he lived in a trench covered with plywood, defending the front line of his city. He was bedridden with hepatitis for six months. When he could paddle the Una River just below his trench, he was under constant threat of sniper or mortar fire. To compete in a 1995 World Cup race, he had to sign a liability release to ride a helicopter out of Bihac over a war zone. Two months later, that same helicopter was shot down, killing the Bosnian foreign minister…

"During his first practice on the Olympic course, the Bosnian's boat, already patched together with epoxy and duct tape, struck a rock, broke in two and sank, seemingly taking Karabasic's dreams with it…

"That's when 25-year-old Scott Shipley became involved in the Bosnian conflict. In an act that was completely reflexive to Shipley and which epitomized the Olympic spirit of sportsmanship, he gave Karabasic the boat he had used to win the 1995 World Cup title. The gesture drew worldwide attention…

"When I gave Samir the boat at the Olympics, a lot of people got interested in contributing to help out the Bosnians," Shipley said. "As we talked with Samir, we found out that things in Bosnia were really tough. Their club had been blown up, along with its 80 boats. The kids couldn't play out in the woods because there were mines there, so they could only play in the river or in town…

"Shipley's agent, Sue Langfit, gathered names and numbers of those offering assistance. When the Olympic Games were over, she organized an aid mission for the paddlers of Bihac. Shipley says that Sue Langfit put the trip together, assembling $40,000 in equipment. In mid-October, Shipley, Langfit, and 19-year-old paddler Sarah Leith flew, courtesy of Delta Airlines, to Munich, and set off on the long drive to Bihac. They drove through five borders to get there...

"Shipley was impressed with the proud people of Bihac and the heroism they had demonstrated during four years of siege. A boy about 14 asked Leith why she came on the trip. One of the reasons she gave was that she had never seen a war before. The boy looked back at her in amazement that she had never been in a war before...

"While the trip was sobering in many ways, there still was time for fun. As might be expected, that came on the rivers. Shipley said the Bihac paddlers were wary of the equipment brought by the Americans. They had never paddled with spray-skirts, which keep water out of the boat. Some wouldn't even wear the spray-skirts, so it turned into a big swimfest, with the Americans fishing the Bosnians out of the water...

"Shipley said he learned more in two days there than in 19 years of kayaking, mentioning the strength of the Bosnian people. He said it gave him a greater appreciation of why Americans need to be involved in world affairs."

After his initial visit, Scott Shipley returned the next year. An excellent video tape was made of his second visit. It is entitled "The Bihac, Bosnia, Kayak Club" and is available from First Run Features. I would recommend it for every whitewater enthusiast.

*****

As for me, I was now in the "Social Security" category of competition, reserved for those 62 and older. There weren't many of us, and of the few, Dave Kurtz of Pennsylvania was easily the best. A year older than I, Dave, a former U.S. national champion and now coach of the Mach One

Team, was still competing and winning races, even against those much younger. I longed to be in my kayak, actually IN the river, whipping through the waves and riding the rapids. Those who've done it know there's nothing quite like it. But my health problems prevented it, and I was stuck on the sidelines.

And yet ... and yet ... it's strange how things work out. As the year's end approached, I was shocked to receive three totally unexpected awards for my efforts. From the Atlanta Olympic Organizing Committee came a beautiful Gold medallion in recognition of my volunteer work with the 1996 Summer Games. From the United States Canoe and Kayak Team came a cute little paddle, engraved with my name, which was the organization's Meritorious Service Award, given in recognition of my many years of coaching and promoting our sport. Finally, at a small ceremony in Asheville, I was given a nice plaque honoring me as Western North Carolina's Humanitarian of the Year. Wow! This was in recognition of my work with the inner-city youngsters in Asheville, which included the kayaking instruction, and my international programming in the Caribbean with the hurricane-stricken residents of Montserrat.

These awards, when added to my Olympic involvement, including the Torch Relay, made the year of 1996 into something beyond special. It was a good way to conclude my 40 years with the YMCA. But just as this was happening, a new door of opportunity was opening. Isn't that always the case?

Chapter Fifteen

"You've just retired from the YMCA, Chuck?"

"That's right. After 40 years. Why?"

"We want you to become vice-president of the Nantahala Racing Club," said Wayne Dickert, looking at me from across the table at the Nantahala Village resort, just down the road from the Nantahala Outdoor Center.

Wayne, or Wayner as everyone called him, had participated in our Asheville YMCA program a decade previously, in the mid 1980s, before moving on. He was now the leader of the Nantahala Racing Club and, with his teammate Horace Holden, Jr., had just competed for the U.S. in C-2 at the 1996 Olympic slalom races on the nearby Ocoee River.

The Nantahala Racing Club was the small, non-profit arm of the Nantahala Outdoor Center, created in 1989 when the latter was designated as a Center of Excellence for training some of our top whitewater athletes. Four Rhino racers had participated in the 1992 Olympics, and four had just competed in the 1996 Olympics on the Ocoee. NRC was ranked as the second-best whitewater racing club in the country, behind only the Bethesda Center of Excellence in Maryland. I had been working with the Nantahala Outdoor Center since the mid 1970s and with the Nantahala Racing Club more recently.

Was I interested in becoming vice-president of the NRC operation? Yes, of course, but there was one small problem. I was already serving as vice-president of the Western North Carolina chapter of the United

Nations Association and was scheduled to move up to the presidency within a few months. I had been active in that organization as part of my international efforts with the Asheville YMCA. I knew I couldn't serve as a leader for both NRC and WNC-UNA at the same time. Which should it be?

I thought about it for all of 30 seconds. "Yes," I told Wayner, "I'd be delighted to become vice-president of the Nantahala Racing Club." And except for my family, that became my main focus over the next several years.

The first president of NRC had been Mike Hipsher. He was followed by "the Wayner" and then by Bob Powell. All three had done exceptional work in developing this small club in a remote corner of Western North Carolina into a true Center of Excellence, where perhaps a dozen top whitewater athletes were training on a daily basis. Mike had then become involved in other activities for the larger Nantahala Outdoor Center operation. Wayner had moved from serving as the volunteer president to the paid position of executive director. Bob had stepped into the presidency, although he was mostly occupied by working as the Center's director of adventure trips. He was gone frequently, leading trips to various countries around the world.

When I attended my first NRC board meeting, Bob was absent. "He's on a trip somewhere," Wayner said, "so as our new vice-president, Chuck, you're in charge of today's meeting."

That was the case more often than not in the following months. I became the club's interim president and then its president pro tem and then, finally, its president in name as well as deed. Okay with me. I had the support of the many outstanding men and women on the NRC board of directors, and we were advancing into several new areas of operation.

First, we wanted to stay connected to the Nantahala Outdoor Center, which was providing the club with a small office and paying the executive director's salary. Without NOC, we really had nothing.

Second, we wanted to make sure our athletes received competent coaching. Former coach Jim Jayes from Great Britain had just departed, so we hired 1992 Olympian Lecky Haller as our new coach.

Third, we wanted to solidify our relationship with Asheville's paddling community. This was, after all, our satellite operation, so we worked even closer with the two Asheville organizations – ACES, which was the Asheville Committee for Excellence in Slalom, and the YMCA, which as always was interested in serving youth – with a goal of doubling the number of participants there.

Fourth, we wanted to improve the club's financial picture, which meant broadening our membership base and conducting a number of fund-raising events.

Fifth, we wanted to do a better job of publicizing our efforts, so we started a newsletter and created a web-site.

Along with these five official goals established by the board of directors, I had two personal goals in the back of my mind: I wanted to upgrade the operation of the NRC board, without which I doubted we could accomplish our official goals, and I wanted to beat the Bethesda Center of Excellence and win the national championship, which BCE had taken for seven or eight years in a row.

When it came to operating the board, I made sure we were conducting monthly meetings with proper agendas, minutes, financial reports, and all the trimmings. When it came to competing against BCE and everyone else, I, as a long-time and successful coach myself, aimed at bringing home The Club Trophy, emblematic of being No. 1 in whitewater slalom racing. Why settle for anything less?

Wayner, who had been serving as NRC's executive director, then accepted a job as director of development for USCKT, posing another small problem. It turned out for the best, however, because Horace

Holden, Jr., replaced Wayner, who remained "on campus" at the Nantahala while working nationally. It was a good scenario, provided we could find more money somewhere.

Wayner's wife, Joanna, an accountant by profession, was serving as treasurer of the NRC board of directors when I arrived, and a year later, she was replaced by Allen Mayers, a national champion Masters kayaker. I relied heavily on both of them to keep us afloat financially. Our budget was, well, on the small side, at least when compared to the larger Nantahala Outdoor Center and the Asheville YMCA and other such agencies and organizations. But I was used to doing a lot with just a little, so I wasn't discouraged. I was sure we would succeed and eventually achieve our various goals and objectives.

Whenever I convened a board meeting, I sat there surrounded by the best of the best in the sport of whitewater racing. This included Olympians John Burton, Wayne Dickert, Lecky Haller, Horace Holden, and gold medalists Joe Jacobi and Scott Strausbaugh. Our liaison person with the Nantahala Outdoor Center was Mark Singleton, on whose judgment I came to rely more and more. As I write this in 2008, Mark is executive director of American Whitewater, the organization which I initially joined when I was at the Des Moines YMCA in 1964. Mark remains a national leader in the whitewater industry.

It would be impossible to overstate the importance of the Nantahala Outdoor Center to outdoor education and recreation in general and to the sport of whitewater kayaking, canoeing, and rafting in particular over the past several decades. Two Atlanta residents, Payson Kennedy and Horace Holden, Sr., had the vision necessary to create NOC. They started with a small office on the banks of the Nantahala River in 1972, with very little capital and just a few employees, and have seen their enterprise grow into what today is probably the leading outdoor adventure operation in the world. For this to happen in the backwoods of Western North Carolina is just plain remarkable.

For a complete history of the Nantahala Outdoor Center and other information, check out their web-site at www.noc.com.

During my active kayaking career, when I was paddling regularly, I ran the Nantahala River perhaps 60 times, practiced frequently at the Nantahala slalom courses, and competed in half-a-dozen races there. Now, as president of NRC, I was there even more often, usually twice or thrice monthly, as we worked at fulfilling our goals and objectives. I have many good memories of driving the 70 miles from my home in Asheville through the scenic mountain passes of WNC to the Nantahala. Serving as the "rhinoprez," which was my email title at that time, was one of the highlights of my entire life, and as I look back over my notes, I see that we were:

* Conducting daily practices for our national-level athletes, and we brought in Shane Murphy, a sports psychologist with the USOC, to work with our racers.

* Hosting a wide variety of camps, clinics, and races, which attracted athletes and coaches from coast to coast and from 18 other countries.

* Organizing two or three fund-raising events annually at the Nantahala and in Asheville and Charlotte, with attorney Jim Chandler, one of NRC's staunchest enthusiasts, serving as master of ceremonies.

* Distributing a very good newsletter and arranging for continuing coverage of our activities through a number of media outlets.

* Increasing our membership to a high of 440, of whom about 40 were active racers, 200 were recreational river-runners, and the remaining 200 were simply sideline supporters.

We were also achieving a lot on the river. After all, that was the bottom line, right? Without minimizing all that the club had accomplished in the past, I felt that 1997 was a "breakthrough" year for the Rhinos. Some of us had been involved with the Junior Olympic Task Force which met at NOC in 1994 and 1995, resulting in the first-ever Whitewater Junior Olympic Championships being held at Wausau, Wisconsin, in 1996. Now it was our turn to host the JO Championships.

Wayne Dickert led the way. As USCKT's director of development, he put his plans into action. Karin Baldzer of Atlanta and I were helping him. We arranged for the NRC-sponsored Junior Olympic races to be included as part of the larger Amateur Athletic Union Games in Charlotte, North Carolina. Over 12,000 youngsters came to Charlotte from 45 states to compete in 20 different sports. There were approximately 30,000 spectators. Media coverage was superb. It was a multi-million-dollar happening, a great way to follow-up the *real* Olympic Games of the preceding year.

To participate at Charlotte, whitewater youngsters had to qualify in regional competition. We held the Southeast Regionals on the Nantahala River, with more than 50 entered. One-third were our own NRC youngsters, who'd been training in our new NationsBank-Nantahala Whitewater Kids Club program. This was the brainchild of Vic Howie, one of my YMCA friends who at that time was a vice-president for NationsBank.

I had known Vic when he lived in Asheville, where he assisted me with the Y's international endeavors. After he moved to Charlotte and I became the Nantahala Racing Club president, I invited Vic to join the NRC board of directors. He was a dynamic addition. With NationsBank's financial help, we expanded our youth program – the one previously operated by the Asheville YMCA and then ACES – to teach the basic skills of the sport to 52 boys and girls from across Western North Carolina in 1997. Gordon Grant and Steve Zarnowski were heading up the youth program in Asheville, and I invited Steve to join the NRC board. He too provided us with instant assistance and inspiration.

On a warm summer Saturday, we hosted a Junior Olympic clinic at Ledges Park, our new Asheville training site on the French Broad River. Over 40 youngsters attended, and there was a long article in the Citizen-Times entitled "Learning from the Best," which said, "Debra McGhee sat calmly with her back to the water at Ledges Park north of Asheville while her 14-year-old daughter, Alexandra, braved the currents of the French Broad River with little more than a small boat and a paddle…

"While some parents would be concerned about the safety of such a situation, McGhee's nerves were settled by the company Alexandra was keeping on the river. Her daughter was being taught the finer points of handling a kayak in the cold, rough waters by Olympic and world-class instructors...

"Alexandra was one of 44 students – all members of the Nantahala Racing Club – who were brought together through the sponsorship of NationsBank for a one-day training session. Team members from the Asheville area and the Bryson City area, who usually train at separate locations, joined forces for a day to receive instruction from kayaking luminaries, including Horace Holden and Wayne Dickert, both members of the 1996 U.S. Olympic Team, and Joe Jacobi, a 1992 Olympic gold medalist...

"According to Chuck Hines, who helped organize the clinic, this was the second time in 1997 that the racing club has gotten all the kids together for a practice. He said many are training for the Southeast Junior Olympic Qualifier at the Nantahala River on July 19."

There was another article in the NationsBank newsletter: "The Carolinas Community Division of NationsBank has partnered with the Nantahala Racing Club to develop the Whitewater Kids Club, which includes disadvantaged inner-city and rural youth who have never previously been exposed to whitewater sports. The young paddlers are working with Horace Holden, Wayne Dickert, and Joe Jacobi, all Olympians, and Chuck Hines, the club's Junior Olympic coach, to learn safety, whitewater fundamentals and skills, and winning techniques and theories...

"Most of the youngsters have improved far enough to become intermediate paddlers and will really test their skills at the U.S. Junior Olympics in Charlotte in early August, also sponsored by NationsBank."

Shortly after this clinic on the French Broad River, our NationsBank-Nantahala racers participated at the Southeast Regionals on the Nantahala, and those who qualified then moved on to the Whitewater Junior Olympic Championships in Charlotte. Wayne Dickert and

Mike Hipsher were directing the JO slalom races, with a helping hand from Scott Strausbaugh. I was coaching the Southeast Team, comprised of 28 youngsters from eight states, with a helping hand from Abel Hastings. I also was arranging accommodations for ALL the participating boys and girls and their families who came to Charlotte from New Hampshire and New Mexico, from Tennessee and Texas, from Florida and Idaho, from Colorado and California, and elsewhere. It was a BIG job!

The slalom and sprint races were conducted at Charlotte's Carowinds Park, which had a narrow whitewater course going through a tunnel at the end. The two days of competition were sunny and comfortable, and the media came out in force to cover the slalom races, which were something new for Charlotte's citizenry. The Southeast edged the Northeast by a few points to win the AAU team title, with the Midwest third and the smaller Far West entry fourth. NRC's 17-year-old David Jacobson, who surprisingly had failed to make the U.S. Junior Team earlier in the year and was so discouraged that he almost didn't enter the JO competition – I spent several hours convincing him to do so – won three Gold medals and the boys' MVP award. Way to go, DJ.

With our junior racers doing so well, it was up to our older athletes to show their stuff, and they did by beating the Bethesda Center of Excellence and 10 other clubs to win the U.S. Men's and Women's Slalom Championships for the first time in 1997. The Rhinos repeated as champions in 1998, 1999, and 2000. Members of our senior slalom squad during this four-year run were Eileen Ash, Adam Clawson, Kari Crowe, Dirk Davidson, Sam Davis, Wayne Dickert, Chris Ennis, Morgan Ford, Frances Glass, John Grumbine, Lecky Haller, Bobby Hartridge, Abel Hastings, Dave Hepp, Horace Holden, David Jacobson, Joe Jacobi, Barry Kennon, Nick Kimmet, Forest King, Lee Leibfarth, Sarah Leith, Allen Mayers, Scott McClesky, Aleta Miller, Andy Padyk, Toby Roessingh, Chris Rush, Lee Sanders, Scott Shipley, Shaun Smith, Hannah Swayze, Matt Taylor, Glen Warner, and Heather Warner. Lecky also served as our coach at the beginning, assisted by Scott Strausbaugh.

While slalom was our primary concern, we also worked hard to promote wildwater racing. Slalom, in which the athletes maneuver through gates hanging above the river, was *the prestigious OLYMPIC sport*. Wildwater, in which the competitors generally race as fast as they can down a five-mile or longer stretch of the river, through Class II, III, and occasionally IV rapids, was not in the Olympics but did have its own world championships. There was also downriver racing, which was similar to wildwater, except that the distance covered was easier, either flat water or Class I-II rapids. This was mostly a local sport.

Many of NRC's wildwater racers had copped national championships in the past, and the duo of Bunny Johns and Mike Hipsher had once won the world wildwater title in C-2M (one man, one woman). We wanted to make sure our club's tradition of excellence in this category of competition continued. Three of the best Rhino wildwater specialists were Bob Powell, Carolyn Porter, and Chris Hipgrave. One summer, our outstanding C-2 Junior duo of brothers Russell and Jeffrey Johnson switched from slalom to wildwater, won the U.S. Team Trials, and went to Europe for international competition.

In slalom, Lecky Haller and Jamie McEwan had represented the U.S. in C-2 at the 1992 Olympics, finishing in fourth place. Lecky and his brother Fritz were favored to get the U.S. spot in tandem canoe for the 1996 Olympics. They had been world champions. But they were upset at the Team Trials by the duo of Wayner and Horace. Always the competitor, Lecky decided to give up coaching and make another attempt at the Olympics, which in 2000 would be conducted at Sydney, Australia. This time, Lecky had Matt Taylor as his partner.

This meant we needed a new coach. After advertising nationally and internationally, we decided to bring in a young, unknown coach from Poland for an interview. There were two other good candidates, but both wanted to go to grad school while coaching for NRC. "No way," our board members said. "We have athletes training for Sydney, and we want a coach now who's going to be a coach full-time. He (or she) can't do anything else, not even compete." The young man from Poland had been a champion kayaker there, with international experience, and he had a college degree in coaching. He spoke very little English. But he wanted to prove himself as a COACH. He was willing to come to the U.S., leaving his wife and young son behind for at least a while, and work with us at NRC for "peanuts," devoting himself to coaching our racers every day, with no distractions. We flew him to the Nantahala for a lengthy interview, and when it was over, our athletes said, "He's the one."

So we hired Rafal Smolen as our NRC Coach for a three-year period. Getting him into the U.S. on a permanent basis was a six-month process, but we managed it. As I write this book 10 years later, he's still here, still coaching the Rhinos. His wife and son have joined him in the U.S., and they are all assimilating into our culture. Apparently we made a good decision in 1998.

We had Rafal on board, but Horace Holden resigned as our executive director in order to pursue a career as a professional airline pilot, which, I might add, is what he's doing nowadays. We hired Heather Warner as our short-term summertime director. She was from New Jersey but had been a participant in the NOC and NRC programs for many years. She did an outstanding job before going back north to college. Then we hired racers David Jacobson and Lee Sanders to be co-directors of NRC. Though young, they both were extremely competent, and with the guidance of the board of directors, they kept us moving forward.

Our youth program, now a growing part of our designation as a Center of Excellence, was attracting new Rhinos. This included Candice Caldwell from Charlotte, along with Becca Red from Chattanooga, Tennessee, and Gwen Greeley from Green Bay, Wisconsin. This gave us the best trio of K-1W junior slalom girls in the U.S. All three won national kayaking titles and competed abroad as members of the Junior Team.

On the boys' side, NRC had the Johnson twins, Jeffrey and Russell, from Franklin, North Carolina, and the Weizenecker brothers, Philip and Seth, from Alabama, giving us the best C-2 junior slalom teams in the country, as well as Clay Wilder from Alabama and James Burris from South Carolina in K-1 junior slalom. All six of the boys were Junior Olympic winners.

It is unlikely any other club or team in the country ever has had such an outstanding array of young talent. When you add our older athletes – the Olympic slalom stars and the wildwater racers – NRC had a once-in-a-lifetime collection of whitewater champions.

Things also were humming in Asheville, which was still our satellite operation, thanks to Steve Zarnowski. The owner of a major home-building company, Steve was the lead instructor in the youth program being held at the YMCA pool, which now was a combined effort of the Y, ACES, NRC, and NationsBank. There was no shortage of participants, and I can recall over 50 youngsters, plus their parents, showing up one night for a demonstration.

Out on the French Broad, Steve was constructing a new and nifty slalom course at Ledges Park. After many months of hard work, the course was opened in October of 1998. The newspaper once again ran a nice article. Entitled "Buncombe County Whitewater Course Nearing Completion," the writer, Nicole Crane, who was to become Lecky Haller's wife a few years later, said, "Without much rain this summer, you'd think kayaking on the French Broad River had all but dried up. But on Thursday evening, Ledges Park north of Asheville was very much alive. The lower water level was enabling Steve Zarnowski to put the finishing touches on a new slalom course…

"Zarnowski, an independent contractor, is building the course in his free time. He expects the cables to be in place by October 23 and the slalom gates hanging by the next week. Once the 25 gates are up, area kayak enthusiasts will be able to practice their skills going upstream and downstream through the gates…

"In anticipation of the course being completed, Chuck Hines, president of the Nantahala Racing Club, invited a couple of national heroes to come and play at Ledges Park. Olympic slalom racer Wayne Dickert and National whitewater freestyle team member Bob McDonough showed the NRC kids a few tricks on Thursday. McDonough, of Asheville, who has dominated the freestyle kayaking scene for nearly a decade, said he loves teaching young paddlers, whether it's basic paddling strokes or freestyle moves…

"Dickert is a Bryson City resident and director of the U.S. Canoe and Kayak Team's national development program. Bryson City is home to some of the world's best paddlers, but Dickert always welcomes the chance to come to Asheville. With the good, new slalom course here and a lot of jobs and schools close by, Asheville would be a neat place for paddlers to live, he said."

Dedication Day for the new slalom course found Bunny Johns and Scott Shipley and many other prominent paddlers on hand. There was extensive coverage by the local newspapers and TV stations. For whitewater racing in general and the Nantahala Racing Club in particular, it was another step forward.

As autumn turned into winter, Steve Zarnowski and I were back at the Asheville YMCA, volunteering our services. He was continuing to teach in the pool, and I was directing a six-lesson classroom course, "Personal Leadership though the Olympic Ideals." Eight of our kaYak kids were enrolled, along with their parents. It was a solid family activity. The lessons were on Vision, Focus, Commitment, Persistence, Self-Discipline, and Good Sportsmanship. After the course was completed, one of the students sent me a note several months later: "Mr. Hines, the Leadership course you gave at the Asheville YMCA has stuck with me, and it will help me throughout my life. You have given me faith and courage to pursue all my hopes and dreams in life. I have chosen my goals, and I am going to achieve them."

Another student in the class was young Pat Keller. His parents, Jerry and Carrie, had met while on the staff of the Nantahala Outdoor Center, where both were expert kayakers. Now they were residing in Asheville. Pat Keller was a kayaking prodigy, whose innate skills reminded me of Becky Weis when she was a young prospect. As a 12-year-old, Pat competed in the Junior Olympic slalom races with our Rhino contingent, placing second to an Atlanta boy in his age group. But slalom wasn't his thing. He later blossomed into an outstanding freestyle kayaker and extreme kayak racer.

*****

We had another exciting event in Asheville when the Torch Relay for the Special Olympics World Games passed through en route to Raleigh, where the 1999 Games were to be conducted. As I had coached a Special Olympics gold medalist in swimming in the past, I was asked to serve as co-chairman, working with my friend and neighbor Ronny Davis. The Torch Relay for this event was sponsored by the police officers worldwide, and Ronny was a local policeman. I rounded up four of our WNC Olympians to greet the runners as they came into the City Square downtown. This included whitewater star Wayne Dickert, swimmers Mary Montgomery and Dr. Steve Rerych, and fencer Dr. Ed Diez.

The Citizen-Times ran a good article with an excellent photo of the torch being carried into town. The article said, "They waited with anticipation as the rain drenched their hair. They giggled and danced the Macarena, but their eyes glimmered with excitement and darted periodically toward College Street as they continued to wait. Then the moment arrived, and the Special Olympics athletes from South Africa jumped with joy and applauded…

"The band blared as a parade of police officers jogged through Asheville on Thursday afternoon, carrying the Flame of Hope in honor of the Special Olympics World Games. The torch is being carried across the state by officers from around the world. The torch's final destination will be Raleigh…

"Special Olympics athletes from South Africa have spent the week practicing and playing in Asheville as our guests while awaiting the start of the Games."

Because of the rain, a pavilion had been erected at City Square, and our four local Olympians were situated there. The South African Special Olympics athletes were there. Our own local Special Olympics athletes were there. Then came the parade of runners trying to squeeze in. Several hundred spectators stood in the rain. The music was loud and boisterous. It was WET and WILD.

The policeman who carried the flame as it arrived at City Square was from the Caribbean island of St. Vincent. He knew the YWCA director there, who had come to work with the YWCA day camp on the isle of Montserrat one summer when Lee and I were there as part of our Asheville-Montserrat project. So the runner and I had a mutual friend. It is indeed a small world.

The Special Olympics World Games at Raleigh was the largest international sporting event in the world in 1999, with 7,000 athletes from 150 countries, plus 2,000 coaches, chaperones, and volunteer officials, plus 30,000 spectators. It was a privilege to play a small role in it.

*****

Returning to the Nantahala Racing Club and our end-of-the-millennium efforts, we were hoping to qualify some of our slalom racers for the 2000 Summer Olympics at Sydney, Australia. NOC or NRC had placed athletes on five U.S. Olympic Teams in the past and on every National Team that competed at the World Championships. Could we continue our successes in 2000?

We brought in a new executive director, Jill Woodruff, thus giving racers Lee Sanders and David Jacobson more time for their training. Jill was working with the board of directors and doing the administrative necessities, while Lee was running the club's numerous camps and clinics and David (DJ) was helping Coach Rafal Smolen with the many races we were hosting. It was a busy, busy time which had its tense moments.

In addition to paying for our day-by-day and month-by-month operation, we had raised $40,000 to help underwrite the travel expenses of our athletes. We were already providing free coaching. Those who came to live at the Nantahala and train there at our Center of Excellence and represent our club in national competition were given free coaching. They could also pick up off-season employment with the larger Nantahala Outdoor Center, which gave them reduced-price meals. It was a good arrangement. The non-profit racing club received support from the Nantahala Outdoor Center, which had a multi-million-dollar annual budget, employed 600 persons each summer, and served tens of thousands of customers in rafting and canoeing and kayaking, hiking and biking and climbing, and other outdoor activities. NOC also offered its elaborate travel adventure trips around the world. It was (is) a huge operation. In return for helping support the Rhinos, NOC received a lot of free publicity, as the media was quick to cover NRC's national championships and Olympic athletes.

Having $40,000 available to help with our athletes' travel expenses caused some friction. This was an unbelievable amount for a small non-profit club like ours. Who should get it? Just the Senior Team members who were aiming at the Olympics? How much? What about the younger kids who would be representing us at the Junior Olympics? Didn't they count? There was the threat of dissention. I appointed a three-man sub-committee comprised of Lecky Haller, Bob Red, and Scott Strausbaugh to study the situation and make a recommendation to the board. Finally we worked it out, with the "top guns" getting most of the money but even our youngest, beginning-level racers receiving $50 to $100 for their travel costs.

As it turned out, Scott Shipley in K-1 and the duo of Matt Taylor and Lecky Haller in C-2 made the U.S. Team for the 2000 Olympic Games. Since NRC had half of the members of the U.S. Team – three of the six – plus several of the alternates – we thought our coach should be going to Sydney, as well. One of the last things I did as club president was send in the paperwork and start the ball rolling to have Rafal Smolen added to the U.S. Team roster as an assistant coach. Once again it took six months to get it done, but Coach Smolen went to Sydney. Job accomplished.

*****

At my final board meeting as president, I was given a stunning silver serving tray that said, "Nantahala Racing Club. National Champions 1997, 1998, 1999. To Chuck Hines. Thank You for Your Leadership, Guidance, and Enthusiasm." I also received a beautifully-framed certificate proclaiming that I had been given a lifetime membership to the Nantahala Racing Club. The club newsletter, published a month later, said, "This year's annual meeting marked the end of Chuck Hines' term as president. Chuck stepped in several years ago after Bob Powell resigned and has led the club through five different executive directors and two coaches. The NRC is truly indebted to Chuck for his service and presented him with a lifetime membership and a silver platter. Chuck had a few going-away presents of his own for the hardworking NRC staff. Thanks, Chuck."

Much to my amazement, there was even a small article in the Citizen-Times: "Chuck Hines has announced that he is not running for re-election for the board president of the Nantahala Racing Club. He thinks it's time for young blood and new, younger leaders to step in and keep things moving ahead…

"Hines made his first trip to the Nantahala Outdoor Center and the Nantahala River in 1976 when he was seeking a new sport to pursue. He then taught kayaking to 1,000 adults and 300 youngsters at the Asheville YMCA. In 1985, when his youngsters won three national championships, the YMCA was chosen as the No. 1 youth paddling program in the U.S. by the American Canoe Association…

"During the 1990s, he was more involved with the Nantahala Racing Club. Now 67, he says he'll still visit the Nantahala River frequently."

Another chapter of my life concluded. A page to be turned. A new door to be opened. Different challenges and opportunities ahead, hopefully. But I was not yet ready to disappear entirely from the whitewater kayaking and racing scene.

Author's Note: In 2000, I wrote a juvenile novel entitled "Kayak Kids." Published by AuthorHouse, it was based on my experiences with the YMCA, the Nantahala Outdoor Center, and the Nantahala Racing Club. It follows the adventures of a teenaged brother and sister who, with their friends, enjoy paddling on a number of rivers and end up competing at the Whitewater Junior Olympics. If interested, you can purchase a copy by logging on to www.authorhouse.com and going to the Book section.

Chapter Sixteen

Back in December, 1990, I retired from full-time employment with the YMCA. Then in July, 1996, I ended my semiretirement and/or part-time work with the Y. Now, as we entered the new century, the new millennium, I was stepping down from my volunteer efforts with the Nantahala Racing Club. No regrets. It was time to retire for real.

I knew one thing for sure. I didn't want to remain directly involved with either the YMCA or NRC. As much as both organizations meant to me – and still do – I resolved not to be some old guy looking over the shoulders of the new leaders and saying, "Yes, but this is how we did it in the past." The past was past. As the newspaper article stated, it was time for young blood.

However, I still had several projects that would keep me close to the sport:

* Locally, with the assistance of Steve Zarnowski, I started a one-week summer pool instructional program for the day camp kids at Eliada Home for Children, just down the road from our house in suburban Asheville. Steve provided the kayaks and helped me with the classes the initial summer. Then he gradually withdrew, first from teaching and then from providing the boats, until I was doing it all by myself.

That was all right with me. Steve, you see, had replaced me as president of the Nantahala Racing Club, and he had his hands full. Under his supervision, the Rhinos kept on winning. They won the National Senior Slalom Championships in 2001 and 2003 and the Junior Olympic Championships in 2001, 2003, 2004, and 2005. Even though the number of slalom racers from the U.S. who were eligible to represent our country at the 2004 Olympic Games in Athens, Greece, was reduced to a bare minimum, NRC came through again and placed Chris Ennis in C-1 and the veteran duo of Joe Jacobi and Matt Taylor in C-2 on the U.S. Olympic Slalom Team.

Author's Note: As I write this in 2008, it's been announced that Joe Jacobi will be serving as an NBC commentator for the Summer Olympic Games at Beijing, China, in August. Joe, you will recall, was a Gold medalist in C-2 at the 1992 Olympics with his boat-mate Scott Strausbaugh. In recent years, both Joe and Scott have been overnight guests at our home here in Asheville. Scott brought his beautiful bride, Melissa. Now residing in Nashville, Tennessee, Scott and Melissa have two lovely young children. This reminds me of a favorite saying from the movie "Cool Runnings," about the Jamaican Olympic bobsled team. Their coach told the athletes, "If you're not enough without the Gold medal, you'll never be enough with it." I can tell you that while Scott and Joe are indeed Olympic champions, they are both ENOUGH without ever having won the Gold. They are men of extraordinary high character. It was my privilege to know them and many other great competitors in whitewater kayaking and racing.

While Steve Zarnowski & Co. at NRC were occupied nationally and internationally from 2001 through 2005, I gave pool instruction for one week each summer to anywhere from 20 to 40 day camp children at Eliada Home, including my grandchildren. Then we'd take them on a rafting trip down the Tuckaseigee River. It was quite low-key, but the youngsters, most of whom were from low-income families, enjoyed it.

* I did some work with Will Leverette and Lecky Haller on the Styrofoam Cup and Warren Wilson College Cup races. Will Leverette has had a long history of involvement with the sport, including many years as coach of the WWC paddling team. Will initiated the Styrofoam Cup, a yearly event held on the Nantahala River, which blossomed into the informal intercollegiate championships. Lecky, of course, was the former NRC Olympian and coach who moved to Asheville, where he replaced Will as the WWC coach and kept on winning races at the local

level. It was my pleasure to present a special award to Will Leverette at one of the races held here in town. As I write this, he continues to serve as one of our sport's greatest ambassadors and historians.

* I also remained involved nationally with the Junior Olympic Program, which Wayne Dickert and I and about 10 others had created in the mid 1990s. At my urging, and with a bit of my financial assistance, the Chuck Hines Cup was awarded to the winning slalom team at the annual JO Championships, starting in 2001. An article that appeared four years later in the Citizen-Times said, "In spite of a coaching switch, a broken wrist, and a burst appendix, the junior Rhinos of the Nantahala Racing Club rocked the 2005 Whitewater Junior Olympic Championships last weekend at South Bend, Indiana…

"Nantahala racers won several events, and Asheville residents Austin Kieffer, 16, and brothers Jeffrey Poe, 15, and Elliot Poe, 13, each placed near the top to add more team points as NRC took the top prize – the Chuck Hines Cup – for the third consecutive year…

"The Junior Olympics took place on a man-made course in South Bend. It was the culmination of the summer season which consisted of the Age Group Nationals at Carlton, Minnesota, and the four-race U.S. Cup series which started in Minnesota and then moved to Wausau, Wisconsin, before finally ending at South Bend…

"Kieffer placed third in K-1 junior slalom. Jeffrey Poe placed second in C-1 junior slalom. Elliot Poe finished third in K-1 cadet slalom…

"The finishes were exceptional, according to Coach Pablo McCandless, considering the young athletes did not have their regular coach, Rafal Smolen, who was coaching elsewhere. Then during the U.S. Cup series, substitute coach McCandless became seriously ill and was rushed to the hospital with appendicitis. But soon after surgery, he was back coaching from the riverbank…

"An injury took out one of the NRC athletes, Zach Bethea, who broke his wrist while bike riding at one of the race sites and was unable to finish the competition. Kieffer himself was coming back from a broken leg which kept him out of his boat for six months…

"While young Elliot Poe finished third, he actually placed first among Americans since the top two finishers were Canadians. This year the Junior Olympics were expanded to include not only those from the United States but also the Canadians. Kieffer welcomed the competition from the Canadians, saying it is great to see how other countries are doing…

"Kieffer has the kind of attitude that makes Chuck Hines smile. The initial Whitewater Junior Olympics were held in 1996 at Wausau, Wisconsin, said Hines, a former NRC president and coach. The driving force behind the inception of the Junior Olympics, Hines is also the namesake for the team trophy, which was begun in 2001…

"This year, second place behind NRC went to Mach One of Pennsylvania. Third place went to the Valley Mill team from Maryland. Twelve states and four Canadian provinces were represented, Hines said, indicating that the Junior Olympics are a step in the right direction for building the sport nationally and perhaps even internationally."

There was also an article about the 2005 JO Championships that I happened to write for the American Whitewater magazine, in which I said, "It started with the rumble on the raceway…

"This was followed by a downriver sprint, and, of course, there was the traditional Olympic-style slalom competition. These events all took place in South Bend, Indiana, as the U.S. welcomed its Canadian neighbors to the USACK International Whitewater Junior Olympics. The tenth annual running of the much-expanded JO Championships was conducted on South Bend's East Race, a multi-million-dollar urban whitewater course. In addition to slalom, there were the freestyle, downriver, and boater-cross events, all designed to attract more young paddlers and provide them with a true international-style experience…

"At the Championships, there were Gold, silver, and bronze medals in each of the four disciplines, with the competing kids further divided into Junior 17-18, Junior 15-16, Cadet 13-14, and Cub Cadet 12-under age categories…

"For the third straight year, the 10-member team from the Nantahala Racing Club of North Carolina won the slalom races and the Chuck Hines Cup competition with 31 points. Trailing were the Mach One Racing Club of Pennsylvania with 20½, Valley Mill Camp of Maryland with 18, Front Range Paddling Association of Colorado with 16½, and six other teams…

"Front Range finished first in the scoring for the new Ray McLain Cup, in which points were accumulated in all four of the aforementioned disciplines. Coached by Chris Wiegand, the 14-member Front Range team totaled 148½ points. This new award memorializes the long-time efforts to promote youth paddling by the recently-deceased McLain from the Green Bay, Wisconsin, YMCA. We miss you, Ray!

"Those of us involved with the Junior Olympics feel we have taken a major step forward in promoting youth paddling and racing in North America. As Olympian Ben Kvanli from San Marcos, Texas, stated while donating his time to help at South Bend, everyone seemed to be finding a way to get along and have fun, and hopefully even more youngsters will be participating in the future."

Led by Dave Kurtz of Pennsylvania, Chris Wiegand of Colorado, and Mike Hickey of Illinois, the Junior Olympic Program kept growing in 2006 and 2007. The 2006 Championships were conducted in British Columbia, Canada, and attracted not only American and Canadian competitors but also a team from China. The 2007 Championships, held in Colorado, were attended by a team of three girls and their female coach from Iran. Kurtz's Mach One kids won both the Chuck Hines Cup and the Ray McLain Cup.

As part of the Cup presentation at the Whitewater JO Championships, there's also a Youth Leadership Award that goes to a deserving coach or mentor of youth. It's a way to recognize those who are continuing to bring youngsters into our great sport of whitewater kayaking and racing. The recipients of this prestigious award have been Wayne Dickert of North Carolina in 2003, Dave Kurtz of Pennsylvania in 2004, Mike Larimer of Georgia in 2005, Tom Long of Idaho in 2006, and Ben and Michelle Kvanli of Texas in 2007. The winner for 2008 is John Brennan of Colorado, who will be honored at the Championships scheduled to be held in Wausau, Wisconsin, where it all began 13 years ago.

Author's Note: the Junior Olympics remain my favorite sports event. In the first half of my YMCA career, I coached Gold medalists in JO swimming and water polo. That was in the 1970s. Then it was my good fortune to coach the winning Gold medal Southeast Team at the 1997 JO Whitewater Championships held in Charlotte, North Carolina. More importantly, I have seen the JO Program in these three sports and various other sports being used to encourage more and more youngsters to participate and to enjoy competition in an atmosphere that emphasizes teamwork and fair play and good sportsmanship.

* I became involved with another Olympic Torch Relay, this one for the Winter Games being hosted by Salt Lake City. Just as the Junior Olympics can bring young athletes together, the Torch Relay can bring different communities and even countries together. The idea for the Torch Relay originated many centuries ago during the ancient Greek Olympics. History tells us that "a Torch relay race is mentioned in ancient Greek stories, dating back to the sixth century B.C.E. The aim of the race is thought to be more ritualistic than competitive, with runners carrying a torch from point to point without extinguishing the flame. The final torchbearer would then light a fire at the Olympic site."

The modern-day Olympic Games were started in 1896, and the first time the flame was used in the modern era was in 1928. There was no relay. The flame was kindled in the Olympic stadium at Helsinki, Finland, and burned throughout the duration of the Games. The flame was lit again at the Los Angeles Coliseum for the Olympics of 1932.

The carrying of the flame in a Torch Relay was initiated as part of the 1936 Olympic Games hosted by Berlin, Germany, and it has become a tradition.

For the 2002 Winter Olympics, I chaired the greeting committee for the Torchbearers as they came into Asheville. Helping me were my family members – wife, daughter, grandchildren – and two former YMCA athletes, Mary Montgomery and Debbie Robinson, and NRC's newest executive director, Lee Leibfarth, and his wife Jean. Afterwards, we all went out to lunch, with Lee and Jean bringing me up to date on the latest Rhino activities.

As I write this in the spring of 2008, the Torch Relay for the Olympic Summer Games to be conducted at Beijing, China, is underway. I am not involved this time, unfortunately.

* Another way I HAVE remained involved with whitewater racing, however, is through my writing. I started editing and distributing "The Whitewater Paddler" bimonthly newsletter immediately after I began kayaking in 1977. In the beginning, I had 60 on my mailing list, mostly Ashevilleans. Gradually the number increased to 100, 200, 300, and finally to a maximum of 360 from coast to coast.

At first, the newsletter focused on river-running and river safety. In later years, it zeroed in more on racing. Each issue contained some type of spiritual message. Other articles were intended to be thought-provoking without being controversial. The underlying theme was teamwork and togetherness.

From time to time, the Nantahala Outdoor Center, whose activities I frequently promoted in my newsletter, sent me a small amount to help with mailing expenses. But I picked up over 90% of the costs myself for 30 years, 1977 to 2006. This totaled thousands of dollars. I was okay with that. As you know if you've reached this page, I like to write, to share adventures and activities and ideas and insights with others, and

"The Whitewater Paddler" gave me an opportunity to fill this need in my life, especially when I could no longer go out into the rivers and rapids myself.

I used "The Whitewater Paddler" to promote the concept of a U.S. Whitewater Slalom Hall of Fame. After completing my term in office as president of the Nantahala Racing Club, I was asked by several Olympians to see if such a Hall could be created. The last time I looked, about four million Americans participated in some form of kayaking annually, half of them being whitewater enthusiasts. When you add the vast array of rafters and the die-hard canoeists, the number is tripled, or more. The toughest task in the sport, at least in my opinion, is whitewater slalom racing, in which, as I write this, about 90 countries compete at the world and Olympic levels. But there's no U.S. Slalom Hall of Fame to recognize our most deserving athletes, coaches, and contributors.

Thus we formed a small committee and divided into two groups, one establishing a list of those who should be considered for possible selection to the Hall, the other seeking a site or facility for the Hall. Both groups met with partial success. We came up with a list of candidates or nominees, and we found a place willing to house and even help finance the Hall. Guess what. It was the Nantahala Outdoor Center.

But when an International Whitewater Hall of Fame was opened in western Maryland, the concept of a separate U.S. Hall just for slalom racers was put on hold. That's where it stands as I write this. Not wanting to see this project fall entirely by the wayside, I made a bold move. In the final edition of "The Whitewater Paddler," distributed on Memorial Day, 2006, which concluded 30 years of publication, I announced the newsletter's own U.S. Slalom Hall of Honorees. It was based on the nominees that had been selected previously.

"The Whitewater Paddler" Hall of Honorees contained 58 members, in commemoration of the 58 years that slalom races have been conducted in this country. Certificates were sent to those whom we chose. Here's the list:

PIONEERS (12) – John Berry, Bill Bickham, Bob Harrigan, Bart Hauthaway, Tom Johnson, Walter Kirschbaum, Bob McNair, Roger Paris, Will Pruett, Dick Shipley, Tom Southworth, Barb Wright.

COACHES/CONTRIBUTORS (21) – Karin Baldzer, Bob Campbell, Wayne Dickert, Abbie Endicott, Bill Endicott, Jay Evans, Don Giddens, Jennifer Hearn, Bunny Johns, Payson Kennedy, Peter Kennedy, Dave Kurtz, Mike Larimer, Tom Long, Ray McLain, David Mitchell, Peggy Mitchell, Silvan Poberaj, Lamar Sims, Mike Sloan, Steve Zarnowski.

ATHLETES (25) – John Burton, Dana Chladek, Adam Clawson, Eric Evans, Kent Ford, Eric Giddens, Rebecca Giddens, Mike Garvis, Steve Garvis, Fritz Haller, Lecky Haller, Linda Harrison, Cathy Hearn, David Hearn, Eric Jackson, Joe Jacobi, Ben Kvanli, Jon Lugbill, Ron Lugbill, Jamie McEwan, Angus Morrison, Bobby Robison, Scott Shipley, Scott Strausbaugh, Rich Weiss.

There are many more who have played major roles in the advancement of our sport over the past 58 years. Hopefully they too will receive the recognition they deserve.

*****

Author's Note: Primarily because of my editorship of "The Whitewater Paddler" for so many years, plus my leadership in developing the YMCA's whitewater program, plus helping with the creation of the Whitewater Junior Olympics, plus serving as president of the national champion Nantahala Racing Club, I received another award in 2005. I was selected as one of the 100 most influential leaders in U.S. Aquatics. It was the first time anyone from the sport of whitewater paddling had been recognized. I knew there were others more deserving than I, but on behalf of everybody involved with our sport, including all those who supported my efforts over the years, I accepted the award. It was presented to me at a small ceremony here in Asheville arranged by Mark Singleton and American Whitewater.

*****

They say that everything that goes around, comes around. Perhaps that's why the last important magazine article I wrote on our sport was about paddling and racing in the pool. Isn't that what initially enticed me into whitewater kayaking, the prospect of developing a curriculum for YMCA members that used a calm, safe pool for basic instruction? Isn't that where we first hung our slalom gates, in a YMCA pool? The article I wrote for the American Whitewater magazine was entitled "Pool Slalom Racing is Gaining in Popularity." It was extremely long and contained seven photos, and here's what I said:

"It's a long, long way from the calm water of the YMCA's indoor pool at Green Bay, Wisconsin, to the raging rapids of the Isere River at Bourg St. Maurice, France, where the World Whitewater Slalom Championships were recently held, but Rebecca Bennett Giddens managed to make the journey. Not only that, but she finished first for the U.S. in women's kayak, no easy feat since racers representing more than 60 countries were entered in the world competition…

"Now 24, Rebecca started kayaking at age nine with her father, mother, brother, and sister at a Green Bay YMCA canoe and kayak camp. Soon thereafter, she began serious practicing under the supervision of Coach Ray McLain, using both the local river and the YMCA pool, where a number of slalom gates were hung…

"The utilization of pools for slalom practices by kayakers and canoeists dates back to 1962, when the first slalom gates were hung in the Dartmouth College pool. The initial pool slalom race was conducted there in the spring of 1963, requiring the competitors to maneuver through 10 gates and perform an Eskimo roll in the process…

"Over the years, many other pools around the country have been used for slalom practices. In 1979, the YMCA in Asheville, North Carolina, hung gates and conducted its first pool slalom, featuring visiting national K-1W winner Linda Harrison. Five years later, Asheville conducted a 'national' pool slalom competition, with races held in various pools and the results then sent to Asheville for comparison. Asheville's young

14-year-old star, Mark Mathews, won the K-1 junior competition, and a year later, he was crowned the 1985 U.S. junior champion at the nearby Nantahala River…

"More recently, USACK, the sport's governing body, began promoting an official National Pool Slalom Challenge. The initial effort came in 1997, under the supervision of Wayne Dickert, a 1996 Olympian, who now serves as director of instruction for the world-famous Nantahala Outdoor Center. Since 1997, USACK's annual pool slalom has attracted every level of athlete, from German Olympic gold medalist Oliver Fix and half-a-dozen U.S. Olympians to absolute beginners. Two years ago, Dickert's doubles canoe partner at the 1996 Olympics, Horace Holden, participated in a pool slalom with his sons Isaac, seven, and Simon, five…

"The USACK Pool Slalom Challenge takes place from mid-January through mid-March each year, and any reasonably-sized pool (or pond) can be utilized. For the several hundred pools in the U.S. already being used for Eskimo roll practices during the winter months, slalom racing can be an added attraction."

The article continued, listing a dozen or more pools from coast to coast that were offering slalom practices and competition. Incidentally, Rebecca Bennett Giddens, who started out in a YMCA pool as a youngster, won not only a Gold medal at the World Championships but also a silver medal in the Olympic Games at Athens in 2004.

Do you recall Pat Keller, whom I mentioned as participating as a youngster in our YMCA-NRC "Personal Leadership through the Olympic Ideals" classroom course while also practicing in the Asheville YMCA pool? Who started out in slalom but moved on to other river excitement? Well, in 2004, as a 17-year-old, Pat won a Gold medal in the World Extreme Kayak Championships at Val Sesia, Italy. The Citizen-Times said, "Keller won first overall in the three days of extreme races on Class V whitewater, which included four separate events."

*****

But you don't have to be a World Champion or a Gold or silver or bronze medalist to benefit from YMCA programming and/or whitewater paddling. My whitewater experiences involved some gratifying moments with racing, but nowadays, when all is said and done, I remember most of all the numerous rivers I ran for fun and the nearness to Mother Nature and to God. I remember my YMCA paddling pals – Will, Jim, Rocky, Anne, and others – and the many hundreds of men and women and boys and girls we introduced to the sport.

I remember Ben Baldwin, the inner-city boy we taught at the Asheville YMCA in the late 1980s, who won a couple of races at the French Broad Riverfest before leaving us and returning to horrific conditions in the slums of Los Angeles. Recently I received a letter from Ben. Now 33 and married and living in Sacramento, California, he wrote, "Dear Mr. Hines, Thank you for always being a true friend. I am glad you continue to work with youth. To my fellow YMCA members and participants, you should consider yourselves blessed to be part of a life-changing organization such as the Y. The programs you take part in will open up the world to you. All you have to do is Listen and give yourself the Chance...

"I was 13 years old and in need of friendship, guidance, and somewhere to vent the passing of my mother. Unable to communicate the pain I was feeling inside, I began to act out my frustration. My grandmother suggested I go down to the YMCA. From there, I was okay. The life skills and people skills I learned in the programs I was involved in helped me grow as a person. They gave me key tools that have helped me as an adult today. The programs at the YMCA are places where youth can learn skills that will benefit them throughout their lives. I am very appreciative of all the people at the Y who are involved in helping youth. Please keep up the good work."

I believe this explains why I made the YMCA my career, my calling, my profession, and I am thankful the Y gave me an opportunity to become a whitewater paddler, teacher, coach, and enthusiast.

When my wife Lee and I celebrated our 50th wedding anniversary – yes, I *am* that old – the newspaper article summarized my life beyond the Family by saying, "Mr. Hines' lengthy career in sports and recreation included coaching numerous national champions for the YMCA and being inducted into the WNC Sports Hall of Fame, and he served as president of the Nantahala Whitewater Racing Club."

Can one's life be summed up in such a few words? I think not. There's so much more to life for each one of us. The ups and the downs. The pleasures and the pain. The calm spots and the turmoil. The eddies and the rapids. The river of life flows on, and on, eventually taking us to the horizon line and over the drop into an unseen and unknown future. For me, it's been an exciting and challenging ride so far, and it's not over yet. My guess, my hope, is that the river of life merges with the never-ending river of the afterlife, churning forward into eternity. So someday, my friends, as the old Spiritual puts it, "We shall gather by the river, the beautiful, beautiful river, gather with the saints at the river, which flows by the throne of God."

Made in the USA
Columbia, SC
24 February 2021